THE FAVROT FAMILY OF LOUISIANA:

A HISTORY OVER THREE CENTURIES

by G. Martin Moeller, Jr.

1 2 3 4 5 6 7 8 9 10

ISBN: 978-0-692-07353-7

Tulane School of Architecture
Richardson Memorial Hall
6823 St. Charles Avenue
New Orleans, LA 70118-5698
architecture.tulane.edu

Book design: Leigh Wilkerson Ayers (10/HALF Studios)
Indexer: Meridith Murray

Front cover: Images courtesy of William Randolph D'Armond, except for lower right, courtesy of Kay Favrot
Back cover: Samuel Augustus Mitchell, *A New Map of Louisiana*, 1853

Printed in Baton Rouge, Louisiana by Moran Printing

for H. Mortimer Favrot, Jr.

CONTENTS

PREFACE

History is a seamless fabric of the extraordinary and the mundane. Wars, natural disasters, technological breakthroughs, and great political speeches punctuate the human narrative, but ultimately tell only part of our collective story. Equally significant are the personal experiences and perspectives of the individuals who witnessed, endured, and sometimes participated in these momentous events, all while going about their daily lives, earning a living, and caring for their families.

Collections of private papers are therefore valuable aids to our understanding of history. Letters, journals, newspaper clippings, and even legal documents such as wills and marriage contracts shed light on contemporary social and political affairs. They also offer glimpses into the aspirations and struggles of the people who composed these documents or saved them for posterity.

One such collection is the Favrot Family Papers, now maintained by the Louisiana Research Collection at the Howard-Tilton Memorial Library of Tulane University. Comprising more than 2,000 documents, the papers serve as a partial but substantial chronicle of a single Franco-American family that arrived in Louisiana in 1728, not long after the region's colonization by King Louis XIV. Covering a period of roughly two centuries, the content of the papers focuses on five generations of Favrot men who pursued military and political careers under four different flags: those of France, Spain, the United States, and the Confederacy.

The collection first entered the public realm around 1910, when the Favrot family entrusted the bulk of the papers to the Louisiana State Museum. In 1936, the Louisiana Historical Records Survey, a program of the New Deal-era Works Progress Administration, launched a methodical effort to transcribe the papers, most of which were handwritten in French or Spanish. The Historical Records Survey issued Volumes I-VII of the transcriptions, along with Volume IX (published out of sequence), between 1940 and 1942. In 1948, the papers were transferred to Tulane, where staff members continued the transcription project as their schedules permitted. Four additional volumes were issued in the 1960s, with the final five volumes released between 1979 and 1984, bringing the total to 17 hefty volumes.[1]

With the transcriptions finally complete—nearly a half-century after the Works Progress Administration began the project—Tulane soon embarked on an initiative to *translate* the French and Spanish documents from the collection in a consistent fashion. This led to the publication, in 1988, of *The Favrot Family Papers: A Documentary Chronicle of Early Louisiana*, Volume I: 1690–1782. That volume included translations of several documents from various archives in France, which proved to be informative complements to the earliest material in the family collection. Tulane went on to publish an additional five volumes of chronological translations, covering the period from 1783 to 1839, along with a few stand-alone publications such as a translation of Pierre-Joseph Favrot's "Education Manual for His Sons," dating from 1798. As of this writing, T. Semmes Favrot, Pierre-Joseph's great-great-great-great-grandson and a son of Tim Favrot, to whom this book is dedicated, is overseeing work on a seventh volume of translations.

While the published translations of the Favrot Family Papers constitute a basic documentary history of the family from the late 17th century to the late 19th century, they provide little historical context for the family's experiences and include almost no material from the 20th century onward. Since that time, not only has the Favrot family continued to grow and thrive, but it has also produced several generations of influential architects and real estate developers who made significant contributions to the physical character and culture of New Orleans and other communities across Louisiana.

This book represents the first effort to present a coherent, contextualized history of the Favrot family from the 1600s to the present day. Using the published transcriptions and translations of the Favrot Family Papers as a foundation, it also draws on material in other public archives, such as the Historic New Orleans Collection, along with various scholarly and popular historical texts, privately maintained collections of architectural drawings and papers, and interviews with a number of living family members. The result is a book that not only traces the story of a fascinating family spanning nearly 350 years, but also offers insights into the complex history of Louisiana, the United States, France, and Spain over that time period.

The book was conceived by Kenneth Schwartz, FAIA, dean of the Tulane School of Architecture, as a tribute to Henri Mortimer ("Tim") Favrot, Jr., FAIA, and his wife, Kay Gibbons Favrot. Tim—who, unfortunately, died before this project was complete—was an architect educated at Tulane and Harvard universities. Following in the professional footsteps of his father, grandfather, and great-grandfather, he went into architectural practice in New Orleans and worked on several prominent buildings before shifting his focus to real estate development, an endeavor in which he was extremely successful. He was a valued member of various boards at Tulane, and, with Kay, a generous donor to the university, as well as to many other civic and cultural organizations in New Orleans.

The research for this book entailed various challenges, some common to such projects, some unique to the Favrots. Handwritten letters are notoriously frustrating sources, often riddled with illegible words and sometimes partially obscured by stains, tears, or smudges. Fortunately for me, the vast majority of the handwritten correspondence had already been carefully analyzed by the scholars who had transcribed and translated the papers. After performing numerous spot-checks of the transcriptions and translations against the corresponding original documents, I was convinced of their overall accuracy, and therefore decided that, in the interest of time, I could rely on the published versions in general. (There were still a number of instances, however, in which I felt it necessary to return to the original documents to verify the exact wording of certain passages. In some cases I made modest revisions to the translations based on additional information I had uncovered, consultation with scholars, or my own judgment.)

Another difficulty in researching historic correspondence is that the paper trail is rarely complete. Some Favrot family members saved letters meticulously, while others did not. Some papers were lost or damaged over the years. This is to be expected, but for the researcher, the effect can be like that of hearing one side of a telephone conversation—sometimes, but not always, one can get the gist of the conversation, but would miss tantalizing details. In several cases, while reviewing the Favrot papers, I encountered a gap in correspondence followed by a letter that suddenly mentioned some recent tragedy or major event, but provided no details, leaving me only to wonder what terrible or wonderful thing had transpired.

One challenge specific to the Favrot family research was the frequency with which certain given names appear in the family tree. The names Joseph, Claude, Pierre, Louis, and others show up in numerous combinations and over multiple generations; indeed, three important figures in the family history—whose lives spanned from 1826 to 2015—all shared the name Henri Mortimer Favrot. To complicate matters further, individuals often had multiple nicknames, and several males in the family were, at different times, referred to simply as "Favrot." For these reasons, in the early chapters of the book, I have tended to rely on the long forms of given names (e.g., "Claude-Joseph," rather than just "Claude"). While the result is sometimes a bit cumbersome, I think it reduces the likelihood of confusion on the part of the reader. In later chapters, I sometimes rely on distinctive nicknames to distinguish key family members. For example, I refer to the 20th-century architect H. Mortimer Favrot, Sr., as "Morty," and to his son, H. Mortimer Favrot, Jr., as "Tim."

In the pre-modern era, the spelling of proper nouns (and, indeed, of many words) was inconsistent. Before the 19th century, the Favrot name often appeared as "Faverot," "de Favrot," or a combination of the two. For simplicity, I use the "Favrot" spelling throughout this book.

Speaking of names, I should note that there are lingering questions about the correct name of Joseph-Claude Favrot (born in France in 1668), the first family member to be discussed in detail in this book. In a letter to Thomas B. Favrot dating from the 1960s, Maggy Carof, whom Thomas had hired to do research on his behalf in French archives, wrote with the astonishing news that "[Joseph-Claude Favrot] was really named Pierre Joseph," based on what she claimed were consistent listings in various documents she had found.[2] Thomas seemed to take Carof's contention as gospel, and thenceforth regularly referred to Joseph-Claude as Pierre-Joseph (not to be confused with the Pierre-Joseph of two generations later, born in Louisiana in 1749) in his notes and correspondence. Nonetheless, various legal documents in the Favrot papers clearly refer to the person born in 1668 as Joseph-Claude. It is certainly possible that his original name was a longer hybrid, such as Pierre-Joseph-Claude, but that is only conjecture at this point. At any rate, based on the preponderance of supporting evidence in the family papers, I have decided to refer to this person as Joseph-Claude from this point onward.

As noted above, the published translations of the Favrot Family Papers end with the year 1839, but most family members continued to use French as their primary language through the late 19th century, meaning that hundreds of pages of documents were still available to me only in their original form or through transcriptions of the French text. Although I never formally studied French, I do read both Spanish and Italian well, and given the similarities between the languages I was able to translate some of the later documents myself. For translations of longer or more complicated documents, I relied on Alexandra Merrill, a graduate student in French at Georgetown University.

Thorough research for a book of this kind could easily take a decade or more of full-time work. In this case, the research phase was a part-time endeavor lasting roughly a year and a half, beginning in the fall of 2013, while I was also working on numerous other curatorial, editorial, and writing projects. Once I began writing the text in the spring of 2015, I discovered that some story lines required additional, focused research in order to clarify certain facts, especially in cases involving conflicting references in the archival material, which were not uncommon. I have no illusions that the resulting book is comprehensive, but I believe it to be as accurate as possible given the numerous gaps and inconsistencies in the original documents, and I trust that it will provide a useful armature for others who wish to investigate the story of the Favrots in greater depth.

I ask the reader to bear in mind several key points before diving into the text. First, the book inevitably focuses on the male lineage of the family. There are several reasons for this, particularly the fact that, for most of the family's history, women did not work outside the home and were not involved actively in political, military, or professional affairs. The vast majority of the material in the archives relates directly to the Favrot men. Even when letters written by women began to appear with greater frequency in the mid-19th century, they tended to focus on relatively mundane matters—the children's health, household tasks, etc.—which, while sometimes critical to the moment, would add little of substance to the overall family story. Owing to my own longstanding interest in the unheralded roles of women in history, I found this disappointing, though hardly surprising given traditional gender roles in western society. Fortunately, there were a few Favrot women who figured relatively prominently in the archives, and whose correspondence and other writing provide some fascinating insights.

Another reason for the preoccupation with the male line is quite simple: this project was conceived as a chronicle of the Favrot family, and given the prevailing family nomenclature system in European-American societies, that obviously entailed a focus on the patriarchal branch of the family tree. This is a shame, because many of the women who married into the Favrot family had extraordinary lineages of their own (related family names such as Freret and Duplantier, to name only two, would be instantly familiar to many New Orleanians). Such limitations were necessary, however, in order to produce a coherent narrative of the Favrot line.

Given the genesis of this book, it also made sense to focus the more recent elements of the story on the multiple generations of architects along Tim Favrot's branch of the family tree. As a result, various other branches bearing the Favrot name are mentioned only in passing or not at all. This in no way should be interpreted to mean that their stories are less important or less interesting than those of Tim Favrot's branch—merely that they were less integral to this particular narrative.

Inevitably, this book deals with some difficult subjects, most notably slavery. As affluent householders and, later, plantation owners in colonial Louisiana and the antebellum American South, the Favrots were slaveholders for more than a century. In reviewing the correspondence from that era, I found it hard to reconcile the seemingly compassionate character of many family members with their ownership—and, on occasion, documented mistreatment—of slaves. Ultimately, of course, it is impossible to make sense of such a senseless institution. As Kay Favrot once said to me during a conversation about this subject, "It happened, and we can't change that. We have to talk about it and learn from it."[3] Throughout the book, including passages about the family's involvement with slavery and support for the Confederate cause (which was actually quite reluctant, at least at first), I have tried to remain as objective as possible, leaving it to the reader to render any ethical judgments.

The Favrot family has bequeathed to the American public a remarkable documentary history that illuminates many details of our shared past. In reviewing this material, one cannot help but wonder what legacy those of us living in the digital age will leave for our successors. Will the nuances, personalities, and sometimes surprisingly raw emotions that are conveyed in handwritten letters be irretrievably lost? With billions of people producing countless electronic documents every day, will society lose the ability—or the will—to sort, compile, and study correspondence in a coherent fashion? Can any compendium of digital documents ever stir the sense of awe that physical papers—with their sometimes quirky handwriting, tinges of sweat, and curious marginalia—inspire in those who have the precious opportunity to handle them?

While the main body of this book concludes with Tim Favrot's generation, there are already three more generations of Favrots alive and making new history. How and whether their own stories are preserved for their descendants will be up to them. As an outsider who has had the privilege of poring over the family's extraordinary archives, however, I sincerely hope that they will all choose to build upon this remarkable legacy.

Acknowledgments

This book is dedicated to Tim Favrot. When I began work on the project, I hoped and somehow fully expected that he would live to see its publication. At the time Tim was already 83 years old and somewhat frail, but he retained a sharp mind. During my interviews with Tim and Kay in late 2013 and early 2014, I was frequently impressed by his clear and precise memory of certain names, facts, and events. (Once, when Kay asked Tim if a certain building in New Orleans had been designed by his father's firm, he said no, and without hesitation accurately recited the rather lengthy name of the little-known firm that actually had designed the project.) Sadly, Tim had a debilitating stroke not long after our last interview in the spring of 2014, and died on May 10, 2015. I was honored to have gotten to know him.

I am very grateful to Kay Favrot, whose sense of humor, candor, encouragement, and unfailing graciousness made her a delightful interviewee and valuable resource throughout the research process.

Numerous other Favrot family members and colleagues kindly agreed to be interviewed for this book. I thank James Favrot, Kathleen Favrot Van Horn, Semmes Favrot, Beverly Favrot Himel, Gervais Favrot, Jr., and Henry Shane for their time and insights.

As stated above, this project was conceived by Kenneth Schwartz, FAIA, dean of the Tulane School of Architecture. I was pleased when Ken asked me to submit a proposal for researching and writing the book, and thrilled when my proposal was accepted. I appreciate his support at every stage of the project.

My research owes a great debt to the scholars involved in the organization, transcription, and translation of the Favrot Family Papers from the 1930s to the 2010s. Particular credit goes to Tulane library staff members Connie G. Griffith, who transcribed many of the documents, and Guillermo Náñez Falcón, who edited several volumes of transcriptions and translations. Their efforts came at a critical time, and helped ensure the continuing viability of the Favrot collection. Their successors were Wilbur E. Meneray, who edited two additional volumes of translations, and Rien T. Fertel, who edited the last volume published so far.

At the time of my research, hundreds of documents in the Favrot Family Papers had yet to be formally translated under Tulane's auspices. I enlisted Alexandra Merrill, a graduate student in French at Georgetown University, to translate selected documents that I deemed important to the family story. The high quality of her work was especially evident in several rhyming verses, which she rendered both accurately and poetically—a true art.

Thanks also go to Sean Benjamin, public services librarian in the Louisiana Research Collection at Tulane's Howard-Tilton Memorial Library, for making vast amounts of material accessible to me and cheerfully responding to my occasionally naïve questions.

Creed Brierre and Tommy Grey of Mathes Brierre Architects kindly opened the firm's archives, allowing me to review first-hand a number of drawings for projects with which Charles Favrot, Morty Favrot, and Tim Favrot were involved.

I was pleased when Lawrence N. Powell, professor emeritus of history at Tulane University, agreed to review the first full draft of the book to ensure general historical accuracy. His comments regarding both content and style were consistently insightful.

I am indebted to Bill D'Armond, a distant cousin of the Favrots, for his help in obtaining photographs of early family portraits. Meridith Murray did an excellent job in preparing the index. Finally, my thanks go to graphic designers Leigh Wilkerson, Madeleine Hawks, and Erin Meekhof, of 10/Half Studios, for their elegant layout of this book.

THE FAVROT FAMILY TREE

K.A. = KNOWN AS
A.K.A. = ALSO KNOWN AS
CA. = CIRCA
BLACK NAME = FAVROT FAMILY MEMBER
GREEN NAME = NON-FAVROT SPOUSE
GRAY NAME = NON-FAVROT PERSON

↓ = UNLISTED CHILDREN

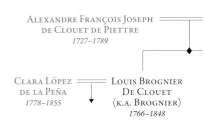

ALEXANDRE FRANÇOIS JOSEPH
DE CLOUET DE PIETTRE
1727–1789

CLARA LÓPEZ ═══ LOUIS BROGNIER
DE LA PEÑA ═══ DE CLOUET
1778–1855 ═══ (K.A. BROGNIER)
1766–1848

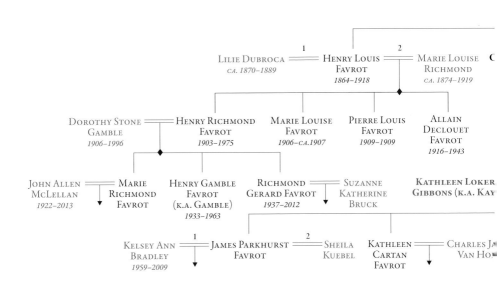

LILIE DUBROCA ═══ ¹ HENRY LOUIS ═══ ² MARIE LOUISE ⊂
CA. 1870–1889 ═══ FAVROT ═══ RICHMOND
1864–1918 ═══ *CA. 1874–1919*

DOROTHY STONE ═══ HENRY RICHMOND   MARIE LOUISE   PIERRE LOUIS   ALLAIN
GAMBLE ═══ FAVROT   FAVROT   FAVROT   DECLOUET
1906–1996 ═══ *1903–1975*   *1906–CA.1907*   *1909–1909*   FAVROT
1916–1943

JOHN ALLEN ═══ MARIE   HENRY GAMBLE   RICHMOND ═══ SUZANNE   KATHLEEN LOKER
MCLELLAN ═══ RICHMOND   FAVROT   GERARD FAVROT ═══ KATHERINE   GIBBONS (K.A. KAY
1922–2013 ═══ FAVROT   (K.A. GAMBLE)   *1937–2012* ═══ BRUCK
1933–1963

KELSEY ANN ═══ ¹ JAMES PARKHURST ═══ ² SHEILA   KATHLEEN ═══ CHARLES JA
BRADLEY ═══ FAVROT ═══ KUEBEL   CARTAN ═══ VAN HO
1959–2009 ═══ FAVROT

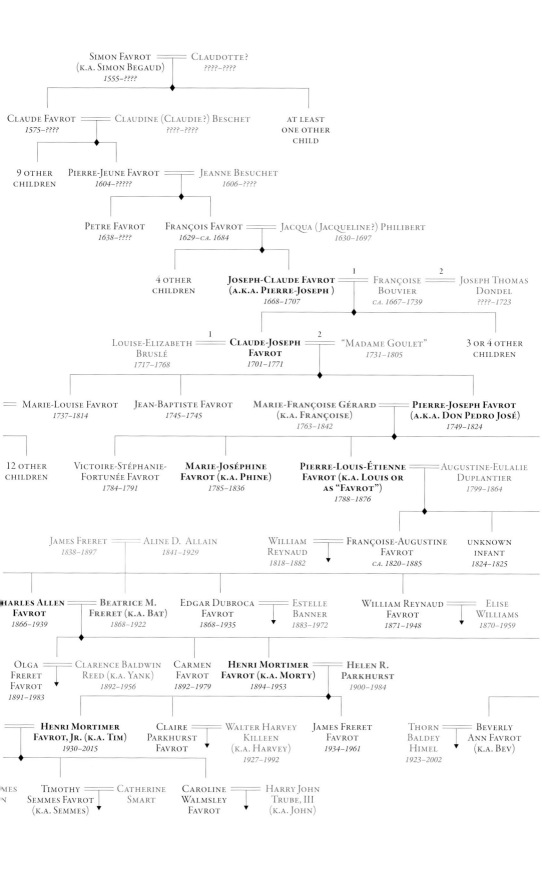

This is a partial family tree that focuses on the direct line from Joseph-Claude Favrot to Henri Mortimer Favrot, Jr., comprising the principal subjects of this book, along with their siblings and closer cousins. Space limitations required the omission of many of their descendants, maternal ancestors, and cousins by marriage.

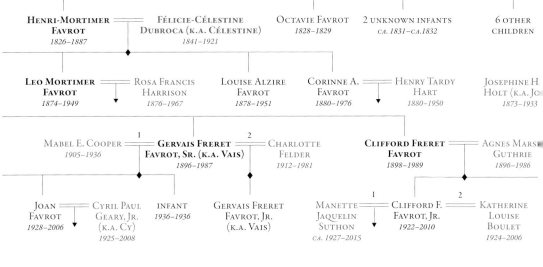

MARIE-LOUISE FAVROT
1789–1790

JOSEPH-PHILOGÈNE-ZÉNON FAVROT (K.A. PHILOGÈNE OR PHILO)
1791–1822

CÉLESTE FAVROT
1792-1794

LOUISE FAVROT
1794–1794

AUGUSTINE-OCTAV... FAVROT (K.A. OCTAVINE/TAV... *1795–1868*

HENRI-MORTIMER FAVROT
1826–1887

FÉLICIE-CÉLESTINE DUBROCA (K.A. CÉLESTINE)
1841–1921

OCTAVIE FAVROT
1828–1829

2 UNKNOWN INFANTS
CA. 1831–CA.1832

6 OTHER CHILDREN

LEO MORTIMER FAVROT
1874–1949

ROSA FRANCIS HARRISON
1876–1967

LOUISE ALZIRE FAVROT
1878–1951

CORINNE A. FAVROT
1880–1976

HENRY TARDY HART
1880–1950

JOSEPHINE H. HOLT (K.A. JO...
1873–1933

MABEL E. COOPER
1905–1936

1

GERVAIS FRERET FAVROT, SR. (K.A. VAIS)
1896–1987

2

CHARLOTTE FELDER
1912–1981

CLIFFORD FRERET FAVROT
1898–1989

AGNES MARS... GUTHRIE
1896–1986

JOAN FAVROT
1928–2006

CYRIL PAUL GEARY, JR. (K.A. CY)
1925–2008

INFANT
1936–1936

GERVAIS FRERET FAVROT, JR. (K.A. VAIS)

MANETTE JAQUELIN SUTHON
CA. 1927–2015

1

CLIFFORD F. FAVROT, JR.
1922–2010

2

KATHERINE LOUISE BOULET
1924–2006

The key at left explains several important abbreviations and symbols used throughout the chart. The principal family members covered in this book and their spouses are highlighted in boldface type.

A downward arrow indicates that the couple above had children, but that the names of those children have been omitted from the chart to save space.

Birth years of family members who are still living at the time of publication are omitted in order to protect their privacy.

In many cases, there is conflicting information about life dates, full names, and official spellings of the names of certain family members. The author made every effort to confirm such information using what seemed to be the most authoritative sources available.

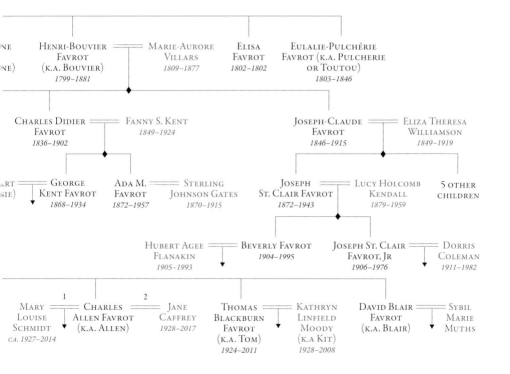

NE | HENRI-BOUVIER FAVROT (K.A. BOUVIER) *1799–1881* ══ MARIE-AURORE VILLARS *1809–1877* — ELISA FAVROT *1802–1802* — EULALIE-PULCHÉRIE FAVROT (K.A. PULCHERIE OR TOUTOU) *1803–1846*

NE)

CHARLES DIDIER FAVROT *1836–1902* ══ FANNY S. KENT *1849–1924* — JOSEPH-CLAUDE FAVROT *1846–1915* ══ ELIZA THERESA WILLIAMSON *1849–1919*

RT ══ GEORGE | KENT FAVROT
IE) | *1868–1934*

ADA M. FAVROT *1872–1957* ══ STERLING JOHNSON GATES *1870–1915*

JOSEPH ST. CLAIR FAVROT *1872–1943* ══ LUCY HOLCOMB KENDALL *1879–1959*

5 OTHER CHILDREN

HUBERT AGEE FLANAKIN *1905–1993* ══ BEVERLY FAVROT *1904–1995*

JOSEPH ST. CLAIR FAVROT, JR *1906–1976* ══ DORRIS COLEMAN *1911–1982*

1

MARY LOUISE SCHMIDT *CA. 1927–2014* ══ CHARLES ALLEN FAVROT (K.A. ALLEN)

2

══ JANE CAFFREY *1928–2017*

THOMAS BLACKBURN FAVROT (K.A. TOM) *1924–2011* ══ KATHRYN LINFIELD MOODY (K.A KIT) *1928–2008*

DAVID BLAIR FAVROT (K.A. BLAIR) ══ SYBIL MARIE MUTHS

INTRODUCTION

The Favrot family is among the oldest and most storied families in Louisiana, with a continuous presence there since 1728.* Indeed, the history of the Favrot family is virtually inseparable from that of Louisiana, from its early days as a struggling French colony, through its four decades under Spanish rule, to its brief retrocession to France and almost immediate purchase by the United States. The shared saga of Louisiana and the Favrots continues through the upheaval of the Civil War, the rigors of Reconstruction, and the development of the contemporary state, with its unique blend of American, French, and Afro-Caribbean cultures.

Although long associated with Louisiana, the Favrot family traces its origins to a rural part of eastern France now known as Franche-Comté. A mountainous region bordering Switzerland, it was one of the last bastions of feudalism in France, still relying heavily on a form of serfdom as late as the 1780s.[1] Feudal practices there were not definitively abolished until 1789, in the wake of the French

---

* Although Claude-Joseph Favrot returned to France permanently in the late 1760s, and his son, Pierre-Joseph, was in France temporarily during the 1770s, Pierre-Joseph's sister, Louise Favrot De Clouet, remained in Louisiana with her immediate family.

Revolution. Given its location near the juncture between traditionally Gallic and Germanic territories, the region has been frequently contested over many centuries, a circumstance that had great implications for the early Favrots.

Very little is known about specific Favrot family members before the late 1600s. The earliest Favrot clearly identified in the family papers was Simon, who was born in the mid-1500s in the village of Gellin in the Jura Mountains, just a few miles from the Swiss border.[2] Even today, Gellin is a tiny community—its population as of 2013 was only 228.[3] In 1575, Simon's son, Claude, was born in the nearby town of Mouthe. Claude married Claudine (or Claudie) Beschet, who, in 1604, gave birth to a son named Pierre. Sometime between 1625 and 1628, Pierre married Jeanne (or Jeannie) Besuchet. They had at least two children, one of whom was François, born in Mouthe in 1629. François married Jacqua (or Jacqueline) Philibert. They had five known sons, all born in Mouthe.[4]

The first section of this book begins with the story of Joseph-Claude Favrot, the youngest of François and Jacqueline's sons, who was born in 1668 and is the first person to be substantially documented in the Favrot Family Papers. Having developed an interest in mapmaking as a teenager, Joseph-Claude joined the army of King Louis XIV in 1690 as a cartographical engineer. He served in two wars: the Nine Years' War (1688–1697) and the War of the Spanish Succession (1701–1714), both of which pitted France against alliances of the other major European powers. These campaigns often exposed Joseph-Claude to great danger, as he traveled behind enemy lines to record the locations of fortifications and the natural features of potential battle sites. Through his distinguished military service and seemingly heartfelt devotion to the French monarch, Joseph-Claude set precedents for several generations of his descendants. His mapmaking skills and loyalty won the acclaim of his superiors, but he struggled to obtain fair compensation and sacrificed his health to grueling military campaigns, dying at the age of only 39.

The story continues with Joseph-Claude's son Claude-Joseph Favrot, who was born at Versailles and became an army cadet at the age of 22. It was he who, in 1728, brought the Favrot family name to the nascent Louisiana colony as an officer in the infantry of King Louis XV. Claude-Joseph served as commandant of several important garrisons in the new French "province," including those at Pointe

Coupée, Natchitoches, and Mobile. He was recognized for his bravery and skill in campaigns against Native American tribes and then against the British during the French and Indian War (1754–1763), the conflict that led to the transfer of Louisiana from France to Spain. Between campaigns, he married Louise-Elizabeth Bruslé, the daughter of one of the richest and most influential men in New Orleans, in the first of many unions between the Favrots and other prominent Louisiana families. Documents from the three decades that Claude-Joseph spent in the colony—he returned to France in the 1760s to seek treatment for his wife's cancer—illuminate the decline of French power in the New World.

Perhaps as a token of gratitude to Claude-Joseph, the governor of French Louisiana awarded his son, Pierre-Joseph, a nominal military commission as a cadet when he was only 18 months old. Pierre-Joseph was already a junior officer when the transfer of Louisiana to Spain in 1763 muddled his career prospects. In 1772, he traveled to France to resume his military service under French sovereignty, but soon became dissatisfied with what he considered unchallenging posts and a lack of promotion. In a pragmatic move, he successfully sought a military commission from the king of Spain, Charles III, and returned to Louisiana in 1779 as a captain in the Spanish army. Like many former French citizens of Louisiana, he adopted the Spanish version of his name, becoming known as Don Pedro José Favrot to his military colleagues and to Spanish officials.

Pierre-Joseph lived to see the retrocession of Louisiana to France—a development that he cheered—as well as the purchase of the colony by the United States and then the elevation of Louisiana to full statehood. Although his father had begun collecting the family's correspondence and important papers, it was Pierre-Joseph who established the tradition of rigorously gathering and preserving as many documents as possible for posterity. Papers from Pierre-Joseph's lifetime chronicle the global geopolitical conflicts that profoundly affected Louisiana in the late 18th century, and on a personal level, the Favrot family's earliest significant investments in real estate, including the Monte Vista plantation in West Baton Rouge and several properties in New Orleans.

At the dawn of the 19th century, during Louisiana's turbulent and rapid transitions from Spanish to French to American sovereignty, Pierre-Joseph resigned from the Spanish army and began his own transition from a military career to management of the family plantation. With the onset of the War of 1812, however, his sons Philogène and Louis enlisted in the U.S. Army, thus continuing the Favrot military tradition under a third nationality (Pierre-Joseph himself also participated in the conflict). Documents from this period reflect the family members' slow but steady Americanization as they began to learn English and took up arms to defend the young United States. The family faced a setback, however, when the young Philogène was killed in a duel, sending his mother and siblings into a lengthy period of mourning and soul-searching.

The Favrots remained a predominantly French-speaking family with strong emotional and cultural ties to France for several generations after Louisiana became part of the United States. They were also Southerners, plantation owners, and slaveholders, however, and when the Civil War began, it was inevitable that Henri Mortimer Favrot (a son of Louis who had already had military training) would fight on behalf of the Confederacy. His diaries attest to the "fog of war"—and the unreliability of mid-19th-century communications—as the family attempted to assess conflicting, incomplete, and presumably biased news about the progress of the war. Henri was ultimately appointed as the historian of Louisiana's troops, and traveled to Richmond near the end of the war to "collect and digest" records related to their service. His diary entries and letters to his wife, Célestine Dubroca Favrot, written during that trip, starkly depict the war's devastation, and convey the emotional toll of Henri's lengthy separation from his family.

The second of the three main sections of this book examines the domestic life of the Favrot family beginning in the very late 18th century—there is little documentation of personal matters before that time—as well as the family's engagement in civic affairs in the 19th and 20th centuries. As one would expect, the careers and activities of male Favrot family members dominate the archives, but this section draws attention to some letters and journal entries that illuminate the views of female family members on both private and public matters. This section also covers a few family members who are outside of the main lineage that is the focus of this book, but whose professional activities were especially notable.

The section begins with a discussion of Pierre-Joseph's primer for his sons, which was written in 1798 and is one of the most intriguing items in the entire Favrot collection. As much a moral guide as an instructional manual, the document articulated Pierre-Joseph's views on the proper conduct of a gentleman, general areas of knowledge with which young men should be familiar, and even effective swordsmanship. The manual provided a foundation for subsequent generations' education and civic involvement.

The Favrots' plantation in West Baton Rouge, known as Monte Vista, was the hub of family life in the 19th century. The second chapter in this section traces the history of the plantation and examines the family's ownership of slaves. Other themes in the chapter on 19th-century domestic life include illness—a frequent topic in family correspondence—and religion. While, as French Creoles—descendants of Louisiana-born Frenchmen—most Favrot family members belonged to the Roman Catholic Church, there were some notable exceptions.

The second section concludes with a chapter about the family's civic and domestic life in the 20th century. Among the numerous family members who were involved in politics and government was George K. Favrot, who was first elected to the U.S. Congress in 1906 and served several non-consecutive terms, despite having admitted to fatally shooting a doctor who had allegedly insulted George's wife—an act for which a grand jury refused to indict him. Leo M. Favrot, a son of Henri Mortimer Favrot and brother of Charles, made his mark as an influential advocate for the reform of "Negro" education in the American South. He held positions with the state governments of Arkansas and Louisiana before being appointed as a field agent for the General Education Board based in New York. Leo's efforts to improve education for African Americans was especially remarkable given that he was the son of a slaveholder, and his work caused great consternation among more conservative factions in his home state.

This section describes the development of "Favrotville," an enclave of houses in Covington, Louisiana, owned by various members of the Favrot family over the past century. It also traces the family's many connections to Tulane University, including the service of four different members on the Tulane Board of Administrators and the family's long history of generous financial support of the university.

The third and final major section of the book focuses on the Favrot family's significant contributions in the realms of architecture and real estate development. Charles Favrot, having received a degree in mechanical engineering from

Louisiana State University, left the family homestead at Monte Vista in 1885 to become an apprentice to his cousin by marriage, the well-established architect James Freret, in New Orleans. After working with Freret—and living with his family—for three years, Charles went off to Cornell University for a graduate degree. He then returned to New Orleans and married Freret's daughter Beatrice, thus linking the Favrot and Freret names in the history of Louisiana architecture.

In 1895, Charles entered into a professional partnership with fellow architect L.A. Livaudais, who also came from a venerable Louisiana family. The firm of Favrot & Livaudais went on to design many exceptional buildings throughout the state, including the Hibernia Bank tower and the New Orleans Cotton Exchange, both in the city's Central Business District; the City Hall in Lake Charles, Louisiana; and literally dozens of elegant houses in the Uptown areas of New Orleans. Charles Favrot also played an important role in the development of New Orleans as chairman of the City Planning and Zoning Commission.

In 1905, Charles and his brother Henry Louis Favrot, along with five other investors, purchased a group of lots in Uptown New Orleans, which they then developed as an exclusive residential enclave called Richmond Place. The firm of Favrot & Livaudais designed the overall layout of the block, as well as several of the individual houses within it, including one each for Charles and Henry. Richmond Place not only marked the Favrots' first venture into large-scale real estate development, but also eclipsed the Monte Vista plantation as the epicenter of the extended family.

Charles's son H. Mortimer ("Morty") Favrot, Sr., apprenticed with his father's firm and helped to engineer an expansion of its scope to include projects in Central America and in Miami (which was, not coincidentally, the winter home of the family of Helen Parkhurst, the woman he loved and eventually married). Following the retirement or death of the original partners, Morty became the senior partner and oversaw the firm's transition to Favrot & Reed (later Favrot, Reed, Mathes & Bergman), which undertook numerous significant projects in its own right, including Tulane University's McAlister Auditorium. That project reflected the broad influence of the Favrot family by the mid-20th century—the auditorium was designed by the firm of Morty Favrot, built by the contracting firm owned by his brother Gervais Favrot, and funded through a generous donation by his second cousin, Amelie McAlister Upshur. Initially, the auditorium building also included a specific room set aside for the storage of the Favrot Family Papers.

The third section concludes with Morty's son, H. Mortimer ("Tim") Favrot, Jr., who studied architecture at Tulane, in Fontainebleau, France, and at Harvard. As an undergraduate he spent several summers working as a draftsman in his father's office. Upon graduation from Tulane, he served two years in the Air Force before returning to New Orleans and his father's firm. It was in that period that he met and married Kay Gibbons. Following graduate school at Harvard, Tim again returned to New Orleans and began working with the prominent architecture firm of Curtis & Davis, later establishing his own practice. In 1964, he rejoined the successor to his father's firm, which accordingly became Mathes, Bergman, Favrot & Associates. Shortly thereafter, however, Tim embarked on his first real estate development project, and in 1970, he formed the architecture and development firm of Favrot & Shane with fellow architect Henry Shane. The firm went on to develop thousands of units of housing in the New Orleans metropolitan area and elsewhere.

The epilogue provides a brief overview of the new generations of Favrots who are beginning to make their mark, while summarizing the remarkable story of a venerable family and its integral connection to Louisiana, the place that it has called home for nearly three centuries.

SECTION I

MILITARY TRADITIONS

CHAPTER 1

ORIGINS IN FRANCE

Franche-Comté, the French region where Joseph-Claude Favrot was born, has a complicated history. Once part of the Kingdom of Burgundy, it was incorporated into the Holy Roman Empire in the 11th century and eventually came under Spanish rule. French King Louis XIV (1638–1715) occupied the area in 1668, the year of Joseph-Claude's birth. The province was soon briefly returned to Spain, but Louis invaded once again during the Franco-Dutch War of 1672–1678. France gained permanent possession of the territory through the Treaty of Nijmegen, which ended that war.

The fluid sovereignty of the Franche-Comté area presaged the changing national identities and loyalties that later would define the Favrot family's experiences in the New World. Yet there is no evidence that Joseph-Claude ever had doubts about his own political allegiance. He was a Frenchman who remained loyal to king and country even as he came to feel that his unique contributions as an officer in the French army were underappreciated. He routinely sacrificed his safety, his health, and ultimately his life in the service of France.

Joseph-Claude's steadfast patriotism is not surprising given that he came of age as the Bourbon dynasty reached the acme of its power. By the early 1680s, when Joseph-Claude was in his teens, France was the world's preeminent nation both politically and culturally. Despite the country's strong position, however, Louis XIV remained wary of potential rivals. Among these were the Dutch Prince William of Orange (1650–1702), who was busy plotting an invasion of England, and the Germanic Habsburg monarchs, including Louis's own cousin, the Holy Roman Emperor Leopold I (1640–1705).

In September 1688, the French army launched the first in a series of assaults on German towns and fortifications along the Rhine River. Thus began what came to be known as the Nine Years' War, which pitted France against the "Grand Alliance" consisting of the Holy Roman Empire, the Dutch Republic, and England, which by then was under the rule of Prince William of Orange, who soon assumed the English throne as King William III.

It was during this war that young Joseph-Claude Favrot built his reputation in engineering and cartography, a skill he had begun to develop as a teenager.[1] He joined King Louis's army in August 1690, and immediately went to work preparing a map of the "Weille plain," an area including the present-day town of Weil am Rhein, situated at the southwestern corner of Germany and bordering both France and Switzerland. In a letter accompanying the finished map that he sent to the Marquis de Louvois (1641–1691), the French secretary of state for war, Joseph-Claude explained that he had worked "day and night, hurriedly" to complete the task. He meticulously documented the locations of natural features such as woods, swamps, gorges, and rivers, as well as all manmade structures, including roads, bridges, and military camps. He also diagrammed the potential formations of the French and enemy armies in the event of battle.[2]

Favrot family lore holds that Joseph-Claude served under Sébastien Le Prestre de Vauban (1633–1707), an innovative military engineer and strategist. The timing of Favrot's association with Vauban is unknown, but it likely coincided with the Nine Years' War, in which Vauban played an active role. Several documents in the Favrot Family Papers also state that Joseph-Claude assisted in the construction of Vauban's design for the fortifications at Verdun, a city in northeastern France that later became famous as the site of a consequential battle during World War I.[3] Although Vauban drew the initial designs for Verdun in 1670, when Joseph-Claude was only a toddler, construction continued fitfully for more than a century, so it is possible that Favrot did contribute to the project at some point during his military service. Unfortunately, the family papers do not provide conclusive evidence of his role, though a portrait of Joseph-Claude shows him pointing toward a fortification in the distance, as if claiming some responsibility for the structure.[4]

According to an entry in a memoir dating to 1695, Joseph-Claude had already spent several years making cartographical sketches of eastern France, Luxembourg, and nearby regions before joining the king's army. He took pride in the scope of his ongoing mapmaking, stating, "I do not believe that there has ever been published a topographic work covering so great an expanse of territory as do these maps, and those that I propose to make." After joining the army, in addition to producing maps of areas as far away as Flanders (in present-day Belgium), he surveyed an extensive stretch of the Rhine River running from Hüningue, a French town across the river from the Weille plain, to Koblenz (in present-day Germany), a distance of nearly 250 miles.

The memoir also reveals some details of Joseph-Claude's cartographic technique. He was careful, for instance, to produce maps of a convenient size, citing an example that was "about five feet square, a fair size and suitable for carrying into camp and for opening in a room." He also ensured that adjacent maps included areas of substantial overlap, thus avoiding the confusion that could arise if the terrain at the edge of a given map proved to be critical to a military campaign.[5] In a letter written much later, after Joseph-Claude's death, Félix Le Pelletier de La Houssaye (1663–1723), a regional representative of the French crown, claimed that Favrot had had a secret method of calculating heights that allowed him to record in a half-hour "what another man would require a day to do."[6]

Several maps by Joseph-Claude Favrot are extant and maintained by the *Service historique de l'armée de terre* at Vincennes, France. Two of them are reproduced in Volume I of the published translations of the Favrot Family Papers.[7] They are beautifully detailed works, with neatly lettered labels and extensive notes in the margins. They employ simple but effective graphic devices to convey changes in elevation, relative densities of trees, and other landscape features. The utility of such skillfully drawn maps for military leaders around the turn of the 18th century is easy to understand even today.

During the war, in 1693, Joseph-Claude married Françoise Bouvier† in Paris. The wedding took place at the Church of Saint-Sulpice,[8] which still stands in the city's sixth *arrondissement*. Françoise presumably remained in Paris as Joseph-Claude traveled to and from the city during ongoing military campaigns, though the couple apparently spent at least some time at Versailles, where their son Claude-Joseph was born and baptized in 1701.[9]

The Nine Years' War concluded in September 1697 with the Treaty of Ryswick, under which France retained the Alsace province but renounced claims to the territory it had occupied east of the Rhine. To Louis XIV's distress, the treaty officially recognized William III and his wife, Mary II (1662–1694), as the king and queen of England. On the other hand, the treaty also legitimized France's claim to Saint-Domingue, the western portion of the island of Hispaniola (corresponding to the modern nation of Haiti), which would prove central to France's colonial activities over the following century.

A New, Wider Conflict

Unfortunately for Europe, the Nine Years' War failed to settle the most burning political question of the era, which was who should succeed the ailing, childless King of Spain, Charles II (1661–1700). Although he was a Habsburg, and thus closely connected to the Holy Roman Emperor Leopold I, Charles ultimately named his great-nephew Philip (1683–1746), the grandson of Louis XIV, as his successor. Because Philip was also in the line of succession for the French throne, other European rulers feared the potential creation of a superpower through a future union of Spain and France.

Following King Charles's death in 1700, the British, the Austrians, and the Dutch reconstituted the Grand Alliance with the goal of thwarting any such union. Louis's refusal to remove his grandson Philip from the French succes-

---

† Françoise's maiden name, Bouvier, appears several times in the Favrot family tree as a male given name. Thomas B. Favrot, who began researching his family's genealogy in the 1960s, was understandably eager to investigate possible familial connections between Françoise and the ancestors of Jacqueline Bouvier Kennedy Onassis. Neither he nor this author was able to confirm any such relationship.

sion led the alliance to declare war on France in 1702. The War of the Spanish Succession soon embroiled most of the European continent. Fighting raged for eight years with few decisive military achievements on either side, but by 1710, France had exhausted its finances, while in England partisan politics were weakening the country's commitment to the conflict. The war officially ended with the signing of several accords, collectively known as the Treaty of Utrecht, in 1713, which recognized Philip as King Philip V of Spain in exchange for his renunciation of any right to the French throne.

Joseph-Claude Favrot continued his vital service as a cartographer to the French army during the brief respite between these two wars and in the early years of the War of the Spanish Succession. His intrepid surveying efforts were facilitated by his fluency in German, which enabled him to infiltrate enemy territory overtly. In a letter to the new secretary of state for war, Michel Chamillart (1652–1721), written in 1702, he reported that he had successfully crossed a bridge over the Weise River [sic, presumably the Wiese River] even though "the road was full of officers and wagons of the enemy, who were coming from Basel [Switzerland]." He subsequently engaged in reconnaissance of the area on the other side of the river, determining that the woods there could provide some protection for French forces in the event of battle, though there was a fort that could pose a threat. He noted that he had personally taken prisoners who had given him information about crossing the river. Lest his superiors assume that the Swiss would remain neutral in any armed conflict at their doorstep, Joseph-Claude's letter included a candid warning: "I can assure Your Honor that the inhabitants of Basel like the enemy better than they do us."[10]

In February 1703, Joseph-Claude was assigned to work directly with Claude-Louis-Hector, the Marquis (later Duke) de Villars (1653–1734), one of Louis's most valued generals and a former ambassador to the Austrian court.[11] Villars had been given the command of all French forces in Germany following his victory over Holy Roman Empire troops in the Battle of Friedlingen in October 1702. Favrot's close association with such an important military leader suggests that he was held in high regard by senior officers.

Growing Frustration with Military Life

While all indications are that Joseph-Claude remained steadfastly loyal to the king and to his military superiors throughout his life, by 1703 he was becoming frustrated with what he regarded as inadequate professional recognition and compensation. In a letter to Chamillart dated May 25 of that year, he made his case for a promotion and other military honors. He began by citing as evidence of his talents the fact that the Marquis de Villars had selected Joseph-Claude's map of the German town of Trier over a similar one made by a group of building engineers. "This proves to Your Honor," he wrote, "that fortification engineers cannot do the work that I do. Yet my work comes easily to me."[12]

He went on to remind Chamillart of the unique dangers he faced on his frequent forays behind enemy lines, without the protection of French troops. In an attachment to the May 25 letter, he related his experiences as a prisoner of war back in 1691, when he was held in a German prison at Rottweil for 14 months. His captors searched him and found documents that described his cartographical skills, whereupon the German troops' leader, Prince Louis of Baden (1655–1707), attempted to recruit him to perform similar services on behalf of the Holy Roman Emperor. When Joseph-Claude refused, he was given only bread and water for the remainder of his captivity.[13]

In the same letter to Chamillart, Joseph-Claude not only protested his failure to be promoted, but also explicitly asked to be awarded the Order of Saint Louis, a military honor established by Louis XIV in 1693 as a means of recognizing outstanding officers who had served the king for at least ten years. "The Order of Saint Louis, which I ask for in order to make my work easier, was given to five hundred people who did not deserve it as much as I do," he protested. "If all the servants of the King worked as hard as I do without rest, very few of them would persist in their work."[14]

Joseph-Claude focused on matters of compensation in a subsequent letter to Chamillart in July. "Your Honor thinks that I have a large income. . .," he wrote. "Yet I assure My Lord that I have no bread for my work." To support his request for higher pay, he attached a general summary of income and expenses, the latter including 1,500 *livres* (the *livre* being the major unit of currency in France at the time) "for five or six horses" and 300 *livres* "for three servants during the campaign."[15] The fact that Joseph-Claude had servants suggests that he enjoyed a relatively high military status even if he did feel underpaid.

By the summer of 1703, Joseph-Claude's complaints had drawn a backlash. "The manner in which I took the liberty to show Your Honor the amount of my necessary expenses did not seem to me to merit such a harsh response as I received on the 23rd of July," he wrote to Chamillart on September 2.[16] By then, he and his wife had as many as five children,[17] and he was feeling the economic pressures of supporting a large family.

Over the next several years, Joseph-Claude continued to write to Chamillart, providing detailed accounts of enemy camps, battle sites, and the physical geography of the theater of war. He also regularly reminded the cabinet minister of his tireless devotion to duty and continuing dissatisfaction with his income. By August 1706, Joseph-Claude held the rank of "reformed half-pay captain," but claimed that he still did not receive a salary commensurate with his skills and position.[18] (The marriage contract of Joseph-Claude's widow to her second husband, written in 1710, indicates that Joseph-Claude died with the rank of captain,[19] but subsequent legal documents refer to him as a brigadier, suggesting that he may have received a posthumous promotion.[20]) Complaints about insufficient or delayed compensation became a persistent theme throughout the military careers of several generations of Favrots.

Succumbing to the Rigors of War

As the war ground on, Joseph-Claude's health declined. More than a quarter of a century of near-constant movement, coupled with the inevitable privations of military campaigns—not to mention the stress that he surely endured while on clandestine missions behind enemy lines—had taken its toll. On October 28, 1707, Joseph-Claude died of an uncertain illness at a site near Hüningue, France,[21] not far from the "Weille plain" he had mapped for the army 17 years earlier.

A remarkably detailed inventory of Favrot's estate, conducted on December 31, 1709, offers insights into his family's social position and way of life. The most valuable single item was a tapestry made by the famed Aubusson weavers. Other notable possessions included a number of upholstered walnut chairs and "seven oval paintings done on canvas in their gilt wooden frames representing the King, the princes and the other lords of the court, another small painting also done on canvas representing the Holy Family, another painting also done on canvas representing Moses and the burning bush in its gilt wooden frame. . ."[22]

While the estate inventory suggests that the Favrot family enjoyed a comfortable household, Joseph-Claude's unexpected death at the age of only 39 years left his widow and children in a state of financial hardship.[23] In 1710, however, Françoise gained a degree of financial security when she married Joseph-Thomas Dondel, Sieur de Longprès. In addition to the dowry that Dondel brought to the marriage, Françoise received from her sister the substantial sum of 10,000 *livres* as a wedding present. The marriage contract also provided for the care and education of each of Françoise's children until the age of 18.[24]

Joseph-Claude Favrot was not the first member of the family to pursue a military career, but his life is the first to be relatively well documented. By virtue of his unique talents and his direct association with several of France's greatest military leaders, he set professional precedents for several generations of his descendants. The Favrot family military tradition had begun.

CHAPTER 2

EARLY YEARS IN LOUISIANA

Claude-Joseph Favrot, born at Versailles in 1701, was not yet six years old when his father died in the line of duty. Although he was the youngest[1] of Joseph-Claude and Françoise's five children,[2] it was he who eventually would carry on the family's reputation—and bring the Favrot name to the New World.

Claude-Joseph had four siblings, including two sisters, one of whom became a nun and later the abbess of a convent. His other sister never married, and presumably had no children. His oldest brother "married below himself" and was supposedly "disinherited" before moving to Germany.[3] Given the tight restrictions on disinheriting a child under the *Coutume de Paris*, or Custom of Paris, which dictated legal standards for marriage and inheritance in France at the time, it is possible that this disinheritance was only figurative, but there is no doubt that the older son had fallen out of favor. Several documents indicate that there was one other son in the family, but provide very little information about him.[4]

The assertion that Claude-Joseph's oldest brother had "married below himself" attests to the Favrots' high social standing. So, too, does a document dated September 15, 1723, certifying that "M. the Chevalier de Favrot"—referring to Claude-Joseph, then aged 21—had enlisted in a military company as a "cadet and volunteer."[5] The term *chevalier*, roughly the French equivalent of the English "knight," was a title typically given to a nobleman in military service, albeit one of minor rank.[6] The document also noted that Claude-Joseph had no formal assignment and was free to withdraw from his military duties whenever he wished, as long as he had his commandant's approval. These stipulations suggest that the initial "enlistment" was little more than a sinecure.

Before long, however, Claude-Joseph apparently had ambitions beyond such light and revocable service. He went on to serve for seven years in the "Battigny [*sic*, probably Bassigny] regiment,"[7] and in 1727, he obtained written permission from his mother to "contract marriage with whomever and in whatever country he shall think fit."[8] The need for such a document implies that the young man was considering opportunities outside of France, presumably a military assignment in one of the colonies.

In August 1732, Claude-Joseph received a commission from King Louis XV as a second lieutenant in the infantry assigned to "the province of Louisiana."[9] The exact date of his arrival in the colony is unknown. Nearly all of the relevant documents in the Favrot Family Papers reflect the assumption that he landed that same year, but there are two critical items that suggest he had already been in Louisiana for four years when he received that particular commission from the king. Claude-Joseph's personal file in the *Archives nationales d'outre-mer*, the Archives of the Colonies, indicates that he "arrived in Louisiana" in 1728, which would have been just a year after he obtained his mother's permission to marry outside of France. Corroborating that assertion is a letter written in 1733 by the then-commandant of Louisiana, Jean-Baptiste Le Moyne, Sieur de Bienville (1680–1767), which stated that Chevalier Favrot had "served five years as a cadet in the colony during the war with the Natchez, in which he performed marvels."[10] Based on these key documents, this book accepts 1728 as the year of Claude-Joseph's arrival in Louisiana. Regardless of the exact date, he reached Louisiana during a critical phase in its history.

Origins of French Louisiana

The colonization of Louisiana had begun as a complement to the French presence in Canada. With English settlements entrenched along the Atlantic Coast of North America, and a vast Spanish empire spanning from South America to what is now the southwestern United States, the French dreamed of creating a buffer colony stretching from the Saint Lawrence River basin, through the Mississippi River Valley, to the Gulf of Mexico. By laying claim to the lower Mississippi Valley, France hoped not only to thwart the colonial ambitions of two of its greatest rivals, but also to establish a naval base to help protect its sugar colonies in the West Indies.

In 1698, Louis XIV assigned the Canadian-born Pierre Le Moyne, Sieur d'Iberville (1661–1706), to lead an expedition to secure the mouth of the Mississippi for France. Over the course of several years, Iberville established a succession of forts that were the earliest permanent European settlements along the central Gulf Coast. Iberville appointed the Sieur de Sauvolle (ca. 1671–1701) as the first commandant of the fledgling colony, which was named Louisiana in honor of the king. Upon Sauvolle's death in 1701, Bienville, who was Iberville's younger brother and also born in French Canada, became the commandant and *de facto* governor at the tender age of 21.

The new colony proved to be a considerable drain on the French treasury, which was already hard-pressed by the wars on the European mainland. The Gulf Coast's poor soil inhibited agricultural production, and at the time the colony offered few natural resources to offset the expense of maintaining a presence there. In 1712, just three years before his death, Louis XIV decided to convert Louisiana into a proprietary colony—a private business enterprise operating under a royal charter. That venture proved equally unsuccessful, so in 1717, the Duke of Orléans—acting as regent for the new king, Louis XV, then a minor—created a joint-stock company called the Company of the West, which later expanded to become the Company of the Indies. A disastrous scheme to pay down the French national debt by selling shares in the company led to a whirlwind of speculative investment later known as the Mississippi Bubble, which burst in 1720, precipitating stock market crashes in France and other countries.

Louisiana limped along under the management of the Company of the Indies until 1731, when Louis XV dissolved the company's charter and restored the colony to royal control. Bienville, by then living in France, was appointed governor, returning to Louisiana in 1733. Although lingering animosities between Canadian- and French-born settlers continued to pose sociopolitical challenges, under Bienville's leadership the colony gradually achieved a degree of economic and administrative stability for the first time.

Military Service in the French Colony

It was during this period of transition from private to royal governance that Claude-Joseph Favrot arrived in Louisiana. His timing was auspicious. More than three decades after its founding, the colony was finally at least marginally viable. Moreover, as Claude-Joseph would soon learn, it offered opportunities for an ambitious military officer to prove himself in battle.

Claude-Joseph's first specific documented assignment in the New World came in 1734, when Bienville made him commandant of Pointe Coupée and the Tunica post, both relatively isolated settlements about 50 miles upriver from Baton Rouge.[11] Such peripheral outposts had become critical to the security of the colony, which faced near-constant threats from certain Native American tribes, especially the Natchez and later the Chickasaw. Meanwhile, the French were cultivating alliances with other tribes, including the Choctaw, which would prove valuable as rivalries with other European colonial powers flared over the coming decades.

By 1735, the French, with the help of the Choctaw, had nearly wiped out the Natchez, and were preparing to launch a major campaign against the Chickasaw. In March 1736, Bienville amassed more than 500 troops, including Claude-Joseph Favrot, in preparation for an assault on a cluster of Chickasaw camps in what is now northern Mississippi.[12] The battle plan called for Bienville's forces to attack from the south, while a contingent of French troops from the Illinois region would launch a coordinated attack from the north. The plan failed. The northern wave of troops, arriving at the site in late March, unsuccessfully attacked a well-defended

Chickasaw village, incurring devastating casualties. The southern wave of troops, joined by several hundred Choctaw warriors, did not arrive until two months later. Their assault on another Chickasaw village was also disastrous, and they soon retreated.

Although the Chickasaw Campaign of 1736 resulted in a costly and embarrassing defeat for the French, for Claude-Joseph Favrot personally it was a career milestone. Wounded in action,[13] he apparently performed bravely during the difficult battle. He was rewarded with a promotion to full lieutenant in October of that year.[14] Perhaps more importantly, the experience prepared him for subsequent assignments in which his familiarity with Native American customs and military strategies would prove valuable.

In 1735, between his initial assignment at Tunica and Pointe Coupée and his participation in the Chickasaw Campaign, Claude-Joseph found time to marry Louise-Elizabeth Bruslé, daughter of one of the richest men in New Orleans. Legal witnesses to the wedding included Bienville and his nephew, Gilles-Augustin Payen de Noyan (1705–1758), who was listed on the marriage certificate as mayor of the city.[15] The marriage to a wealthy local woman not only enhanced Claude-Joseph's financial and social position, but also firmly anchored the Favrot family to New Orleans for the first time.

In accordance with the Custom of Paris, the couple entered into a marriage contract in advance of the wedding ceremony. The document listed both the bride's and the groom's parents by name and affirmed that the parents consented to the union—in Claude-Joseph's case, the blanket permission he had obtained from his mother before coming to Louisiana presumably served as proof of such consent. The contract also enumerated the dowry to be provided by the bride's parents, including a fixed annual income of more than 176 *livres* derived from earnings on a Parisian municipal bond, as well as an advance payment of "2,000 *livres* in cash, furniture, linens, wearing apparel, and cattle, which will be delivered to the said future husband on the eve of the wedding." Under the terms of the contract, half of that dowry would become "part of the community property" of the couple, while the other half would be held in escrow "for the children that may be born of the future marriage." At the same time, Claude-Joseph would bring a dower of 2,000 *livres* to the marriage, once again with the stipulation that it would remain intact for the benefit of the couple's future children. Such provisions were in keeping with French legal custom, which sought to secure the wellbeing of the offspring of a marriage involving people of means.[16]

Following the Chickasaw Campaign, Claude-Joseph resumed command of the Tunica post. The few extant family papers from the late 1730s make no mention of his wife, but it is likely that she remained in New Orleans during that time. The couple's first child, a daughter named Louise, was born in the city in 1737.

By 1739, the king and Bienville were determined to try again to conquer or destroy the Chickasaw nation. Toward that end, Noyan, the New Orleans mayor, ordered Claude-Joseph to travel by boat to the Illinois territory to pick up a load of supplies for use in the new campaign. Noyan's highly detailed instructions dictated the precise complement of people who were to accompany him: "one sergeant, thirty-six privates, ten Indians, and twenty-six Negroes." Such a voyage was risky, exposing the crew to potentially hostile Native American tribes along the way. Somewhat ominously, Noyan's orders urged Claude-Joseph to "exercise the utmost diligence during the trip and in loading provisions."[17]

Bienville, still chastened by the calamitous 1736 conflict, sought to bolster his chances in the new campaign by building a new fort near the Chickasaw stronghold and assembling a significantly larger force—roughly 1,200 French troops plus 2,400 warriors drawn from their Native American allies. The campaign was hampered, however, by widespread illness, coupled with heavy attrition among the Native Americans. The French-led contingent engaged the Chickasaw in several battles, but the results were inconclusive. A face-saving peace treaty between the French and the Chickasaw was signed in 1740. The intensity and frequency of conflicts subsequently diminished, though a degree of hostility lingered.

No further documentation of Claude-Joseph's 1739 journey to the Illinois territory is extant, but he must have completed the assignment successfully, because in February of 1740, he was placed in command of the French garrison at La Balize. Located near the mouth of the Mississippi, La Balize was a remote but vital post—the Louisiana colony's first line of defense against infiltration by other naval powers. Here again, Claude-Joseph apparently performed admirably, as he went on to command five other garrisons over the following decade and a half: first at Pointe Coupée again, then at English Turn (a few miles downriver from

New Orleans), followed by Natchitoches (in the northern part of the present-day state of Louisiana), Mobile, and finally New Orleans. In 1750, while serving in Natchitoches, he was promoted to captain.[18] The previous year, his wife had given birth to their second child, Pierre-Joseph Favrot, born a dozen years after their daughter Louise.

The relative calm that prevailed in the Louisiana colony following the treaty with the Chickasaw evaporated in the late 1740s, when English colonists began settling in the upper Ohio River Valley under a land grant from the British crown. The French, who claimed the Ohio territory as their own, saw the English incursion as a direct threat to the sovereignty of New France. Recognizing the potential for a major new conflict, the European powers established a commission to address the territorial disputes in North America, but it failed to reach a resolution.

The French and Indian War and the Decline of French Power

In the early 1750s, the French launched a concerted effort to protect their claim to the Ohio region through a build-up of troops and the construction of a series of forts there. Inevitably, French and British soldiers began to encounter each other with greater frequency. On May 28, 1754, British troops under the command of Lieutenant Colonel George Washington (1732–1799), the future U.S. president, accompanied by a small number of Native Americans, engaged a group of French Canadian soldiers in a very brief battle in what is now southwestern Pennsylvania. Known as the Battle of Jumonville Glen, the seemingly inconsequential skirmish is now widely regarded as the opening conflict of the French and Indian War, so named because the French were, by then, closely allied with several major Native American tribes against the British. The North American war would soon escalate into a trans-European conflict that came to be called the Seven Years' War.

During the lead-up to the war, Claude-Joseph Favrot was an experienced officer in his early 50s. His excellent reputation earned him the immediate confidence of the new colonial governor, Louis Billouart, Chevalier de Kerlérec (1704–1770), who assumed office in 1753 and was responsible for Claude-Joseph's assignment as commandant of the New Orleans garrison that same year. With trouble brewing in the Ohio Valley, however, Kerlérec soon decided that Claude-Joseph's services were more badly needed elsewhere.

In August 1754, Kerlérec dispatched Claude-Joseph to lead a vital convoy of reinforcing troops from New Orleans to the Illinois garrison, which was under the command of Major Jean-Jacques Macarty Mactigue (1698–1793?). The orders came in the form of a lengthy and remarkably detailed letter with instructions regarding tactical matters, crew welfare, rules of engagement with other parties, and even religious duty. The letter encouraged Claude-Joseph, for instance, "to have prayers said regularly at night and in the morning," and "to be inflexible, to all possible degree, against certain habitual blasphemers." Despite the letter's almost parental tone, Kerlérec clearly had faith in Claude-Joseph's abilities, writing that "[t]he proofs of experience and zeal given by M. de Favrot on many occasions in the King's service are known in the whole colony. . . . I know that I may rely entirely on his judgment in all unexpected circumstances."[19]

There is a two-and-a-half-year gap in the Favrot Family Papers after Kerlérec's letter. It is therefore unknown whether Claude-Joseph returned to New Orleans immediately after the expedition of 1754 or stayed in the Illinois territory. The latter scenario is more likely, however, given that in February 1757, Macarty Mactigue assigned him to command another supply convoy, this time leaving from Illinois and headed to Fort Duquesne, on the site of present-day Pittsburgh.[20]

Macarty Mactigue's orders, like those of Noyan and Kerlérec previously, were very specific, including instructions regarding the exact amount of gunpowder and lead to be carried, as well as the timing of the ammunition's distribution among the crew. One section of the letter offers some insights into the fluid relationships among the French and the various Native American tribes at the time:

> Should M. de Favrot meet some Indian nations, he shall treat them in a friendly manner, especially the Chaouanon [Shawnee] Indians. He may even give them some little presents and tell them that I would have been pleased to see them here. He will have them smoke the calumet [peace pipe] with the Illinois Indians who might be in his convoy. Should he be able to bring some chiefs or prominent leaders on his return, that

would contribute to the welfare and tranquility of our residents. M. de Favrot will also make peace with the Flat Heads, who ask for peace with earnestness.[21]

In April 1758, when Claude-Joseph was stationed in the French settlement of New Chartres, in present-day southern Illinois, he received orders to lead another mission to investigate the British presence "above the falls of the river of the Cherokees [the Ohio River]." Should he discover any British troops building fortifications, he was instructed to engage them in battle and destroy the fortifications if possible. Furthermore, in what appears to have been a completely unrelated directive—as well as an indication that old enmities often endure—he was instructed to "strike a blow at the Chickasaws" by attacking their camp near the falls.[22]

The mission apparently was not a success. In June 1758, Claude-Joseph wrote to Kerlérec with an account of the expedition, and while that letter is lost, Kerlérec's response suggests that the Native Americans in Claude-Joseph's crew had somehow sabotaged the mission. His wording serves as a reminder that, despite the warm diplomatic relations between the French and many native tribes at the time, the former continued to view the latter as barbarians. "I can see better than ever now that it is hardly possible for you to expect to succeed when one is dependent on the whims of the red man," Kerlérec wrote, adding that "the savage [is] naturally deceitful." The letter also indicated that Claude-Joseph was seeking a transfer away from the area as soon as possible, but Kerlérec assured him that he was still needed in Illinois, and asked him to be patient.[23]

Claude-Joseph was back in New Orleans no later than May of 1761, when his daughter, Louise, married Alexandre De Clouet.[24] De Clouet, a lieutenant in the colonial military, had arrived from France in 1758 and, like Claude-Joseph, was to be the forebear of a distinguished Louisiana lineage.[25] The marriage contract between Alexandre and Louise is the first extant document in the Favrot Family Papers to mention slave ownership within the family. The contract stated that Louise's maternal grandmother, Marthe Frémont Bruslé, was giving the bride "a little mulatto girl named Jeanne." At the same time, the future husband was listed as bringing the substantial sum of 31,000 *livres* to the marriage, along with two

African slaves and two Native American slaves, among other "property."[26]

Claude-Joseph's last known military mission was in September of 1761, when he was charged with leading a detachment of troops to pursue and capture 15 deserters from the garrison at La Balize. The fugitives had stolen a merchant ship and escaped into the Gulf of Mexico. To fulfill his orders, Claude-Joseph was given command of the naval vessel *Le Cerf,* though another officer with more experience on the open sea was given direct responsibility for navigation and maneuvers. Unfortunately, the results of the mission are unknown.

The French and their Native American allies had scored a number of important victories against the British in the early days of the full-fledged war, but by 1758, the tide had turned. Over the following two years, the British took the Ohio territory and defeated the French in their stronghold of Quebec. New France, once a monolithic colony spanning from maritime Canada to the Gulf Coast, had been broken to pieces. Although the French and Indian War was effectively over by 1760, the official end did not come until the signing of the Treaty of Paris on February 10, 1763. By then, Britain and its Germanic allies had also claimed victory in the war on the European mainland.

The End of French Control of Louisiana

The key provisions of the Treaty of Paris entailed profound geopolitical shifts that changed the course of North American history and left French inhabitants of the continent in shock. Britain won possession of Canada and all French territory east of the Mississippi River, while Spain—an ally of France in the Seven Years' War—took possession of the Louisiana territory west of the Mississippi. Ostensibly, the latter provision was intended to compensate Spain for its losses during the war (only later did the world learn that France had already promised to give Louisiana to Spain in a secret agreement known as the Treaty of Fontainebleau, signed in November 1762). To the colonists, the fact that Louisiana was ceded to a country on the *losing* side of the European conflict revealed how little France valued the colony it had struggled to nurture for more than six decades.

In September of 1763, as Spain was reorganizing the formerly French troops in Louisiana, Claude-Joseph retired from military service.[27] In February 1764, he was admitted to the Royal and Military Order of Saint Louis, thus achieving a goal that had eluded his father. King Louis XV had actually bestowed the honor upon Claude-Joseph in 1759, but the original paperwork was lost on its way to Louisiana. Curiously, the reissued royal decree of 1764 instructed Claude-Joseph to appear before Governor Kerlérec in order to take his oath as a knight, even though Kerlérec had already been recalled to France at that point. Nonetheless, given that the first Spanish colonial governor did not arrive until 1766, it is safe to assume that Claude-Joseph managed to find a suitable French official to administer the oath before the transfer of power was complete.

Any plans Claude-Joseph may have had for a tranquil retirement were interrupted when his wife Louise-Elizabeth developed breast cancer.[28] Seeking the best possible treatment for her, the couple left Louisiana for Paris in August of 1767.[29] She died in April 1768, a few months short of her 51st birthday.[30]

In their haste to get to France, Claude-Joseph and Louise-Elizabeth had left most of their physical possessions and other assets in Louisiana, and after her death, it took some time to settle the estate. Meanwhile, Claude-Joseph was living off of his military pension, which he found inadequate for the cost of living in Paris.[31] In 1771, he married a woman now known only as Madame Goulet, who, according to Favrot family lore, was a widow roughly 30 years his junior. The marriage, which was troubled from the start, failed to improve Claude-Joseph's financial position, and they later separated, but did not divorce.[32]

By 1772, Louise-Elizabeth's estate was essentially settled, and Pierre-Joseph, the son who had remained in Louisiana, arranged for the family's personal property to be shipped to Paris. Disaster struck when the ship carrying that cargo, the *Marie-Thérèse*, sank somewhere in the Gulf of Mexico, possibly during a storm.[33] Claude-Joseph was left destitute. "All my belongings and monies, the fruits of my labors in the service of His Majesty, have been lost in the shipwreck of the *Marie-Thérèse*," he later wrote. "It is a calamity from which I will never recover."[34]

Sadly, his prediction proved to be correct. Frequent entreaties to the government for a post-retirement promotion to lieutenant colonel and an increase in pension were refused.[35] Although his son, Pierre-Joseph, was able to provide some financial assistance when he was in France temporarily in the early 1770s, both father and son had difficulties making ends meet in the aftermath of the Spanish takeover of Louisiana and the loss of the family's valuables in the shipwreck.[36]

Claude-Joseph spent his last years as an indigent resident of the Convent and Charity Hospital of Senlis, roughly 25 miles north of Paris. At the time of his death there on November 6, 1777, he was heavily in debt to the convent.[37] After an auspicious beginning in the New World, marked by Claude-Joseph's marriage to a New Orleans heiress, his distinguished military career, and his admission to the prestigious Order of Saint Louis, the Favrot family's prospects for the future were now in doubt.

CHAPTER 3

THE SPANISH COLONIAL ERA

There was every expectation that the male children of French military officers under the *ancien régime* would follow in their fathers' footsteps. It was not unusual, in fact, for minor children to receive nominal military commissions. Pierre-Joseph Favrot, Claude-Joseph's second child and only son, was commissioned as a "fusilier cadet" on January 1, 1751. As of that date, he was a mere toddler, not yet 18 months old.[1]

In January of 1759, Pierre-Joseph, then nine years of age, received a somewhat more substantive commission as *cadet à l'aiguillette*.[2] Named for the *aiguillette*, a braided cord worn on the cadet's uniform, the term essentially designated an officer in training. The rank was commonly used throughout New France, and was regarded as a step in the professionalization of the *Compagnies Franches de la Marine*, the branch of the French military assigned to the overseas colonies.

Pierre-Joseph completed his training by October of 1761, when he was awarded a commission as a second ensign in the infantry.[3] At the time, the French and Indian War was winding down, and the teenage officer must have wondered about the implications of a French defeat—by then inevitable—for his life and career. Less than two years later, the Louisiana troops were reorganized in the wake of the Treaty of Paris, and in September 1763, he received notice that he had been retired from the French military at half-pay, with an annual pension of 200 *livres*.[4] He was 14 years old.

The transfer of power in Louisiana was far from instantaneous, of course, given the slowness of communication and transportation at the time, coupled with the complexity of such a major administrative shift. A document in the Favrot Family Papers from April 1764 sheds light on the mechanics of the lengthy transition. Written in Pierre-Joseph Favrot's hand, it is a copy of a letter from Étienne-François, Duc de Choiseul (1719–1785), King Louis XV's chief minister, to Jean-Jacques Blaise d'Abbadie (1726–1765), who, as director-general of Louisiana, was charged with overseeing the colony's transfer to Spain. Choiseul announced his expectation that Spain soon would be sending ships to take possession of its new territory, and that Abbadie's responsibilities would probably be complete by September 1764. He also noted the French king's expectation that "the Spanish government may have some trouble in keeping the necessary harmony and understanding with the Indian tribes and with the Europeans scattered in the different sections of the colony. . .," and therefore offered to keep a small number of experienced French troops in service in and around New Orleans for as long as the Spanish king might wish.[5]

Contrary to Choiseul's prediction, September came and went with no sign of the Spanish officials. Abbadie continued to administer the colony until his death in February 1765. He was succeeded by Charles-Philippe Aubry (1720?–1770), who technically served as acting governor with the expectation that his responsibilities would end along with French rule in short order.

In fact, the first Spanish governor, Antonio de Ulloa (1716–1795), did not arrive in Louisiana until March 1766, more than three years after the signing of the Treaty of Paris. Furthermore, it was not until 1767 that Ulloa finally conducted an official ceremony to mark the transfer of sovereignty to Spain. In the interim, the French flag continued to fly over most public buildings and squares, and the colonists—many of whom had already convinced themselves over the preceding several years that the transfer might never take place—understandably grew confused about who was really in charge of the province.

Pierre-Joseph's Reentry into Military Service

Aubry, who retained an authoritative role under Ulloa, ordered Pierre-Joseph Favrot in December 1767 to return to active duty by joining the Arkansas post, where he would serve under his brother-in-law, Alexandre De Clouet, for roughly two years.[6] In the fall of 1769, De Clouet ordered Pierre-Joseph to deliver a packet of official mail to the commandant of the Illinois post, accompanied by only two Native American guides. He was captured on the return trip by the Chickasaw and held for an unknown period of time. While in captivity, according to later correspondence, "[h]is life was at stake several times."[7]

Pierre-Joseph somehow managed to return safely, and by August 1770, he was back in New Orleans. In that month, he entered into an "act of mortgage"—in this case, a simple loan agreement—relating to his lending 500 *pesos* to a married couple in the city. The mortgage document is significant as the earliest personal item in the Favrot Family Papers to be written in Spanish, and the first to refer to Pierre-Joseph by the Spanish version of his name, Don Pedro José Favrot.[8]

The political situation in Louisiana while Pierre-Joseph was stationed at Arkansas had been tumultuous. Ulloa attempted to impose restrictions on long-standing French trading practices, raising the ire of Creole merchants. Prominent colonists began circulating petitions against Spanish rule. The situation came to a head in October 1768, when the Superior Council—a judicial and administrative body held over from the French period—voted for the ouster of Ulloa and all other Spanish officials. Ulloa fled the following month.

The Spanish king, Charles III (1716–1788), responded by sending several thousand troops under the command of Irish-born general Alejandro O'Reilly (1725–1794), who became colonial governor upon his arrival in August of 1769. O'Reilly quickly asserted control, ordering the arrest and, in several cases, the execution of the leaders of the insurrection. He replaced the Superior Council with a Spanish-style town council known as a *cabildo*, which later gave its name to the famous building facing Jackson Square in the heart of New Orleans. With remarkable speed, O'Reilly established formal contacts with Native American leaders, instituted new trade regulations, and made important improvements to the infrastructure of New Orleans and remote military posts. He left Louisiana in

1770, just half a year after his arrival, having firmly established Spanish authority over the colony.

Pierre-Joseph's Visit to France

The transfer of colonial sovereignty, perhaps inevitably, caused social and economic upheaval among well-to-do Creole Louisianians. Many French colonists' military careers were interrupted, while currency and property were devalued. By 1772, Pierre-Joseph's professional and financial situation had become so dire that he decided to travel to France, where he could join his father while seeking a new post in the French military. A letter written by one of his supporters and addressed to the secretary of state for the navy described Pierre-Joseph's plight:

> [Favrot] is coming to France to appeal for himself and to beg of you to consider the events, following the change of government, that reduced him to poverty and unemployment. This officer and, unhappily, many other families, were forced to leave their belongings. They preferred this sacrifice rather than to be made to obey the laws of a king who was not theirs, but for whom, however, it would have been advantageous to work had his promises been kept.[9]

In July 1773, Pierre-Joseph received a commission as first lieutenant assigned to "one of the companies of the regiment for America garrisoned at the port of Rochefort,"[10] on France's west coast. Within a few months, however, he was already seeking a leave of absence from his post in order to "take care of" some of the family's remaining possessions in Louisiana, possibly relating to the continuing disposition of his mother's estate.[11] The king granted the request in December of the same year.[12] Before his departure, Pierre-Joseph obtained from his father a written permission to marry whomever he wished, much as Claude-Joseph had done a half-century before.[13]

Having agreed to allow Pierre-Joseph to return to Louisiana, his military superiors realized that he could still be of service during the journey. He was assigned to command a detachment of some 200 new recruits being transported to Saint-Domingue, the French outpost in the Caribbean, aboard a ship called *La Bricole*. His orders, dated January 20, 1774, provide a grim reminder of the ever-present concern about disease during that era. Much of the text is devoted to procedures he should follow in the event of illness or death among the recruits.[14] Pierre-Joseph officially "delivered" 97 recruits to Port-au-Prince, in Saint-Domingue, on May 24, 1774.[15] The fate of the other roughly 100 troops is unclear, though the ship stopped in Martinique on the way and at least some of the soldiers were hospitalized there and presumably stayed behind.[16] At the end of the voyage, the ship's captain attested to Pierre-Joseph's "diligence in maintaining order among his men and keeping peace between them and the crew."[17]

At some point either before or during the voyage, however, Pierre-Joseph was reprimanded for complaining about remarks made to him by "M. de la Perelle." A letter from Louis Legardeur de Croisil, Chevalier de Repentigny (1721–1786), then-commander of the American Regiment, mentioned the reprimand and gently chided Pierre-Joseph for his "marked streak of vanity" and pride. "Rest at ease, my dear Favrot," wrote Repentigny. "I am as sure of your desire to do well as I am certain that you will succeed if you work diligently to obtain the experience that your age and tenure allowed me to assume you had already acquired." Repentigny admitted that he believed de la Perelle to be a "scoundrel and a wag," but felt that Pierre-Joseph had overreacted.[18] The letter is one of several documents in the Favrot Family Papers suggesting that Pierre-Joseph was an ambitious, if impatient, officer who expected much of himself and of others. It also illuminates what historian Lawrence N. Powell calls the "prickly sense [of] honor" that shaped many interactions between aristocratic military officers of the era.[19]

Pierre-Joseph traveled onward to Louisiana to deal with the pressing family matters, but there is no documentation of his activities during that time. He was back in France by January of 1775, when King Louis XVI (1754–1793), who had assumed the throne while Pierre-Joseph was away, assigned him to a newly established recruiting station at Île de Ré,[20] an island not far from Rochefort, where he had been stationed in 1773. The young lieutenant was eager, however, for a more senior position, with the greater responsibilities—and higher salary—that would come with it.

A letter written on Pierre-Joseph's behalf to Antoine-Raymond-Jean de Sartine (1729–1801), the secretary of state for the navy, and believed to date from January of 1775, asked that he be awarded a captaincy in Saint-Domingue or Martinique. The letter cited Pierre-Joseph's military lineage and personal dedication to the king's service, but emphasized his financial need, based on the series of misfortunes that had befallen the family:

> In the past [Pierre-Joseph] Favrot possessed a respectable revenue from his mother's fortune. When Louisiana was transferred to the Spanish, however, the laws of the new masters, the troubles, the sad ending, the resulting desire to emigrate, destroyed the product of his labors and the value of his possessions. M. Favrot could get only a small price for what was left of his properties, and even that is gone with the loss at sea of the ship . . . which was carrying Favrot's goods from Louisiana to Saint-Domingue.[21]

The letter concluded, "M. Favrot's only hope lies in the military service. It is the only vocation proper to his birth and compatible with his age. Can this sole, just way be forbidden or rejected?"[22] Unfortunately, a promotion in the French service was not forthcoming.

In September 1776, Pierre-Joseph received an assignment similar to that of 1774. He was given command of 120 recruits—the number apparently later increased to 250[23]—being transported aboard the ship *Le Père de famille* to Martinique.[24] When the ship reached its destination, Pierre-Joseph learned that the camp there had been closed by new orders from the crown. He asked the local authorities for permission to go to Saint-Domingue and join the regiment there, which was granted,[25] but when he arrived, he was told that there were no vacancies for an officer of his rank, and he subsequently returned to France.[26]

During the initial voyage on *Le Père de famille*, Pierre-Joseph had been appalled by the poor quality of the food being served to the recruits in his charge. He confronted the ship's captain, who denied responsibility and claimed that he had no better provisions available. Upon arrival in Martinique, Pierre-Joseph submitted a report explaining the problem to the lieutenant governor-general of the

Windward Islands, Comte Robert d'Argout (1724–1780). The report was blunt and detailed, describing the prevalence of mold on the bread and vegetables, the substitution of rotten pigs' heads and feet for bacon, and the serving of "an inferior, sulfurated wine, more likely to create rather than quench thirst."[27]

Pierre-Joseph continued to pursue the matter after his return to France. In May 1777, he wrote a memorandum to Sartine, the secretary of state for the navy, and enclosed a copy of the previous report to Argout.[28] The secretary responded promptly, citing other evidence that the ship's captain was indeed responsible for adulterating the food supplies, and promising that he would be interrogated upon his return to France, and punished if appropriate.[29] While the results are unknown, there is evidence that an inquiry did take place, and that Pierre-Joseph submitted written testimony refuting statements made by the captain.[30]

Claude-Joseph Favrot's death in November 1777 apparently somehow exacerbated Pierre-Joseph's financial troubles, though the reasons are unclear, since by then his father had been surviving for some time on the charity of the convent where he was living. Regardless, Pierre-Joseph began to pursue several strategies to improve his financial position. Most notably, he repeatedly petitioned the crown to award him a portion of his father's pension. Those requests were consistently denied. He also bought several slaves—presumably during one of his trips to the West Indies—with the intention of "renting" them out for a profit to a notary on Saint-Domingue. The notary later sold the slaves himself, pocketed the money, and fled the island, leaving Pierre-Joseph with a loss of some 10,000 *livres*.[31]

A Transfer of Allegiance and Return to Louisiana

Claude-Joseph's death left Pierre-Joseph with no immediate family in Paris. At some point, perhaps homesick for Louisiana and missing his sister, he began to explore the prospects for returning to the land of his birth by entering the service of the Spanish king. While the documents from this period reveal few details of Pierre-Joseph's emotional state, it must have been very difficult for such a patriotic Frenchman even to consider abandoning his citizenship. Nonetheless, a change of allegiance increasingly seemed to be the only path that would allow him to advance his career, regain financial security, and reunite with his one remaining close relative.

Pierre-Joseph had several powerful friends among the French elite, including Marie Claudine Sylvie de Thiard de Bissy, Duchesse de Fitz-James (1752–1812), one of Queen Marie Antoinette's (1755–1793) ladies in waiting. The duchess wrote letters to the Spanish ambassador to France, Pedro Pablo Abarca de Bolea, Conde de Aranda (1718–1798), seeking his help in securing a Spanish military commission for Pierre-Joseph.[32] A favorable response came in August 1778: the king of Spain was willing to grant Favrot a commission in Louisiana, provided that it be at the same rank he held in France.[33] For Pierre-Joseph, then still a lieutenant, it was therefore imperative that he obtain a promotion to captain before leaving the French service, in order to ensure that he would enjoy a higher salary upon his return to Louisiana.

For the French court, perhaps weary of Pierre-Joseph's repeated pleas for higher pay and rank, these developments presented an easy out. In September 1778, King Louis XVI issued a pair of orders, both retroactive to the beginning of that year, simultaneously promoting Pierre-Joseph to captain and approving his retirement from the French military.[34]

Pierre-Joseph traveled to Madrid, where, in November 1778, he was granted an audience with His Catholic Majesty King Charles III.[35] On the 20th of that month, Pierre-Joseph—now officially Don Pedro José Favrot—received his royal commission as a captain in the Spanish Louisiana infantry.[36] He set sail soon thereafter, and was back in Louisiana by April 1, 1779, when his commission was recorded in the office of the royal comptroller in New Orleans.[37]

He had returned to a colony that was once again preparing for war. That same month, Spain and France signed the Treaty of Aranjuez, under which the Spanish formally joined the French alliance with the American colonists in their fight for independence from the British. The governor of Louisiana, Bernardo de Gálvez (1746–1786), had already been covertly aiding the American rebels since his appointment in 1777. Following Spain's official declaration of war against Britain in June 1779, the governor began preparations for full-scale armed conflict.

By the late 1770s, the mutual animosity between the French Creole colonists in Louisiana and the Spanish provincial administrators had, if not disappeared, at least subsided. Gálvez, in fact, placed a great deal of trust in some of the Creole military officers now under his command. When, on July 13, 1779, he convened a war council to discuss military strategy, one of the 11 men in attendance was Pierre-Joseph Favrot.[‡] One participant, the future governor Esteban Rodríguez Miró (1744–1795), favored launching an immediate attack on Fort Bute, the British garrison at Bayou Manchac, near the Mississippi River. All of the others agreed, however, that the Spanish forces were insufficient for such an offensive, and that the priority should be the defense of New Orleans.[38]

At Gálvez's request, Pierre-Joseph offered his detailed strategic recommendations in a letter dated two days after the conference. He focused on the need to prevent possible British incursions into New Orleans either from further inland or from the Gulf of Mexico. He suggested specific points that should be fortified, such as the Chef Menteur Pass, connecting Lake Pontchartrain to Lake Borgne, and English Turn, between the city and the outlet of the Mississippi River into the gulf. He concluded with a candid assessment of the situation: "Despite the prudence and intelligence of which a military commander may be capable, I see much difficulty in the defense of this province, unless enough troops are available to guard the posts of Manchac, English Turn, Chef Menteur, and Bayou Saint John."[39]

Gálvez, perhaps mindful of an intercepted communiqué from British King George III (1738–1820) instructing his generals to attack New Orleans as soon as possible, decided to disregard the cautionary advice of his war council. In August 1779 he began gathering hundreds of soldiers and officers, Pierre-Joseph among them, for a campaign against the British garrisons inland of New Orleans. The first target was Fort Bute, which the Spanish troops took surprisingly quickly in early September. (What Gálvez's advisors could not have predicted was that the British commander, upon learning of Spanish intentions, decided to evacuate most of his troops from Fort Bute, which was in poor structural condition, leaving only a skeleton crew that was no match for the Spanish forces.) Emboldened by

---

‡ For consistency and clarity, this book will continue to refer to Pierre-Joseph Favrot by his French name. Over the course of his life after joining the Spanish army, he himself alternated between the French and Spanish versions of his name.

the easy victory, Gálvez's troops soon advanced to the British stronghold at Baton Rouge—on the eastern bank of the Mississippi, in British territory—which fell on September 21. In less than a month, the Spanish had significantly strengthened their hold on the lower Mississippi Valley.

In the aftermath of the campaign, Pierre-Joseph was appointed commandant of the Baton Rouge fort and surrounding district. Just 30 years old, he apparently took to the leadership role quite readily, earning even greater respect from the Spanish authorities. In a letter from October 1779, Gálvez wrote to him, "I am very favorably impressed with the steps and activity you have taken in repairing the fort, which duty has been entrusted to you."[40] In November, Miró, the future governor, wrote a personal note at the bottom of an official letter, saying, "I am one of your sincere friends, although I am not very attentive in answering your letters. I await an occasion to prove the desire I have to serve you. The governor is very well pleased with your work."[41] The personal note was written in French, rather than Spanish—a small gesture indicative of the fondness that Miró, a Spaniard, felt for the Creole officer.

Pierre-Joseph's authority at Baton Rouge extended to civil affairs. In that capacity, he presided over the infamous trial of Marie Glass (?–1781), a mulatto woman from nearby Brown Cliffs, who was accused of murdering a white indentured servant girl and torturing an adult white woman and a young mulatto boy.[42] Although evidence suggested that her sanity was in question, Glass was found guilty and condemned to death. Pierre-Joseph announced the sentence and relayed the decision to the governor's office for final disposition. Glass was likely the first woman to be legally executed in the Louisiana colony.[43]

Marriage and Real Estate Investments

In August 1781, Pierre-Joseph relinquished command of the Baton Rouge post,[44] and returned to New Orleans. He apparently had managed to save a substantial sum of money following his return to Louisiana, since he soon went on something of a buying spree. In September he bought a house at the corner of Bourbon and Dumaine streets, measuring "50 by 34 feet with a front balcony."[45]

In December and in February of the following year, he bought two young male slaves in separate sales.[46] Then in June 1782, he bought another house, this one at the corner of Royal and St. Philip streets. The second property was much larger and included several structures. The main house, measuring 60 feet by 35 feet, was "divided into three large rooms and six smaller ones, with a balcony in front, raised upon five-foot brick walls that house various storerooms." The property included a wing measuring 84 feet by 25 feet, containing a kitchen, storage rooms, and slave quarters. Another structure, at 40 feet by 20 feet, contained "a stable and a room with a stone floor." At 3,600 *pesos*, the entire property cost twice as much as the one at Bourbon and Dumaine.[47]

It is unclear which, if either, of these houses became Pierre-Joseph's principal residence, but it is likely that the string of major purchases was related to the fact that he was actively planning to get married. While serving as commandant at Baton Rouge, he had met and courted a young woman named Marie-Françoise Gérard, from nearby Pointe Coupée, where Pierre-Joseph's father had been stationed in the 1730s and '40s. Marie-Françoise was also from a prominent Creole family: her father had been surgeon at the Pointe Coupée post during the French period, and her maternal grandfather was once the post's commandant.[48]

Marriage was hardly a perfunctory matter, however, for a Spanish military officer in the late 18th century. By law, any marriage involving an officer required the direct approval of the king himself, and obtaining that approval entailed substantial documentation of the future bride's "purity of blood and good character."[§] Pierre-Joseph and Marie-Françoise spent several months in late 1781 and early 1782 compiling the necessary paperwork, including a personal statement by the bride-to-be and written testimony by four witnesses. The bulk of the documentation was devoted to questions of lineage and the "legitimacy" of births in the prospective bride's family. The following passage from Marie-Françoise's own statement illuminates the overtly racist underpinnings of the process:

§ Efforts to ensure *limpieza de sangre* (purity of blood) in Spanish society date to the *Reconquista*, the nearly eight-century campaign by Iberian Christian kingdoms to retake the peninsula from Muslim Moors, which concluded with the fall of Granada in 1492. Proof of European Christian heritage before marriage was intended to root out Muslims and Jews, including those who had publicly converted to Christianity but continued to practice their own religions in secret.

[I]t is true that I, and my aforementioned parents and grandparents, paternal and maternal, are true Christians, free of all evil and free of the blood of any newly converted race, of Moors, Jews, mulattoes, or Indians, and have never been tried for any infamous crimes, but, on the contrary, have enjoyed those honorable employments with which are distinguished persons of quality and good habits.[49]

It would be nearly another two years before Pierre-Joseph and Marie-Françoise would marry, and even then, they did so without yet having received formal permission from the king. Perhaps growing impatient, the couple had a church wedding in December 1783, but did not draw up a marriage contract until a full year later, by which time the king's approval had finally been granted. They may have exploited a loophole, arguing that it was the *marriage contract*, rather than the wedding itself, that required royal consent. Given that the couple's first child, Victoire-Stéphanie-Fortunée Favrot, was born less than eight months after the wedding, however, it is possible that Marie-Françoise had become pregnant and that she and Pierre-Joseph felt it was better to risk the ire of the king than to endure societal scorn for bearing a child out of wedlock. (It is also possible that the first child, who did not live to adulthood, was born prematurely.)

Command of the Mobile Post

By the time of the wedding, the Treaty of Paris of 1783 had marked the end of the American Revolutionary War, and a series of separate treaties had ended hostilities between Great Britain and the colonists' allies, including Spain. Under the terms of the various agreements, Britain retained its territory in Canada, but the new United States of America gained all British territory east of the Mississippi River except for East and West Florida, which Britain ceded to Spain. Because West Florida (spanning the southern portions of the present-day states of Alabama and Mississippi) extended westward to the Mississippi River, the lower Mississippi Valley—including the Baton Rouge area—was now entirely under Spanish control, at least on paper. Unfortunately, the precise borders of West Florida were not consistently or precisely described in the various treaties, an oversight that would lead to numerous disputes in the following decades.

Pierre-Joseph received his next assignment in October 1783—a month after the signing of the latest Treaty of Paris—when Miró, who had succeeded Gálvez as governor, sent him to Mobile in West Florida.[50] Although Spain had occupied Mobile during the last few years of the war, it was now legally Spanish territory and its defense took on a greater significance. Pierre-Joseph assumed interim command of the post when its previous commandant, Enrique Grimarest (life dates unknown), was granted a four-month leave of absence for health reasons.[51] As Grimarest's illness dragged on, however, Pierre-Joseph ultimately remained in command of the post until 1787, exercising both military and civil authority over the Mobile region as he had done previously in Baton Rouge. During that time, his wife also gave birth to their second child, Marie-Joséphine Favrot, who was usually called either Joséphine or simply Phine.

Despite Spain's territorial gains in the wake of the American Revolution, its grip on the Mississippi Valley and Gulf Coast was tenuous. American settlers were flooding into the area seeking land and resources, while both the United States and Britain were considering possible assaults on New Orleans in order to secure control of the primary trade route into the North American interior. Many of the American settlers were ruffians—perhaps attracted by the relative lawlessness of the frontier—who occasionally attacked and robbed other residents of the area.[52]

To counter the growing American presence, Miró sought to create a buffer around Spanish territory through alliances with local Native American tribes. Toward that end, Pierre-Joseph, as acting commandant at Mobile, established a warm relationship with Alexander McGillivray (ca. 1750–1793), the son of a Scottish father and Creek Indian mother, who proved to be a valuable intermediary. McGillivray offered candid advice regarding relations with the Americans, British loyalists, and other Native Americans.[53] Pierre-Joseph also successfully secured the loyalty of several Native American chiefs formerly allied with the British by issuing them nominal Spanish commissions and giving them official medals on behalf of the Spanish crown.[54]

Pierre-Joseph's leadership at Mobile earned him the respect and affection of the area residents. In October 1786, upon hearing rumors that he was to be assigned to a different post, 14 prominent inhabitants of the Mobile territory sent a petition to Governor Miró asking that Pierre-Joseph remain in charge there, stating:

> We have enjoyed great satisfaction since we have been under M. Favrot's command. We have proofs of his justice and fairness. He has been able to keep the savages quiet and contented. This is the essential requisite for the tranquility of our homes, which would be ruined by the evils of war. He has made our lot a happy one. We are satisfied with M. Favrot's administration and, therefore, we would be most grateful if it please Your Lordship to grant the continuation of his command at the post.[55]

A few months later, a similarly enthusiastic petition was signed by 62 inhabitants of the Tensas and Tombigbee river valleys within the Mobile territory.[56] Despite the residents' pleas, however, Miró decided to bring Pierre-Joseph back to New Orleans. He officially relinquished command of the Mobile post at the end of June 1787.[57]

Disaster Strikes Again

That October, Pierre-Joseph requested a leave of absence to attend to family matters in France.[58] The exact reason for the request is unknown, given that his father had died nearly a decade earlier and he had no other close relatives in that country. In December 1788, he finally received word that King Charles III had granted him "permission to go to Paris for one year,"[59] but there is no evidence that he ever left Louisiana again.

Pierre-Joseph had bought at least six slaves during his tenure at Mobile and just after his return to New Orleans, including at least three children.[60] This steady series of purchases suggests that he was doing well financially despite occasional complaints to his superiors about his salary.[61] Meanwhile, he continued to own the two properties in New Orleans, which presumably provided a steady rental income.

On March 21, 1788, any sense of financial security that the Favrot family may have had was shattered once again. That afternoon, a fire broke out in a house on Chartres Street, not far from the Plaza de Armas (now called Jackson Square), in the heart of New Orleans. It spread quickly. By that evening, the fire had heavily damaged or destroyed more than three-quarters of the structures in the city, including the two properties that Pierre-Joseph owned. For the second time in 16 years—the first being the loss of the family's possessions in the sinking of the *Marie-Thérèse*—much of the Favrots' physical assets had suddenly and irretrievably disappeared. To make matters worse, during the fire, someone stole a chest containing money that Pierre-Joseph was holding for the soldiers in his company, which he was later required to pay back out of his own funds.[62]

Pierre-Joseph still had financial resources, however, and soon set to rebuilding what he had lost. In July 1788 he signed a contract with a carpenter to build a new kitchen and chicken coop on one of his properties.[63] Later that same month, he bought yet another slave.[64] Meanwhile, his family was continuing to grow— in April 1788, not long after the fire, Marie-Françoise gave birth to their third child and first son, Pierre-Louis-Étienne Favrot, who was generally called Louis or sometimes just "Favrot." Their fourth child, Marie-Louise Favrot, was born in March 1789, followed by Joseph-Philogène-Zénon Favrot (alternately called Philogène or Philo) in May 1791.

Louisiana After the French Revolution

There is relatively little material in the Favrot Family Papers from the period between 1787, when Pierre-Joseph left Mobile, and 1792. This is unfortunate, given that it was such a consequential era in European and colonial history. Charles III, the dynamic king who led Spain into a cultural and political revival while strengthening its colonial empire, died in December 1788. He was succeeded by his son Charles IV (1748–1819), a weak monarch who delegated most affairs of state. The royal succession in Spain was soon followed by a far more significant event with worldwide ramifications: the French Revolution of 1789, which marked the end of the *ancien régime* that had framed the lives and careers of Favrot family members for centuries, and the beginning of a period of political upheaval that would soon reshape colonial America.

For the first few years after these profound events, the administration of the Louisiana colony continued much as usual. In 1791, Francisco Luis Héctor, Barón de Carondelet (1748–1807), became governor. A seasoned Spanish colonial administrator of Burgundian descent, he was fluent in French and initially managed to cultivate warm relationships with many influential Creoles. Under his leadership, the Spanish government made welcome improvements to the colony's infrastructure while successfully fending off incursions into Spanish territory by Anglo-American settlers. His good relations with the colonists later soured, however, after he banned the importation of African slaves and granted new legal protections to existing slaves—actions that were driven not by ethical concerns but by fears of a potential slave revolt like the one that began in Saint-Domingue in 1791.

In 1792, Carondelet assigned Pierre-Joseph to serve as commandant of the Natchez post in present-day Mississippi. After an 18-day journey up the river by barge, Pierre-Joseph arrived in Natchez on August 6, 1792.[65] He returned to New Orleans at Christmastime to pick up his wife and children, sailing with them back to Natchez in early 1793. He formally assumed command of the Louisiana Regiment there on February 5.[66]

Pierre-Joseph's tenure at Natchez coincided with the first of a series of wars between the revolutionary French government and various European monarchies, most notably Great Britain and Spain, the latter of which struggled under its disengaged and ineffectual new king. The diminishing fortunes of the Spanish crown were evident in a remarkable letter to Pierre-Joseph written by Colonel Francisco Bouligny (1736–1800), head of the Louisiana Regiment, in July 1793. The letter outlined the solicitation of "donations" from Spanish soldiers—most of whom already barely survived on modest pay and meager rations—to aid the war effort:

> The gracious Royal clemency of His Majesty [Charles IV] has been pleased to accept the various donations that have been voluntarily offered by his faithful subjects of Europe and America, who are moved by a spirit of patriotism and zeal for the glory of His Royal armies. The following solemn decision has been officially communicated to me. His Majesty

authorizes the government of this province to receive donations that are offered. . . . I am convinced that you and the other officers of your garrison will gladly consider and participate in this gift . . . Advise them that they are free to extend their generosity beyond their individual shares, if their financial conditions permit them to do so.[67]

At the time of this campaign for "voluntary" contributions to Spain's coffers, there was indeed a resurgence of patriotism among the colonists—but it was directed toward France. Much of the revolutionary rhetoric resonated with Creoles who still spoke French at home and avidly followed French political affairs even after decades under Spanish rule. Pro-French fervor increased in the wake of the Citizen Genêt Affair, in which Edmond Charles Genêt (1763–1834), who had been appointed France's minister to the United States in 1793, used his diplomatic position to solicit privateers to seize British ships in direct violation of U.S. neutrality policies. Although the French government recalled Genêt in 1794, he remained in the U.S. under the implicit protection of President George Washington, who assumed that Genêt would be executed if he returned to France, where a more radical faction had assumed power.

The Spanish administrators of Louisiana feared that Genêt's presence in America could give rise to an insurgency among the Creoles. There were rumors that France was poised to attack Louisiana from the Gulf of Mexico, and that Genêt—who had adopted the epithet "Citizen" to emphasize his revolutionary credentials—might lead an expedition against New Orleans via the Mississippi River. An undated, unsigned letter to Citizen Genêt written in Pierre-Joseph's hand, probably dating to 1794, suggests that, even if their fears of invasion were unwarranted, the Spanish certainly could not count on the loyalty of Louisiana residents:

> You [Citizen Genet] arrive in a colony inhabited by Frenchmen like yourself. The same blood flows through their veins. The same spirit moves them. Long separated from their mother country, they lament their abandonment in secret. . . . Notwithstanding all indications to the contrary, they dare to hope that one day they shall return. This longed-for

day has at last arrived, and we have become again the children of France, our country. . . . It is under such circumstances, Citizen General, that you are coming to organize this colony and to reunite the spirit of the people, which Spanish rule believed it must divide.[68]

It is uncertain whether Pierre-Joseph wrote the letter himself or merely copied a letter written by someone else, but the existence of such a document in his own hand leaves little doubt as to his political sentiments. Even as he had faithfully served numerous Spanish officers and administrators, consistently earning their praise, trust, and friendship, Pierre-Joseph had remained a Frenchman at heart. Even so, it appears that he was still willing to work with Spanish officials to improve relations with Creole colonists if the hoped-for rescue by Genêt did not come. The Favrot Family Papers include another anonymous letter, also in Pierre-Joseph's hand, addressed to Governor Carondelet, offering advice for regaining the affection of the people:

> You will frequently see the intendant [another Spanish colonial official] receive the blessings of the people. This intendant, Sir, during the great fire was not hidden away at some fort. He was with the citizens in the midst of the conflagration. He was offering his sympathies for the misfortunes that he could not prevent. . . . It is in such critical moments that he gained the goodwill and confidence of the people. . . . But you, Sir, if your administration were to end, would you not find yourself wholly isolated?[69]

Despite frequent rumblings about possible French threats to Spanish Louisiana, no attacks were forthcoming, but in December 1794, New Orleans suffered another disaster—a second great fire. While less extensive than the conflagration of 1788, the second fire also damaged the Favrots' properties, apparently including a third house that Pierre-Joseph owned by then.[70] It is unclear whether Pierre-Joseph was still in Natchez at the time of the fire. A letter from Bouligny dating to April 1794 states that Pierre-Joseph was about to be relieved of his post there,[71] but there is no documentary evidence that he was back in New Orleans until late 1795.

Meanwhile, the Favrot family continued to grow, with a daughter named Augustine-Octavine Favrot, called Octavine or Tavine for short, born in 1795. Unfortunately, the Favrots' oldest child, Victoire-Stéphanie-Fortunée, had died in 1791 at the age of seven. Marie-Louise had died in infancy. A daughter named Céleste, born in 1792, died at the age of five. Another child either was stillborn or died within a day of birth in 1794.

Command of the Plaquemines Post

The relationship between the United States and Spanish Louisiana changed considerably in October 1795 with the signing of Pinckney's Treaty, also known as the Treaty of San Lorenzo. The treaty explicitly delineated the previously disputed border between the U.S. and the Spanish colonies of West Florida and East Florida, and established the middle of the Mississippi River as the official boundary between Louisiana and the U.S. from the 31st parallel (about 40 miles north of Baton Rouge) to Canada. More importantly, the agreement also opened up the river to American shipping. The Mississippi had been restricted to Spanish vessels since 1784.

In 1795, Pierre-Joseph received a long-sought promotion to lieutenant colonel,[72] and in July 1796, he was appointed commandant of Fort San Felipe, or Saint Philip, at Plaquemines, a position he held—except for a one-year hiatus—until the end of the colonial period. Located on the East Bank of the Mississippi River not far from its mouth, the fort had long been critical to Louisiana's defense. With the opening of the river to American traffic, its role became even more important—and more delicate, since it was now the gateway for American ships traveling to and from the westernmost U.S. territories. As commandant, Pierre-Joseph would have to exercise careful judgment to ensure that the provisions of the Treaty of San Lorenzo were honored without compromising the security of the colony. His civil and military jurisdiction included not only Fort Saint Philip, but also the surrounding territory on both sides of the river from La Balize (the settlement at the very mouth of the river that was repeatedly destroyed by hurricanes and rebuilt) to Pointe à la Hache, which still exists and is the current seat of Plaquemines Parish.[73]

While strategically significant, Fort Saint Philip was isolated and rustic. It was surrounded by swampland, teeming with disease-bearing mosquitoes, and buffeted by heat, humidity, and frequent storms. It was an uncomfortable place for soldiers, and even more so for civilians, including Pierre-Joseph's wife and young children, who joined him there in October 1796 once it became clear that his assignment was a long-term one.[74]

The Plaquemines post was undoubtedly Pierre-Joseph's most challenging to date. Rampant illness was a constant problem, and during his first few months there, Pierre-Joseph devoted a great deal of attention to securing a qualified doctor to replace the garrison's surgeon, whom he considered incompetent.[75] At one point, Carondelet offered the seemingly hopeful news that a surgeon named Ursule might accept the position, but the news was tempered by the governor's warning that Pierre-Joseph would "have to control his drinking, which is his shortcoming."[76] Regardless, Ursule ultimately refused the assignment, and the best that Carondelet could do was to send an intern instead.[77]

Smuggling was rampant during the Spanish colonial period, and Plaquemines was one of its primary hubs. La Balize, in particular, was a chokepoint for illegal trade. Many high-level Spanish officials in Louisiana, including Miró, were implicated in smuggling and bribe-taking. While there is no direct evidence that Pierre-Joseph personally engaged in, or benefitted from, such illegal activity, there can be no doubt that he was constantly exposed to temptation, and almost certainly faced administrative challenges arising from the illicit commerce.

Pierre-Joseph's responsibilities at Plaquemines included overseeing improvements to Fort Saint Philip and the reconstruction of its companion, Fort Bourbon, which had stood just across the river before it was destroyed by a hurricane in 1795. The construction and repair work was largely done by convicts, whose presence in the settlement frequently caused unease among the other residents and posed disciplinary problems for Pierre-Joseph.[78] Even as work on Fort Saint Philip was under way in the late summer of 1796, another hurricane struck, inflicting damage to the garrison and surrounding earthworks.[79] The same storm also damaged the settlement at La Balize.[80]

Meanwhile, the political situation in Europe continued to shift. In July 1795, Spain and France signed the Peace of Basel, a treaty under which Spain ceded the eastern portion of the Caribbean Island of Hispaniola to France, in exchange for the return of territory in northeastern Spain that French revolutionary forces had captured over the previous year. Then, in August 1796, Spain did a political about-face, entering into an alliance with France, its recent enemy, against the British. The British responded in 1797 by blockading Spanish ports, seriously inhibiting the country's communications with its colonies in the New World and frequently depriving Louisiana of badly needed money from the mother country.

The new conflict made Pierre-Joseph's job even more difficult. When several British vessels were spotted marauding off the Gulf Coast in early 1797, Governor Carondelet believed that La Balize was at risk of imminent attack. He warned Pierre-Joseph that the British might surprise the post by sneaking into the mouth of the river on a captured Spanish ship.[81] Pierre-Joseph responded shrewdly to the possibility of such deceit, issuing a blanket order that any ship approaching La Balize at night must first anchor two leagues (about six miles) below the fort, then send a small launch to Fort Saint Philip to present the vessel's identification papers to the commandant himself. Ships approaching by day were ordered to anchor "under the fire of Fort Bourbon" (then still under reconstruction) and send a launch to Fort Saint Philip to present their papers.[82] While such precautions were certainly prudent, the widely-feared British attack never materialized.

Carondelet and Pierre-Joseph exchanged letters frequently during this period, and it appears that they had developed a mutually respectful and effective working relationship, despite the concerns expressed in the anonymous letter to Carondelet written in Pierre-Joseph's hand in the mid-1790s. In March 1797 came the news that Carondelet would be leaving his post in Louisiana later in the year to assume "the presidency and captaincy general of the Kingdom of Quito,"[83] officially known as the Royal Audience of Quito, an administrative division of the Viceroyalty of Nueva Granada whose territory included the present-day country of Ecuador and parts of Columbia, Peru, and Brazil. The new position was clearly a significant promotion for Carondelet, who proudly noted that "[t]he capital alone contains 58,000 inhabitants,"[84] likely more than the European population of the entire Louisiana colony at the time. As he was leaving Louisiana in September,

Carondelet stopped by Fort Saint Philip, where Pierre-Joseph apparently hosted a good-bye celebration.[85]

Carondelet was succeeded as Louisiana governor by Manuel Gayoso de Lemos (1747–1799), formerly district governor of Natchez. Pierre-Joseph promptly sent a congratulatory note to the new governor, who responded that he had heard excellent reports from Carondelet about Pierre-Joseph's service.[86] In the fall of 1798, after he had been in office more than a year, Gayoso had come to his own very positive assessment of Pierre-Joseph's leadership: "I am extremely well satisfied with the painstaking care and zeal with which you manage your garrison. It is to your particular attention that I attribute the good discipline and health of the men under your command."[87] Given the boredom-inducing isolation of Fort Saint Philip, coupled with the constant threat of epidemic disease in the marshy, mosquito-infested setting, Gayoso's remarks constituted very high praise.

Earlier that year, Pierre-Joseph played host to a trio of very high-profile visitors: Louis Philippe, Duc d'Orléans (1773–1850), and his brothers Antoine Philippe, Duc de Montpensier (1775–1807), and Louis Charles, Comte de Beaujolais (1779–1808). Louis Philippe would later reign as king of the French from 1830 to 1848, but at the time the three siblings were in exile from the revolutionary government. Their father, despite having been a vocal supporter of the revolution, had been guillotined during the Reign of Terror. In 1796, after traveling all of Europe with revolutionary sympathizers at his heels, Louis Philippe ended up in Philadelphia, where his two younger brothers soon joined him. The trio visited Boston and New York before embarking on a voyage down the Ohio and Mississippi rivers. They arrived in Louisiana in February 1798, spending several weeks there. Eventually, they boarded an American vessel bound for Havana, which stopped at Plaquemines, where Pierre-Joseph entertained them.[88] Once at sea, their ship was intercepted by a British vessel, whose crew detained the brothers but soon deposited them in Cuba. They were finally able to sail to England in 1800, remaining there until 1815, when they returned to France following the downfall of Emperor Napoléon Bonaparte (1769–1821).

Despite Gayoso's praise and the thrill of hosting royal dignitaries, Pierre-Joseph was nonetheless increasingly unhappy with the deprivations of the Plaquemines post. Like his father and grandfather before him, he also grew frustrated by what he perceived as the slow pace of his promotions and salary increases. In November 1798, he wrote directly to King Charles IV asking to be placed in command of the militia of the "German Coast,"[89] an area along the east bank of the Mississippi above New Orleans that had originally been settled by Germans in the early 18th century. That petition came to naught, but beginning in March 1799, Pierre-Joseph was granted a leave of absence to return to New Orleans "to recover his health."[90] In August of that year, Marie-Françoise gave birth to the couple's ninth child, Henri-Bouvier Favrot, whose middle name recalled his great-grandmother, Françoise Bouvier.

By September of 1799, Pierre-Joseph was posted at Baton Rouge again. The circumstances of his transfer are not directly documented, but he apparently received a temporary assignment as commanding officer of the troops stationed there, with the promise from Gayoso that he would become commandant of the entire post when that position opened, as was expected soon. Anticipating a long-term assignment, Pierre-Joseph not only moved his family to Baton Rouge,[91] but at some point over the next year, also purchased property nearby in West Baton Rouge, on the other side of the Mississippi River. That property would become the family's plantation, Monte Vista.

Unfortunately, Gayoso died in office in July, leaving Pierre-Joseph's future position at Baton Rouge in doubt. He and his family managed to stay at the post for a year before the acting governor, Sebastián de la Puerta y O'Farril, Marqués de Casa Calvo (ca. 1751–ca. 1820), finally ordered him back to Plaquemines.[92] Pierre-Joseph gently protested the reassignment, but Casa Calvo responded that it would be improper for an officer of his rank "to remain with an undermanned detachment away from [his] own company."[93] He reluctantly returned to Fort Saint Philip in November 1800, followed by his family a few weeks later.[94]

The Retrocession of Louisiana to France

During Pierre-Joseph's stint in Baton Rouge, the political situation in France once again changed dramatically. On November 9, 1799, General Napoléon Bonaparte, who had gained fame for his audacious and decisive military victories in a recent campaign against Austria, staged a *coup d'état*, bringing the French Revolution to an abrupt end. Napoléon was named first consul, ostensibly sharing executive authority with two other men in a body known as the Consulate, but in reality wielding almost exclusive political power. Just five years later, he would be crowned emperor.

Napoléon moved quickly to exploit other countries' weaknesses. Knowing that Spain—France's ally since 1796—was nearly bankrupt from the continuing war against the British, he sensed correctly that King Charles IV might be willing to relinquish Louisiana, which had been a drain on Spanish finances. Representatives of the two countries entered into secret negotiations in 1800, and on October 1 of that year, signed the Third Treaty of San Ildefonso, under which the entire Louisiana colony would be retroceded to France. In return, King Charles's son-in-law was to be made king of a new state later named Etruria, roughly corresponding to the modern-day Italian region of Tuscany—a token gesture in comparison to the vast territory that France was to gain in North America. The terms of the Third Treaty of San Ildefonso were affirmed and expanded by the Treaty of Aranjuez in March 1801. At that time, the French representatives supposedly promised their Spanish counterparts that, should France ever decide to give up control of Louisiana, the territory would automatically revert to Spain, but no such provision was included in the written treaty.

As early as 1797, there had been rumors within Louisiana about a possible "transfer" of the colony, presumably to France, but the Spanish administrators dismissed such notions, perhaps out of fear that they might foment a Creole insurrection.[95] By the time that word of the Treaty of Aranjuez reached Louisiana years later, most colonists probably regarded the news with some skepticism. Daily life continued much as usual. Casa Calvo, though technically only interim governor, ended up remaining in office until mid-1801, when Juan Manuel de Salcedo (ca. 1743–?), whose arrival had been delayed by illness, finally relieved him. Salcedo would be the last Spanish governor of Louisiana.

There is no documentation of when Pierre-Joseph learned of the treaties or how he felt about the pending retrocession. In the meantime, however, he continued to seek a transfer out of Plaquemines to another, less Spartan post elsewhere in still-Spanish Louisiana,[96] but to no avail.[97] The reality of the looming transfer of sovereignty—with its profound implications for Pierre-Joseph's military career—was beginning to sink in by early 1802. In January of that year, Marie-Françoise Favrot's brother-in-law, Armand Allard Duplantier (1753–1827), wrote to Pierre-Joseph that while "retrocession is still uncertain . . . should this occur, there is no middle way. You must accept your regiment's fate, or quit." He added: "I do not believe that you could count on being employed by the French Republic."⁹⁸ For Pierre-Joseph, the prospect of retrocession must have posed a terrible dilemma: remain in the Spanish service, which would require that he leave Louisiana, or resign his commission and run the risk of unemployment under the restored French administration that he had longed to see.

Meanwhile, the colonial government of Louisiana, already hampered by inadequate funding and the constant threat of attack from British forces, deteriorated further under Salcedo. Widely despised by the colonists and probably corrupt, Salcedo delegated much authority to his equally unpopular son, Manuel María de Salcedo (1776–1813), who later served as colonial governor of Spanish Texas. Pierre-Joseph, who had cultivated good relations with a series of Louisiana governors, worried that his position at Plaquemines was threatened by the senior Salcedo's favoritism. In a letter to Casa Calvo, then living in Havana, he wrote: "Those of us who know you would gladly have you in exchange for our present acting [sic] governor, who only annoys us more every day, and who, if you do not interpose your influence, I am afraid will relieve me of the post to which you so kindly assigned me."⁹⁹ As eager as Pierre-Joseph was to leave Plaquemines, he may have feared that any other options under Salcedo would be worse.

The mechanics of the retrocession of Louisiana to France proceeded slowly but inexorably. In October 1802, King Charles IV issued orders officially authorizing the transfer, which would also entail the withdrawal of Spanish troops from the colony. Spanish administrators and military officers began planning in earnest for the handover of all forts, public buildings, and other governmental assets to French authorities, though the exact date of the formal transfer remained uncertain.

Pierre-Joseph was still stationed at Plaquemines in early March 1803, when the ship carrying Pierre Clément de Laussat (1756–1835), Napoléon's appointee as "prefect" of soon-to-be-French Louisiana—the equivalent of the Spanish governor—anchored off La Balize. Fog and uncooperative wind patterns off the Louisiana coast delayed the final leg of the ship's journey, up the Mississippi River to New Orleans, by a couple of weeks.[100] During that time, Laussat exchanged several letters with Pierre-Joseph, laying the foundations for a warm relationship even before the prefect had set foot in his new land. Laussat sensed in Pierre-Joseph a kindred spirit—a fellow Frenchman who shared his eagerness to make Louisiana an integral part of the French empire once again.[101] When Laussat's ship reached Fort Saint Philip on March 24, he and his family went ashore. In his memoirs, he recounted his meeting with Pierre-Joseph: "M. Favrot, an old Frenchman and loyal soldier, received us in the midst of his family. He was candor and hospitality personified. Joy beamed in this good man's face upon seeing us."[102]

Laussat finally reached New Orleans on March 26.[103] He soon issued a lengthy proclamation intended to set the political tone for the future administration of Louisiana under the Napoleonic regime. The extraordinary document, with its aspirational language and multiple pledges to the colonists, warrants lengthy quotation:

LOUISIANIANS:

Your separation from France marks one of the most shameful times of our history under a government already weak and corrupt, after an ignominious war following a dishonorable peace.

Facing this cowardly and unnatural abandonment, you offered the contrast of heroic love, loyalty, and courage.

All French hearts were moved by this and have never forgotten it. They exclaimed with pride, and have never since that time ceased to repeat, that their blood flowed in our veins.

As soon as they had recovered their dignity and reconquered their glory, thanks to the Revolution and a prodigious series of triumphs, they turned their attention toward you. You entered their first negotiations; they wanted your retrocession to be a part of their first peace treaty.

The time had not yet come. It was necessary that a man appear for whom nothing that is national, grand, magnanimous, and just, is foreign or impossible. . . .

Today, this man [Napoléon] is in charge of our destiny, and from this moment on, he guarantees yours. . . .

To live in peace and friendliness with all of your neighbors, protect your commerce, encourage your culture, populate your deserts, encourage work and industry, respect properties, customs, and opinions, render homage to religion, embrace probity, preserve the laws of the empire, and, if you guide them, do so with moderation and in the light of experience, maintain an alert and firm police force, introduce a permanent order and economy in all branches of public administration, and constantly strengthen the ties that common origin, customs, and desires have established between this colony and her mother country. . . .

In every way, you will be gratified for having become French again; more and more every day, you will feel the value of this beautiful title envied throughout the world. . . .[104]

The next month, Napoléon sold the Louisiana territory to the United States.

CHAPTER 4

THE AMERICANIZATION OF LOUISIANA

News of the sale of Louisiana to the United States took several months to reach North America. When it did, in the summer of 1803, the colonists were flabbergasted. Laussat, the French prefect who had arrived in March but had not yet formally taken office, was incredulous. Even the American president, Thomas Jefferson (1743–1826), who had initiated the negotiations that led to the sale, was surprised by the scope of the agreement, which greatly exceeded his own directions and expectations.

Jefferson recognized that the free passage of American ships along the Mississippi River was vital to the economic wellbeing of the U.S. states and territories lying west of the Appalachian Mountains. Since the signing of the Treaty of San Lorenzo in 1795, Spanish authorities had allowed U.S.-flagged ships to navigate the river largely unhindered. With the retrocession of Louisiana to France, Jefferson worried that this relatively open trade route might be shut off. France under Napoléon was, after all, an increasingly ambitious and belligerent nation. While a renewed French presence in North America was potentially troublesome, Jefferson's primary concern was less about the sovereignty of Louisiana *per se* than about French control of New Orleans, the gateway to the Mississippi.

With that in mind, Jefferson instructed the U.S. minister to France, Robert Livingston (1746–1813), to begin negotiations with the French government for the purchase of New Orleans. The president authorized Livingston to offer as much as ten million dollars for a limited area—the city and its environs perhaps—and nothing more. With talks proceeding slowly, in January 1803 Jefferson dispatched future U.S. president James Monroe (1758–1831) to assist Livingston. Then, in April, just before Monroe arrived, the French stunned Livingston with a surprise offer to sell the entire Louisiana territory—measuring some 530 million acres—for just 15 million dollars, or less than three cents per acre. Fearing that a refusal could jeopardize any further negotiations, Livingston accepted the offer. The purchase document was finalized on April 30 and signed by the American and French representatives on May 2. When word of the agreement reached Washington, D.C., the new American capital, it triggered a fierce debate about the president's authority to execute such a purchase—a power that was not expressly addressed in the Constitution. Even Jefferson had his doubts, but ultimately he decided to proceed, and the Senate ratified the agreement—technically a treaty— in October.

Initially unaware of the Anglo-French negotiations and resulting treaty, Spanish and French authorities in Louisiana spent the spring of 1803 working through the logistics of the ongoing retrocession to France. Among the most critical issues were the protocols regarding the rights and responsibilities of the colonists after the transition. Governor Salcedo and former governor Casa Calvo, who had returned to New Orleans to assist with the administrative details of the transfer, issued a proclamation in May stating that all Spanish citizens of the colony would be free to stay in Louisiana and become French citizens should they so desire. Those wishing to remain subjects of the Spanish king were advised to leave the colony and go to Havana or another Spanish possession. The proclamation also promised that the king would still honor military pensions for retired Spanish soldiers or widows.[1]

Meanwhile, Pierre-Joseph Favrot, 53 years old and suffering from poor health, was confronting the profound uncertainty that retrocession posed for his future career and livelihood. In January 1803, he wrote to the Spanish king yet again, this time asking for a paid, two-year leave of absence "in order that he may sell his property and collect the money due him from residents of this colony and thereby save his property, which consists of land, slaves, and other possessions."[2] He also requested a two-year leave for his son Louis, by then a Spanish cadet. The nature of the request suggests that Pierre-Joseph had concluded that his best option was to retain his military commission, liquidate his assets in Louisiana, and presumably move his family either to Spain or to another Spanish colony.

Apparently, however, Pierre-Joseph was also entertaining the possibility of retiring from the Spanish army. In a letter believed to have been written in May 1803, Casa Calvo informed him that Baton Rouge, which was technically a part of West Florida rather than Louisiana and therefore not included in the territory being ceded to France, was expected to remain under Spanish control. Casa Calvo added that he intended to encourage the king to retain a full regiment of troops in Pensacola, the territorial capital of West Florida. Sensing a continuing career opportunity for Pierre-Joseph there, Casa Calvo advised him not to retire—advice that suggested that the two of them had previously discussed that option.[3]

The realization that Baton Rouge would continue to be in Spanish territory raised Pierre-Joseph's hopes that he could find a way to retain his military commission while moving closer to his plantation, allowing him to keep and develop the property. He soon wrote to Governor Salcedo saying that "so long as Baton Rouge remains in Spanish hands, I am under the orders of the king of Spain." He noted, however, that if he were to join the Spanish regiment at Pensacola, he would have to abandon his plantation, a move that he argued would be economically disastrous for his family. He hinted that he would welcome "some post not with the regiment," presumably allowing him to settle in Baton Rouge or nearby, though the vague language indicated that he had no idea what sort of post that might be.[4]

There is no record of a direct response from Salcedo, but Casa Calvo wrote to Pierre-Joseph again on June 15, 1803. In that brief letter, he alludes to some unspecified but significant news, and advises Pierre-Joseph to delay any decisions regarding retirement "until the reports are confirmed."[5] It is likely that the "reports" to which he was referring were those regarding the sale of Louisiana to the United States.

Even as such reports were becoming more authoritative in the summer of 1803, Laussat maintained that there was no substance to them. In a letter to

Pierre-Joseph in early August, he wrote: "As to the rumors being circulated by the Anglo-Americans, do not believe a word of them. It is the fodder needed by the rabble of their little schemers, to feed the naïve people of the wilderness in order to succeed in their petty intrigues and narrow political ambition. It would be surprising if sensible persons fell into such foolish traps."[6] Then, sometime in August, Laussat received definitive confirmation of the sale from Paris. He could no longer deny the reality. Just three weeks after his previous letter to Pierre-Joseph, a chastened Laussat wrote to him once again: "I could not believe, Sir, in the cession of Louisiana up to the moment when doubt was no longer possible."[7] Laussat now recognized that his tenure as prefect of Louisiana would be a very short one.

Although Laussat had been in Louisiana since March 1803, the official transfer of the colony to French control did not take place until November 30 of that year. On that day, he issued another lengthy proclamation to the people of Louisiana, but in contrast to the triumphant tone of the statement he published upon his arrival in March, this one was tinged with resignation and regret. While embracing the colonists as fellow Frenchmen, Laussat also addressed them as future Americans. He outlined the various political freedoms and economic opportunities that Louisianians would enjoy as citizens of the United States, but wistfully begged them never to forget the "mutual feeling of tender emotion" that they should feel for their "brothers," the French.[8]

On the same day, Laussat dissolved the *Cabildo*, the Spanish town council that had governed New Orleans for more than three decades, and established an interim government for the city, including a mayor and a municipal council. Several of the council members' surnames—including Destréhan, Villeré, and Fortier—would be familiar to many New Orleanians even today.[9] Given the obvious tenuousness of a government that was expected to exist for only a short while, Laussat pledged to lend his own money to cover the interim administration's expenses, rather than rely on formal funding from France, which might never reach the city during the brief period of French control, thereby delaying necessary civic actions and services.[10]

The transfer of the Spanish forts in the lower Mississippi Valley soon followed in early December. Pierre-Joseph was ordered to hand over the forts under his jurisdiction—Saint Philip, Bourbon, and La Balize—to a representative of the

French navy.[11] During the transfer ceremony at Fort Saint Philip, Pierre-Joseph lowered the Spanish flag and gave the keys to the fort to the French officer. Then the French flag was raised to the sound of a 21-gun salute and shouts of "Long live the Republic! Long live Bonaparte!" A similar ceremony took place simultaneously at Fort Bourbon across the river.[12]

France's second possession of Louisiana was not to be long-lived, however. On December 20, 1803, just three weeks after officially taking office as prefect of the colony, Laussat formally ceded the territory to two American "commissioners" appointed by President Jefferson: William C.C. Claiborne (ca. 1775–1817), governor of the Mississippi Territory of the United States, and James Wilkinson (1757–1825), senior officer of the U.S. army. The ceremony took place in the Cabildo, the building that had housed the Spanish town council of the same name. Built in the 1790s after its predecessor was destroyed in the great New Orleans fire of 1788, the building still stands today on Jackson Square, and is one of the architectural highlights in a city full of landmarks.

Upon accepting the transfer of sovereignty from Laussat, Claiborne became governor general and intendant of the new Louisiana Territory of the United States. Among his first acts was to retain, on a temporary basis, all of the "public officers" of New Orleans who had been appointed by Laussat. In addition, he declared that all of the municipal ordinances the mayor and council had enacted would remain in effect.[13] As with the cession of Louisiana from France to Spain in 1763, and with retrocession back to France, which began in secret in 1800, the transfer to full American control would be a gradual process.

Pierre-Joseph's Transition to Civilian Life

During the final few months of Spanish rule of Louisiana, Pierre-Joseph had received good news on two fronts. First, in September 1803, his wife Marie-Françoise, who had traveled to New Orleans for the occasion, gave birth to the couple's 11th, and last, child.[14] The baby, named Eulalie-Pulchérie Favrot (and later alternately called Pulchérie, Toutou, or Toutoute), was robust and healthy, which came as a great relief to her parents, who had lost their tenth child, Elisa, just two months after her birth in 1802. In total, five of their 11 children had died in infancy or early childhood.

Pierre-Joseph also learned in September that both he and his son Louis had been granted the leave he had requested the previous January.[15] Since he had made that request, of course, the situation had become much more complicated. As Casa Calvo had correctly noted in an earlier letter to Pierre-Joseph, West Florida, which stretched to the East Bank of the Mississippi River below the 31st parallel, was not part of the territory ceded by Spain to France, and therefore was not included in the sale of territory to the United States. Therefore, as of December 1803, Baton Rouge and West Baton Rouge—site of the Favrot plantation—were technically in different countries. That would prove to be a thorny problem for Pierre-Joseph as he tried to balance the needs of his plantation with his obligations to the Spanish military.

The period immediately following the transfer of Louisiana to the U.S. was marked by frequent jurisdictional confusion. Shortly after the transfer ceremonies at the Cabildo, for instance, the American commissioners asked Laussat about the boundaries of the Louisiana territory, which they assumed included West Florida.[16] He disabused them of that notion, but essentially abdicated responsibility for such critical details, which he believed would have to be worked out directly between Spain and the United States based on the provisions of the Third Treaty of San Ildefonso, the initially secret agreement by which Spain retroceded Louisiana to France.[17] Unfortunately, as previously noted, that document was vague in its description of the boundaries of the Louisiana colony. Ownership of the West Florida territory continued to be disputed by American and Spanish authorities over the next decade.

In April 1804, Pierre-Joseph received a passport allowing him and his family to leave New Orleans for Baton Rouge. Here again, some jurisdictional ambiguity was evident. The passport was issued not by the American authorities, or even by the French, but by Casa Calvo, the former Spanish governor, representing a regime that had been superseded not once, but twice already. Casa Calvo was still in New Orleans at that point, continuing to represent the Spanish crown on issues relating to "the demarcation of boundaries and other matters pertaining to the province of Louisiana."[18]

The confusion that prevailed in the aftermath of the two momentous territorial transfers in rapid succession placed Pierre-Joseph in an awkward position. Although Casa Calvo, a Spanish official, had issued the passport allowing Pierre-Joseph to go to Baton Rouge in West Florida, technically speaking, the terms of his leave of absence—also authorized by Spain—required that he remain in *Louisiana* during the period of the leave. While one might assume that the Spanish authorities would be pleased to have Pierre-Joseph residing in Spanish territory, at least one key official was not.

Juan Vicente Folch y Juan (1754–1829), the Spanish governor of West Florida, considered Pierre-Joseph's presence in Baton Rouge a direct violation of the terms of his leave, and informed Charles de Grand-Pré (1754–1809), the commandant of Baton Rouge and a close friend of the Favrots, that he would not tolerate it. Folch instructed Grand-Pré to "urge [Pierre-Joseph] to rejoin his army without further delay or vacate and enjoy his leave of absence in Louisiana in the place for which it was granted."[19] It seems that, for Folch, there could be no flexibility in the interpretation of the terms of the leave, which, after all, had been granted by the king of Spain.

Pierre-Joseph, upon learning of Folch's demands, replied to Grand-Pré that his health prevented him from rejoining the army. He also stated: "I believe that Louisiana comprises the entire province, although the dividing line has separated the western bank of the river on which all of my property is located. I could not abandon it under any circumstances, because this would mean the ruination of my entire family." He added that he was convinced that the king would not mind his living on his plantation until he could sell the property.[20]

The situation grew more ominous over the summer. In August, Folch sent word through Grand-Pré that if Pierre-Joseph's son Louis did not report back for duty at the end of his furlough, he would be demoted.[21] A subsequent letter to Pierre-Joseph from Charles Howard (1739–?), another Spanish official at Pensacola, indicated that some sort of legal charges against Louis might be forthcoming.[22]

While Pierre-Joseph's earlier response to Grand-Pré might have seemed naïve or even disingenuous, it is possible that his comments reflected the common, if delusional, belief among many Creoles that the transfer of Louisiana to the United

States might be invalidated. Ever since the announcement of France's decision to sell the territory to the U.S., Spanish authorities had questioned the legality of the sale, citing Napoléon's admittedly unwritten promise to the effect that, should France ever decide to give up the colony, it would automatically revert to Spain. Several disputes between the American and Spanish governments emerged and intensified during 1804, stoking rumors among the Louisiana populace that somehow the various territories along the Gulf Coast might be reunited under Spanish rule. Writing in December of 1804, Pierre-Joseph's nephew Louis Brognier De Clouet reported:

> Letters dispatched from Cádiz [a port city in Spain] on October 20 assure us that the right [western] bank of the Mississippi River decidedly remains in Spain's possession. One has even added that the Marqués de Casa Calvo has been appointed captain general of the Texas provinces united to these provinces on the bank of the Mississippi. By the first mail, no doubt, we will have confirmation of the news. May God grant our wish![23]

De Clouet's optimism was misplaced, of course, but it would be some time before many Louisianians fully accepted the permanence of the colony's transfer to the United States. Meanwhile, the territory continued to face political threats as described later in this chapter.

Pierre-Joseph was back in New Orleans by December 1804, perhaps having failed to convince his superiors to allow him to stay in Baton Rouge. In January 1805, he decided to pursue a different course with the Spanish authorities. He wrote to the king again, this time requesting retirement with the rank of colonel—a promotion from his current rank of lieutenant colonel—and the active salary of a captain. He asked to be allowed to live with the garrison at Baton Rouge.[24] This implies that he still had hopes of keeping and managing his plantation across the river in Louisiana, but did not yet intend to live there full-time.

Several documents indicate that Pierre-Joseph returned to the Baton Rouge area in 1805 while still awaiting a response to his request for retirement. It is unclear whether he and his family were living with the garrison in Spanish territory or on their plantation in American territory. Louis must have been absolved of any legal charges and returned to active service in the Spanish military at some point during that year, since in February 1806 he was granted another leave of absence for unspecified reasons,[25] though in subsequent correspondence Pierre-Joseph refers to Louis's separation as retirement, rather than a leave of absence.[26] Louis was 17 years old at the time. Pierre-Joseph's second-oldest son, Philogène, also held a cadet's commission until September 1804, when he was discharged at the age of 13.[27]

Pierre-Joseph was finally awarded retirement at half-pay, apparently sometime in late 1807.[28] Thanks to bureaucratic delays and political events in Spain, however, it would be years before he would ever see any payments on the pension he had been promised.

The Favrots in Service to the United States

Soon after its purchase of Louisiana, the United States government embarked on a concerted effort to assimilate the new territory culturally, politically, and militarily. Keenly aware of New Orleans' strategic vulnerability, President Jefferson in 1806 drafted legislation that would provide land grants to young white males willing to live in the Orleans Territory—the name adopted in 1804 for the portion of the Louisiana Territory south of the 33rd parallel (corresponding to the present-day northern boundary of the State of Louisiana). Grantees would be required to live in the territory for at least seven years, during which they would spend at least two years on active duty in the militia. The plan would have the added benefit of attracting large numbers of American settlers to the territory, which, Jefferson hoped, would speed its cultural integration. The militia plan never won Congressional approval, however, and was finally dropped in 1808.[29]

Another of Jefferson's priorities was converting the territory's legal system, a mélange of French and Spanish civil law, into one based on English common law consistent with that of the rest of the United States. The two legal traditions differ in numerous ways, including the nature of court proceedings and the basis for rendering legal judgments. Civil law relies on explicit, written codes that dictate which cases may be brought to court, how they are to be tried, and what punishments should be rendered. Common law, on the other hand, is largely uncodified, and relies heavily on judicial precedent as a guide for court procedures and sentencing. Among the common law practices that Jefferson was eager to introduce to the Orleans Territory were the right to trial by jury and the writ of *habeas corpus*, which allows a detainee to sue for release from unlawful imprisonment.

Louisianians, accustomed to the French and Spanish legal traditions under which they had lived for generations, resisted efforts by the Jefferson administration to impose common law in the Orleans Territory. Their stalwart opposition posed great difficulties for Governor Claiborne. Charged with implementing Jefferson's policies, Claiborne was also personally skeptical of the existing legal system, which was plagued by delays and corruption. Recognizing that a rapid transition to the American system would be politically untenable, the governor adopted a gradual, cautious strategy of integration. He established courts that operated in accordance with common law traditions, but initially vetoed bills passed by the territorial legislature that sought to declare civil law as the law of the land.

In 1808, the legislature adopted *A Digest of the Civil Laws Now in Force in the Territory of Orleans, with Alterations and Amendments Adapted to its Present System of Government*, which accepted the civil law tradition in the territory. Published in both French and English, the digest was not a legal code *per se*, but a catalogue of existing Louisiana laws reflecting a mix of French, Spanish, and even Roman precedents. In the wake of Congress's failure to pass Jefferson's militia-and-settlement plan, Claiborne realized that an immediate, substantial influx of American settlers was unlikely, and that the cultural and political assimilation of the territory would be a much longer-term proposition than Jefferson and he had hoped. In a pragmatic gesture, he signed the legislation, and the *Digest* became the basis for the hybrid legal system that distinguishes Louisiana to this day.

An 1808 letter from Claiborne to Judge William Wikoff (1750–1821), while not directly related to the Favrots, is included in the family papers and is noteworthy because it illuminates his rationale for approving the legislation. In his letter to the judge, a fellow American, Claiborne affirmed his general preference that the laws of the Orleans Territory be consistent with those of the rest of the United States. "We ought to recollect, however, the peculiar circumstances under which Louisiana has been placed," wrote Claiborne, "and we ought not to be unmindful of the respect due the sentiments and wishes of the ancient Louisianians who compose so great a proportion of the population." Claiborne assumed that American-style laws eventually would work their way into the Orleans Territory code. Meanwhile, he told the judge, "I fear you will continue to experience difficulty in the faithful discharge of your official duties; the aversion of the ancient Louisianians to our courts of justice and particularly their dislike of lawyers, the *mutual jealousy* [emphasis original] between the French and American population, together with the great dislike of the latter to the principles of the civil law, which for the present will be your guide, cannot fail to render your situation unpleasant. . ."[30]

This period of political transition in Louisiana included an important milestone for the Favrot family. In October 1807, Louis was commissioned as an ensign in the Seventh Regiment of Militia in the Territory of Orleans.[31] This was an American unit under the command of territorial governor William C.C. Claiborne. Following generations of military service under French and Spanish kings—and briefly under the French first consul, Napoléon—a member of the Favrot family was now pledged to fight on behalf of the United States.

Even as Louisiana Creoles were becoming integrated into American society, events in Europe continued to interest and concern them. Since Napoléon's "election" as emperor of the French by means of a dubious plebiscite in November 1804, he had embroiled the European continent in a near-constant series of military conflicts collectively dubbed the Napoleonic Wars. In March 1808, his armies invaded Spain, forcing the abdication of King Charles IV and then that of Charles's son and successor, Ferdinand VII (1784–1833). Napoléon then installed his own brother, Joseph-Napoléon Bonaparte (1768–1844), on the Spanish throne. Pierre-Joseph, in a letter to a Spanish officer at Pensacola in December 1808, mentioned "the unfortunate troubles in Spain" and called Napoléon a "monster" who "causes much trouble in all four parts of the world."[32]

The overthrow of the Bourbon dynasty in Spain fostered consternation and confusion in the country's colonies. Most of the colonial governments began operating under provisional authorities called *juntas*, with varying degrees of success. In West Florida, Spanish control was gradually undermined by an influx of

American settlers, many of whom actively conspired to have the territory incorporated into the United States. The situation came to a head on September 23, 1810, when rebels successfully attacked the Spanish garrison at Baton Rouge. The victors then declared the establishment of the independent Republic of West Florida, with its capital at St. Francisville, a small settlement on the East Bank of the Mississippi River that is now the seat of Louisiana's West Feliciana Parish. The putative republic comprised only the westernmost portion of the West Florida territory—the eastern portion, centered around Mobile, remained in Spanish hands for the time being.

The rebellion not only engendered a new wave of political confusion along the Gulf Coast, but also brought personal tragedy to the Favrot family. Louis de Grand-Pré (ca. 1787–1810), who was the son of the late commandant of Baton Rouge, a close friend of Louis Favrot, and the fiancé of Joséphine Favrot, was mortally wounded in the battle. He died in Louis Favrot's arms. Pierre-Joseph eulogized the young Grand-Pré, saying, "This martyr, or rather, this model of honor, was 23 years old. . . . His loss was even mourned by the enemies of his government, who delivered public testimonies of veneration by giving him funeral honors that were marked most touchingly by all that sorrow and mourning could offer."[33] It is unclear why Louis, an ensign in the U.S. militia of the Orleans Territory, was at the Baton Rouge fort—in Spanish territory—during the battle. As for Joséphine, she was never engaged again and never married.

The American government refused to recognize the Republic of West Florida as an independent nation. In late October 1810, President James Madison (1751–1836) unilaterally announced the annexation of the region by the United States and its incorporation into the Orleans Territory. The rebels did not accept the annexation, hoping instead for direct admission to the union as a state. Governor Claiborne subsequently led troops into the wayward territory, taking St. Francisville on December 6 and Baton Rouge on December 10. The rebels acquiesced, and the short-lived Republic of West Florida was dissolved. The region became part of the Orleans Territory as Madison had initially decreed. (The U.S. gained control of the remainder of West Florida from Spain in 1813, during the War of 1812.)

Pierre-Joseph remained bitter about the attack on Baton Rouge, which he blamed on Spanish authorities' removal of Charles de Grand-Pré from command of the post in 1809 and his replacement by a well-intentioned officer who, unfortunately, delegated most authority to a corrupt deputy named Raphael Crocker (life dates unknown). In a letter to the Marqués de Someruelos (life dates unknown), the captain general of Cuba, in January 1811, Pierre-Joseph did not mince words: "[Crocker's] boundless cupidity has caused the downfall of this place. . . . No affair was transacted except through bribery. Persons attached to the Spanish government for twenty-five years have been cheated. . ." He backed up his assertions with several specific, detailed descriptions of Crocker's nefarious dealings. Pierre-Joseph concluded by stating his belief that the rebellion resulted not from dissatisfaction with Spanish rule in general, but from anger over the "mercenary" behavior of one key official.[34] His argument is notable because it contradicts prevailing historical views regarding the causes of the insurrection.

The upheaval in West Florida coincided with growing tensions between the United States and Great Britain. The British, already at war with French forces under Napoléon, had issued in 1807 the Orders in Council, a series of proclamations that supported the country's blockade of France. As a neutral party in the Anglo-French conflict, the U.S. objected to the orders as an unreasonable restraint of international trade. The American government was also angered by the British navy's increasingly frequent habit of kidnapping American seamen and forcing them to serve on British vessels—a practice known as impressment. Adding to the friction were British efforts to arm Native American tribes as buffers to potential American expansionism toward the north and west.

As the U.S. and Britain careened toward war, Pierre-Joseph's two eldest sons were preparing to help defend their new country. Louis received a promotion to captain in June 1811. In awarding the commission, Governor Claiborne noted his "special trust and confidence in [Louis's] patriotism, valor, fidelity, and ability."[35] Philogène joined his brother as an American soldier in March 1812, when he was commissioned as an ensign of infantry in the Army of the United States.[36]

On the eve of war came another momentous event in the history of Louisiana. On April 30, 1812, the Orleans Territory, including the former portion of West Florida as far east as the Pearl River, was admitted to the union as the State of

Louisiana. The granting of statehood followed years of fierce debate in Congress about the constitutionality of expanding the union, the voting rights of free men of color, and the potential disloyalty of Louisiana citizens, given their tradition of close association with two European powers. As Louisiana became a state, to avoid confusion, the portion of the former Louisiana Territory north of the new state line was renamed the Missouri Territory.

A special election to choose the state's first governor was held in July 1812. The campaign revealed a continuing cultural and political rift between the Creoles and the Americans in Louisiana. Claiborne, the American territorial governor, was pitted against two Creole candidates: Jacques Villeré (1761–1830) and Jean Noël Destréhan (1754–1823). The Favrots' sympathies were with their fellow Creoles, though apparently they did not have a strong preference between them. In a letter to his brother Louis, Philogène wrote, "I hope, my dear friend, that being a Creole, you voted for one of your fellow citizens."[37] The family was disappointed when Claiborne, who had gradually earned the trust of the citizenry during his term as territorial governor and twice married into Creole families, won the election with more than 70 percent of the vote. Four years later, Villeré would become the state's second governor.

America and Britain at War Again

By the time of Claiborne's election, the U.S. was already officially at war with Great Britain. Neither side was well prepared for the conflict—the American military was small and poorly trained, while the British were preoccupied by the ongoing war against Napoléon. Both sides in what came to be called the War of 1812 entered into alliances with various Native American tribes. Most of the early battles in the war occurred either at sea, in British Canada, or in the far northern U.S. states and territories, far from Louisiana.

Louis, Philogène, and other Louisiana soldiers nevertheless readied themselves for possible action. Philogène, whose personal letters often reflected a youthful cockiness, was in classic form when he wrote to his brother regarding his training around July 1812: "To the right face—This is all I have learned up to now; you see that I have profited a great deal since the time I left you!" After that introductory joke, he went on to say that he planned to seek an appointment as an aide-de-camp to General Wilkinson,[38] the officer who, with Claiborne, had formally accepted Louisiana from France in 1803.** He was unsuccessful in obtaining that position, however, due to his youth and lack of fluency in English, despite the efforts of his father to intervene on his behalf.[39] By October of 1812 he was stationed at Plaquemines, where his father had served as commandant years earlier.[40] Philogène was reasonably satisfied with the posting, in part because the circumstances there encouraged him to improve his English.[41]

Philogène kept a journal during the spring and summer of 1813, in which he noted that he was studying medicine,[42] a development that made his family very proud.[43] He also received a promotion to second lieutenant.[44] As the weeks passed, however, the young man, who turned 22 on May 4, became increasingly restless and eager for a more active military assignment.[45] He devoted much of his free time to writing letters to his family at the plantation near Baton Rouge, and eagerly awaiting their replies.

Philogène soon became involved in a dispute between two other officers at the post. He overheard a lieutenant named Stergus make disparaging remarks about a Captain Miller, commander of volunteers, whom Philogène respected. Out of a sense of duty and honor, he decided to inform Miller, who thanked him and stated that he "would obtain redress," suggesting the possibility of a duel. Instead, Miller asked that a superior officer have Stergus arrested, which happened immediately. Philogène considered this a cowardly act on Miller's part, and declared that he would no longer take orders from the captain. When he directly challenged Miller's authority in front of other troops, he was placed under arrest and confined to his room. Miller and Stergus subsequently reconciled, but that did not satisfy Philogène, who now considered Miller insufficiently brave to

---

** Wilkinson had a reputation for duplicity and was the subject of several Congressional and military inquiries, but he was never convicted of any wrongdoing. After his death, however, historians found documents proving that he was a longtime agent of the Spanish crown, to which he had sworn allegiance in 1787. Known by the code name "Number Thirteen," he continued to receive payments from Spain in exchange for American military secrets until at least 1800. Wilkinson was also implicated in the Burr Conspiracy of 1804–1807, a still-murky affair in which former vice president Aaron Burr allegedly sought to establish his own empire by taking control of parts of the Louisiana territory and possibly Mexico. Burr was captured and tried for treason in 1807, but was acquitted.

command others. Meanwhile, the garrison received orders to leave for Tennessee, where Philogène's regiment was to merge with another one. With that mission pending, Philogène was released from confinement and returned to active duty.[46] There is no record of his ever informing his family of the incident.

The regiment reached Nashville by September 1813. Philogène was surprised by the quality of the architecture and infrastructure there. "I did not expect this little city to be so well built," he wrote to his mother after he arrived. "The streets are paved, all of the houses are made of bricks with elegant cornices painted white, and the roofs are red. In the center of a large square, in the upper part of town, stands the city hall, which is a very beautiful two-story building."[47]

While Philogène was assigned to visit a nearby town to recruit new soldiers to the regiment, other troops were massing for a campaign against the Creek tribe. Some 5,000 volunteers from Tennessee were expected to join a similar number from Georgia to form an overwhelming force that would attack Native American settlements. In an echo of strategic statements made by French authorities in Louisiana during the time of his grandfather, Philogène stated bluntly that the troops' mission was "to exterminate all of [the Creeks] at the same time."[48] He later wrote to his father regarding the details of the battles between the volunteer regiments and the Creeks, touting lopsided victories for the former, with relatively few casualties.[49] His account bore no hint of sympathy for the defeated Native Americans, who, at the time, were still almost universally regarded by whites as "savages."

Philogène's regiment left Nashville in November, arriving at Lexington, Kentucky, in December. The journey was an interesting one for him. "We crossed a little river whose banks were formed by a perpendicular rock three hundred feet high," he wrote in a letter to his mother. "This spectacle is rather new for a Louisianian who has never seen anything higher than a cypress tree."[50] From Lexington, the regiment moved on to Newport in northern Kentucky, across the Ohio River from Cincinnati.

Meanwhile, in Europe, the tide of the Napoleonic Wars was turning. French forces had invaded Russia in 1812 and soon captured Moscow, which had been nearly abandoned by the citizenry and partially burned, leaving little food and few other resources for the occupying army. The Russians steadfastly refused to capitulate, resulting in a stalemate lasting several weeks. When the French troops began to retreat, they were caught in grueling winter weather for which they were inadequately prepared. Tens of thousands of French soldiers died from hypothermia or starvation. An embarrassed Napoléon returned to Paris with only a fraction of the force with which he had begun.

The disastrous Russian campaign emboldened the anti-French coalition, which by then included not only Great Britain and Russia, but also Austria, Prussia, Sweden, Spain, and Portugal, among other countries. As the ranks of the coalition armies swelled, French forces were increasingly outnumbered. In March 1814, France finally surrendered, and the following month Napoléon was exiled for the first time to Elba. The Bourbon dynasty was restored when the grandson of Louis XV, Louis Stanislas Xavier (1755–1824), assumed the French throne as Louis XVIII. Ferdinand VII, who had been ousted by Napoléon in 1808, had already been restored to the throne in Spain.

The news of these events was presumably welcomed by Pierre-Joseph, who had called Napoléon a "monster," though there is no remaining record of his reaction. His nephew Brognier De Clouet was certainly excited, if perhaps overly optimistic, about the news, writing, "You know about the grand and happy events which took place in Europe: the Bourbons, our dear Bourbons, have been restored with all of their rights and have become the idols of France and Spain again. Everything is going well in those two kingdoms."[51]

Philogène, however, did not share his father's and his cousin's views. Upon learning of Napoléon's exile, he wrote to Pierre-Joseph: "[France], by declaring itself in favor of Louis XVIII, Duke of Angoulême, showed itself ungrateful toward the one to whom it owed all its glory and splendor. French people have always been fickle and probably will always remain so. The hair of the politicians in Baton Rouge must be standing on end now that they have learned of the fate of their god, Napoléon."[52]

The apparent conclusion of the pan-European Napoleonic Wars—which would flare up again briefly following Napoléon's escape from Elba and return to power—freed up British troops for the ongoing war in North America, which intensified in the spring and summer of 1814. During that period, Philogène was gradually moving closer to the front lines of the conflict. From Newport, Kentucky, he marched with 70 men through Ohio to Fort Sandusky, near the shore of Lake Erie, where he "practiced medicine" while posted there for a month.[53] He then traveled through part of Canada, and finally to Detroit, arriving by June. He began lying about his location in letters to his immediate family, in fear that they would worry about his proximity to Canada, the site of so many prominent battles during the war.[54]

Philogène's well-intentioned deception was exposed when his cousin Fergus Duplantier (1783–1844), to whom he had written more candid letters, spread a rumor that Philogène had, in fact, seen battle, and that supposedly both his "servant," Manuel, and his horse had been killed during one skirmish. The rumor confirmed the suspicions of his brother Louis, who had noticed that Philogène's recent letters were postmarked from Detroit, and not from Fort Meigs, Ohio, where he had claimed to be stationed.[55] Philogène later informed his brother directly that he had indeed participated in an unsuccessful attack on Fort Michilimackinac, near the juncture of lakes Huron and Michigan, and that his regiment suffered 66 casualties in the battle. The rumors about his slave Manuel and horse, however, were false—Manuel was not present at the battle site, and Philogène did not have a horse with him at the time. "You should have believed only half of what Fergus told you," he wrote to Louis, "or nothing."[56]

In the late summer of 1814, British troops launched new assaults on the Chesapeake Bay area in an effort to divert American military assets from the more northerly battlefronts. The so-called Chesapeake Campaign culminated on August 24 when the British swept into the poorly defended capital of Washington, D.C. They set fire to the Capitol building, the Executive Mansion, and other key public buildings, leaving much of the city in ruins. News of the destruction of the young capital shocked Americans and even elicited condemnation from some leaders of other European nations, who considered it an unnecessary act of vandalism.

British forces then went on toward Baltimore, where in mid-September they launched a series of attacks on the city and its surrounding defenses. This time, they encountered much stronger resistance from American forces. After several days of battle—immortalized by Francis Scott Key in his poem "Defence of Fort McHenry," which later became the basis for the American national anthem—the British withdrew.

The War Comes to Louisiana

Even as Americans were celebrating the victory at Baltimore, there were signs that the war was about to spread to a new theater: the Gulf Coast. "News from Pensacola states that the English are making big preparations to capture New Orleans," wrote Pierre-Joseph to Philogène that same month. "People say that they have landed about three thousand men and eight hundred Negroes at the Appalaches [Apalachicola], that they have equipped Savages with uniforms at Pensacola, and that they expect reinforcements."[57] The letter's explicit distinction between "men" (i.e., white men) and "Negroes" and "Savages" starkly illuminates the common view among early 19th-century European Americans that black Africans and Native Americans were not merely inferior races, but somehow not quite fully human. The alarmist language also reflects the common fear among Louisianians that an advancing British army might offer slaves refuge behind its lines and, if victorious, would abolish slavery completely.

Pierre-Joseph added that the Louisiana militia had been ordered to form an army of 1,000 men, and that Louis, who had been promoted to major the previous year,[58] volunteered to join. He also recounted rumors that the British intended to recapture Louisiana and return the territory to Spain, and that the Native Americans accompanying the British troops "had been ordered not to harm anyone who has a French or Spanish flag in front of his house."[59]

The Favrot family was comforted to learn in September that Philogène was being transferred back to Nashville, far from any of the frontlines of the war.[60] Their relief was short-lived, however. In October, as tensions along the Gulf Coast grew, Philogène's regiment was ordered to Mobile to reinforce the garrison there.[61] Although New Orleans was widely recognized as the most likely target of the British vessels prowling nearby, the family had good reason to fear that Mobile was also threatened.

Pierre-Joseph had continued to play a prominent role in Louisiana's military and political affairs since it achieved statehood. In the summer of 1814, he was elected to the state legislature. He would have preferred that Louis serve instead, but Louis had "neglected to show that he was a property owner"—a requirement for statewide elective office at the time. Nonetheless, Pierre-Joseph fully expected that Louis would take his place the following year.[62]

Amid the growing specter of a British invasion of Louisiana, Pierre-Joseph offered his views on the defense of the state in a memorandum written in November 1814. He began by addressing the need for Fort Saint Philip and Fort Bourbon to be in the best possible condition, armed, and ready—not surprising, given his intimate familiarity with those forts, which he had commanded for a total of six years. Other recommendations included sending an old, "disabled" ship, *La Louisiana*, to La Balize, where it could be scuttled if necessary to obstruct potential entry points for British ships to the Mississippi River. He concluded by advising that all necessary preparations be executed in one week, lest Louisiana forces run the risk of being taken by surprise.[63] It is unclear whether Pierre-Joseph wrote the memorandum on his own initiative or at the request of a military official, or whether the document was ever sent.

In December 1814, Major General Andrew Jackson (1767–1845), commander of the Seventh United States Military District, which covered the Gulf Coast, arrived in New Orleans to take charge of the defense of the city. The first military engagement in the area came on December 14, when British ships broke through an American blockade to enter Lake Borgne, just east of New Orleans. Two days later, with invasion appearing imminent, Jackson used his military authority to declare martial law in New Orleans and its environs. No one was allowed to enter the city without first reporting to military officials, and no individual or boat was permitted to leave without written permission from Jackson or a member of his staff.[64] Jackson, his troops, and the citizens of New Orleans steeled themselves for a battle that they believed could begin at any moment.

The British used their free access to Lake Borgne as a conduit for bringing troops ashore, eventually setting up camp several miles downriver from New Orleans. All indications are that they expected to take the city quickly and with little resistance. Jackson, however, learned the position of the British camp and launched a surprise nighttime attack on December 23. While the ensuing battle was indecisive, it may have convinced the British that the campaign would not be as easy as anticipated, and that they should await reinforcements. The delay allowed the Americans to strengthen their physical defenses substantially. Jackson used slave labor to widen and deepen the Rodriguez Canal, near the Chalmette Plantation, to form a sort of moat. He then ordered the displaced dirt to be piled into an embankment, which was reinforced with wood. When finished, the barrier stretched roughly a mile from the river to a nearly impenetrable swamp.

With reinforcements on hand, the British advanced toward New Orleans early on January 8, 1815. When they reached the Rodriguez Canal, they came under heavy fire from the Louisiana troops, who were reinforced by large numbers of volunteers from Tennessee and Kentucky. The American contingent also included a number of Choctaw warriors—now U.S. allies—and even some pirates loyal to Jean Lafitte (ca. 1780–ca. 1823), the notorious smuggler, who lent their assistance in exchange for federal pardons for their crimes. The British launched charge after charge, most of which failed dramatically as their soldiers were wounded or killed in horrifying numbers. Their commander, General Edward Pakenham (1778–1815), was hit multiple times by grapeshot—small projectiles fired from a cannon—and died on the battlefield. In roughly a half-hour, the British suffered more than 2,000 casualties, while Jackson's forces had lost anywhere from about a dozen to 100 men, based on different accounts.

The next day, British ships that had been anchored near the mouth of the Mississippi commenced a last-ditch attack on Fort Saint Philip, where both Pierre-Joseph and Philogène Favrot had been posted previously. The garrison withstood ten days of fire before the British vessels finally retreated. Louisiana, after less than a month of intense conflict, was out of imminent danger.

The irony of the Battle of New Orleans was that it took place after the U.S. and Britain had signed a peace treaty on December 24, just as Jackson's forces were retreating from the initial land battle with the British. Because the treaty was signed in Ghent, a Flemish city in what is now Belgium, confirmation of the agreement took a couple of months to reach the United States. President James Madison ratified the document on February 17, 1815, in the Octagon House, his temporary residence after the burning of the Executive Mansion (and later the headquarters of the American Institute of Architects). The treaty officially went into effect upon its approval by the U.S. Senate the following day. So, while the Treaty of Ghent was signed before the Battle of New Orleans began, technically it was not yet in effect at the time. Even after the treaty was ratified, there were rampant rumors in Louisiana that the British might abrogate the agreement and attempt another assault on the Gulf Coast.

The news of the battle itself, of course, reached Baton Rouge more quickly. Joséphine Favrot was moved to write a tribute to the defenders of New Orleans titled "A Louisianian Speaking for Her Women Contemporaries." The essay, dated January 15, 1815, not only captured the sense of relief and pride that swept over the state, but also reflected the gradual but steady emotional assimilation of Creole families into the American fabric:

> Inspired by the sublime example [the American troops] left us, as well as by the desire to aid our country's courageous defenders, we [women] would have won our enemy's admiration by telling them we knew how to combine advantages people concede that we have: high spirits and courage which usually do not belong to such naturally weak and timid creatures. But when we saw complete security rapidly following a moment of turmoil and more soldiers coming from every direction than were needed to defeat an even more formidable force than the British army, we felt pity for the enemies who were already enslaved. Today, when their defeat justifies our foreboding, being guided by compassion, we forgive their audacity. We can only lament the disastrous consequences of their presumptuousness. . . .
>
> How did [the British] not reject the fantastic hope of triumphing simultaneously over Louisiana courage, American patriotism, French intrepidity and the ability of our generals?.... [T]hey regret too late, no doubt, that after having surmounted so many obstacles, they went forth to sacrifice the elite of their troops at the gates of New Orleans. . . .
>
> And you, illustrious and magnanimous Jackson, filled the adversary's soul with terror and the hearts of Louisiana women with gratitude. . . . Your name will forever be pronounced by us with veneration and Fame will publicize your sublime conduct everywhere. . . .

Flee, presumptuous English, flee quickly; it is your only recourse; but before withdrawing, in order to leave us a souvenir of your work, do not forget to follow Hercules's example of erecting a column above your encampment and have engraved upon it this inscription: *Non plus ultra....*[††][65]

Governor Claiborne referred to the practical and emotional engagement—but gendered role—of women in the conflict in a printed broadside he issued on January 26:

The honorable manner in which heads of families behaved has already been mentioned, but there is another circumstance we will never forget: it is the interesting and truly admirable conduct of this amiable sex whose smiles soothe life's misfortunes and whose charms add another price to the benefits of liberty. The sincere wishes and the fond memory of that enchanting sex accompanied soldiers to battlefields; it was thanks to their delicate hands that a sentinel during cold wintry nights had his protective clothes; it was those same hands that brought comfort to soldiers who were still suffering from bloody wounds.[66]

Philogène's regiment, after two months of marching from Nashville, had arrived in Mobile the day after Christmas, and he was still there when the British launched the January 8 attack on New Orleans.[67] Frankly eager for military action, he was disappointed to have missed the battle. He later wrote to Louis: "I would have given anything I owned to have been there."[68] In a letter to Louis dated February 27, 1815, Philogène stated that Pierre-Joseph had said that Louis was in camp on the day of the battle,[69] but this was apparently incorrect. In a letter to his brother dated March 29, Louis wrote, "You must have heard that I took part in

---

†† *Non plus ultra* is a Latin phrase meaning, in this context, "nothing further." Joséphine was referring to the legend that the phrase was somehow inscribed into the Pillars of Hercules—a pair of mountains framing the opening of the Mediterranean Sea into the Atlantic Ocean—as a warning to ancient sailors against venturing into the unknown of the open ocean.

the campaign."[70] Louis's obituary in 1876 also stated that he had participated in
the battle.[71]

Post-War Life

Shortly after the British withdrawal from Louisiana, Philogène was appointed to an administrative military position as assistant adjutant general.[72] He was
stationed at Camp Mandeville, on the northern shore of Lake Pontchartrain.[73]
Although the job involved a good deal of bureaucratic paperwork, he relished the
authority that came with it. He wrote to Louis in late February: "I had the pleasure of arresting a brigadier general and taking his sword from him; that was nothing to sneeze at!" He also noted in a matter-of-fact tone that he had sent seven
men to the firing squad following their convictions under a court martial, and had
seen "that a saber was broken over the head of a militia officer who had been given
this sentence by the same court."[74]

Philogène was transferred back to Mobile in March, which disappointed him.
"You are aware," he wrote to his family, "that [I think] Mobile is the dullest, most
insipid, most boring place in the world."[75] His boredom was soon relieved, however, because he was back in New Orleans by April 7. The circumstances of his departure from Mobile are unknown, though he noted that he had left "hurriedly."[76]

He quickly resettled into New Orleans social life and once again enjoyed access to relatively reliable information and gossip from around the world. In May
1815, he wrote to his father with the surprising news that Napoléon Bonaparte
was back on the throne of France.[77] His account of the events leading to the restoration was reasonably accurate. Napoléon, who had been exiled to the small
Mediterranean island of Elba, escaped in February of that year aboard a French
ship accompanied by hundreds of local men whom he had recruited to form a
personal army. After landing on the French mainland, he and his men were confronted by King Louis XVIII's troops. Napoléon approached them with a small
group of his own soldiers and offered his life to whomever might wish to take it.
Instead, the royal troops yelled *Vive l'Empereur!* and escorted him to Paris. The
king and his court fled as soon as they learned that Napoléon was on his way.

The reaction in New Orleans to the news of Napoléon's return to the throne revealed the continuing cultural affinity between the city and its former mother country. Philogène reported to his father that "a bust of Bonaparte was carried through the streets, with candles and music and shouts of '*Vive Napoléon!*'" A specially composed play was presented at a theater in New Orleans to mark the occasion.[78]

The other major European powers, however, which had lost hundreds of thousands of troops in their past conflicts with Napoléon, quickly resolved to stop him from regaining and consolidating power. They formed yet another military coalition and began assembling troops for a possible invasion of France. In June, just two months after retaking the throne, Napoléon attempted to ward off such an invasion by launching a campaign against coalition forces in a part of the Netherlands that now lies within modern-day Belgium. The campaign ended with the infamous Battle of Waterloo on June 18, 1815, when British and Prussian troops resoundingly defeated Napoléon's army. The emperor abdicated for the second time on June 22. He was exiled again, this time to the extremely remote South Atlantic island of Saint Helena, where he remained for the rest of his life. Napoléon's attempt to have his four-year-old son succeed him as Napoléon II was thwarted by the country's provisional government. Louis XVIII soon returned to Paris and resumed his reign, which continued for another nine years until his death in 1824.

A letter from Philogène to his father written in September 1815 relates to a New Orleans legend that has been told—with varying degrees of accuracy—to countless tourists over the years. "Today's news," he wrote, "states that Bonaparte left Paris for America on June 29."[79] Indeed, there were rumors afoot that Napoléon was bound not only for the United States, but specifically for New Orleans—a story that had a certain logic, given the city's French roots and the continuing prevalence of the French language there. The rumors were false, of course, but they gave way by 1821 to a deliberate campaign on the part of a former mayor of New Orleans, Nicholas Girod (1751–1840), to bring the exiled emperor to the city. Girod even went so far as to refurbish the building he owned at the corner of Chartres and St. Louis streets as a future home for Napoléon. The exiled emperor's death in May 1821 ended the scheme, but the building, dubbed the Napoleon House, still stands today and houses a popular bar of the same name.

After the war, both Louis and Philogène were appointed to political positions. Governor Claiborne named Louis collector of taxes for West Baton Rouge Parish in January 1816.[80] Louis did not give up his military commission, however, and in fact, was promoted to colonel in February of the following year.[81] Two years after that, his brother Philogène was appointed parish judge for West Baton Rouge Parish[82] despite having no known legal education or experience, though he may have learned something about legal procedure during his brief assignment as assistant adjutant general at Camp Mandeville.

April 1819 brought the first marriage of one of Pierre-Joseph and Marie-Françoise's children when Louis wed Augustine-Eulalie Duplantier, his first cousin on his mother's side. Because of their close blood relationship, the couple had to obtain special permission to marry from the vicar general of Louisiana.[83] Perhaps in anticipation of his upcoming wedding and plans to raise a family, the previous month Louis had bought a plot of land in East Baton Rouge Parish in an area known as the German Highlands (now called the Dutch Highlands as derived from the German word *Deutsch*) because its earliest European settlers were largely German. The property was 24 *arpents* by 40 *arpents*,[††] or about 812 acres. The topography of the site was advantageous, since it included a swath of fertile land along the river abutting higher ground atop a bluff, where houses and other structures could be built without risk of flooding.[84]

In June 1819, with his 70th birthday approaching and his eyesight failing, Pierre-Joseph decided it was time to entrust the family papers he had so meticulously collected over the decades to Louis, his eldest son. In a cover letter accompanying the box of original papers, he wrote, "Preserve these honorable documents so that they may be handed down to your posterity, who will respect the memory of your ancestors." The letter also expressed his regret that he had been unable to provide for his family as well as he would have liked: "Please believe, my son, that . . . I have never been able to recover from the loss I suffered in two

---

†† An *arpent* was a measure of length and of area. In length, an arpent was equal to about 191.834 feet, while in area, it was equal to 0.84628 acres.

fires. Twenty-two thousand dollars was the amount I lost." The first line of the concluding paragraph suggests that Pierre-Joseph believed that his death was imminent: "Accept, my dear son, the everlasting farewell of an affectionate father who loves you." Pierre-Joseph also made copies of the most important documents, such as his military commissions, for each of his other male children, Philogène and Bouvier.[85]

A Disagreement Turns Deadly

As Marie-Françoise and her children were steeling themselves for the death of the increasingly frail Pierre-Joseph, an unexpected tragedy befell the family. It began with an insult, though the details are unknown. Extant documents in the Favrot Family Papers suggest that Philogène had made remarks to, or about, Sébastian Hiriart (1774–1850), a West Baton Rouge planter and state senator, that the latter considered defamatory. Hiriart, in response, challenged Philogène to a duel.[86]

While technically illegal in Louisiana since the initial French colonial period, dueling was still a common practice in the state—and elsewhere in the American South—in the early 19th century. The impetus for a duel was often astonishingly trivial. When an aggrieved party issued such a challenge, however, it was difficult for his opponent to refuse, lest he be accused of cowardice or dishonor—allegations that could, in extreme cases, make it impossible for him to do business or obtain credit in his community. Once a challenge was accepted, elaborate rules governed the preparations for the confrontation. Typically, each of the opponents would choose at least one "second," whose responsibilities might include selecting the time and place of battle, inspecting the chosen weapons, and—perhaps—talking the duelers out of the confrontation. Should the seconds fail in that last duty, they would monitor the fight for fairness, tend to survivors' wounds, and report the outcome to the public if necessary. The most infamous duel in American history was undoubtedly that in which Aaron Burr (1756–1836), the sitting vice president of the United States under Thomas Jefferson, fatally wounded Alexander Hamilton (1755–1804), one of the framers of the Constitution and a former secretary of the Treasury under George Washington.

Evidence suggests that Philogène and Hiriart tried to negotiate an alternative to battle through Hiriart's second, Louis Esnault (1779–1831), who, like Philogène, was a judge.

"It is infinitely disagreeable for me," Philogène wrote to Esnault, "to again have to speak to you of an affair, which I thought had ended, but because of my reputation, I am forced to adopt the only means possible to hush this calumny and malice. A few lines from you relating the facts concisely would fully satisfy me and put an end to any other difficulties.[87]

The events related to the dispute from that point forward are muddled. Philogène apparently refused to fight Hiriart directly, but declared that he was prepared to fight Esnault instead, if Esnault were willing to "espouse the interest of Mr. Hiriart." Esnault claimed that he accepted Philogène's counter-challenge, "but upon learning from Mr. Favrot himself that he bore [him] no ill will personally," proposed that the matter be dropped.[88] It was not.

Philogène and Esnault met each other for the duel at Pinckneyville, a small town in what is now southwestern Mississippi, on February 11, 1822. Sabers were the chosen weapons. In a frantic battle, Esnault incurred four wounds, but survived. Philogène, however, was killed.[89] He was 30 years old.

Philogène's parents and siblings were devastated by his death. A newspaper obituary, presumably written by a close relative, since it mirrors that language of the inscription on his tomb, referred to him as the "support and idol" of his family. "Hero of filial devotion, of fraternal love, of friendship; judge, honest and conciliatory; man, upright and beneficent; citizen, patriotic and courageous; he made himself distinguished in the society by the combined possession, not so common, of all that can make a man respectable and worthy of being loved."[90] Philogène was initially buried at Pointe Coupée, not far from the site of the duel, but his body was later exhumed and reinterred in Baton Rouge.[91] A memorial service, held at the cathedral in New Orleans on May 11, drew "a large assemblage of citizens."[92]

Louisiana governor Thomas B. Robertson (1779–1828) quickly appointed Louis Favrot to succeed his dead brother as judge of West Baton Rouge Parish.[93] He also became judge of the Court of Probates, and among his first responsibilities was overseeing the disposition of Philogène's estate.[94] Later, Louis would also find himself embroiled in a continuation of his brother's dispute with Hiriart, as discussed later in this chapter.

The End of an Era

On June 26, 1824, Pierre-Joseph, the Favrot patriarch whose life had spanned Louisiana's French and Spanish colonial periods, its brief return to French rule, its purchase by the United States, and its elevation to full statehood, finally succumbed to the various maladies that had afflicted him for so many years. Besides his contributions as a soldier, an elected official, an advisor to military and political leaders, and progenitor of a large and prominent Louisiana family, he earned a place in history as the spearhead of one of America's great familial archives. More than a century after his death, his great-great-granddaughter-in-law, Helen Parkhurst Favrot, would dub him "the Creole Pepys,"[95] a reference to Samuel Pepys (1633–1703), the English Member of Parliament whose extensive diaries provide vital first-hand accounts of some of the most significant events of the 17th century, including the Great Fire of London of 1666. The Favrot Family Papers similarly provide a unique perspective on 18th- and 19th-century Louisiana history.

There is relatively little material in the family archives from the period just after Pierre-Joseph's death, perhaps because his heirs had not yet developed the habit of collecting documents as faithfully as their father had. Louis nonetheless assumed the mantle of family leader, and in March 1825, his surviving siblings, Joséphine, Octavine, Bouvier, and Pulchérie, all sold their rights to land in their father's estate to him.[96] Louis thus became the sole owner of the plantation in West Baton Rouge, which would remain the family homestead for decades to come. Like Joséphine, neither Octavine nor Pulchérie ever married. Both Joséphine and Octavine lived at the plantation for the rest of their lives.

Louis and his wife, Augustine-Eulalie, had their first child, a daughter named Françoise-Augustine Favrot, in 1820. A son born in 1824 died the next year. Then, in 1826, Augustine-Eulalie gave birth to Henri Mortimer Favrot (nicknamed "Alot"), who, as the eldest surviving son, would later inherit the Favrot family plantation. Three daughters born later all died in infancy or early childhood.

The simmering feud between Louis Favrot and Sèbastien Hiriart reached a boiling point again in 1830, fully eight years after the dispute that led to Philogène's death in the duel. This time, the battle was waged entirely in words, though in a highly public fashion that implicated many Baton Rouge-area citizens beyond both families. In May of that year, when Hiriart was running for reelection to the Louisiana State Senate, the *Baton Rouge Gazette* published a letter to the editor, which, without mentioning Hiriart by name or expressly accusing him of specific wrongdoing, posed a series of rhetorical questions as to whether an unnamed political candidate was improperly trying to manipulate the electoral process.[97] The letter was signed under the pseudonym "Verbumsat," a play on the Latin phrase *verbum sat sapienti est*, meaning "a word to the wise is sufficient."

It is likely, but uncertain, that the letter to the editor was actually written by Louis Favrot, because the next month Louis published under his own name a broadside "in support of his accusations against Sèbastien Hiriart." The broadside contained sworn statements by six people accusing Hiriart of judicial improprieties. The statements alleged that Hiriart had solicited and accepted bribes, and that he had tried to persuade a witness to commit perjury in testimony related to the duel between Philogène and Louis Esnault in 1822.[98]

Louis Favrot published two other broadsides around the same time, including one in which he responded to accusations by Hiriart that Louis had charged excessive fees related to his judicial duties. Some 18 citizens contributed statements to that flyer, some of whom certified that Louis had charged them fairly for court services, while most of them stated that, in fact, he had not charged them anything at all for basic judicial procedures such as estate settlements and marriage ceremonies.[99] Yet another broadside published at about the same time listed the names of more than 100 citizens of West Baton Rouge—surely a substantial portion of the area's eligible voters at the time—who pledged that they would not vote for Hiriart in his State Senate race.[100]

Hiriart, inevitably, retaliated with his own broadside, which included some extraordinary allegations. Louis, he claimed, "bearing a hideous and sinister soul, and it is a notorious fact, tried, on the night of June 5–6, 1822, to kill me and my family; and, everyone knows, it was only by the stroke of good fortune that myself and some member of my family were not victims of his guilty attack." A statement later in the document suggested that that shocking accusation may have been at least partially metaphorical: "On the aforementioned night, this vile character, wrapping himself in the shadows of mystery, sought to murder me by destroying my reputation." The lengthy, rambling document, which reiterated the allegations about Louis's charging excessive fees, was riddled with sensationalistic language, referring to Louis as a "venomous reptile" with a "filthy and impure mouth" that had "vomited perfidious invectives."[101]

In September 1830, Louis filed a libel suit against Hiriart in court, citing the broadside in which he was accused of attempted murder, whether literally or figuratively. Louis claimed that he had already suffered $20,000 in damages as a direct result of Hiriart's accusations. The case ground on for years. Louis partially blamed the slow progress of the lawsuit on Hiriart for certain "subterfuges," such as his attorneys' repeated efforts to postpone the trial either because they needed more time to prepare their case or wished to lodge protests against specific potential jurors. Other, clearly unrelated hurdles arose, such as an outbreak of cholera in 1832, which led to the suspension of judicial proceedings in the fall of that year.[102] Louis frequently noted during this period that Hiriart had never countersued *him* for libel, suggesting that Hiriart knew that he did not have adequate evidence to prevail in such a suit.

It was not until 1836—more than six years after the lawsuit was filed and 14 years after the duel that killed Philogène—that the case was finally dropped. Louis agreed to withdraw the suit when Hiriart retracted his principal accusation. An addendum to the court order dismissing the case stated: "Mr. Hiriart has since more carefully & deliberately examined the facts & circumstances on which he made that charge [and] finds that he cannot in justice to Judge Favrot persist in making it. He therefore without reserve withdraws that accusation, & exhonerates [*sic*] Judge Favrot."[103]

The drawn-out legal battle between Louis and Hiriart must have caused great stress among other Favrot family members, especially Louis's mother, Marie-Françoise, and sister Joséphine, both of whom were predisposed to often debilitating bouts of anxiety and depression compounded by frequent physical illness. While the resolution of the case was certainly a relief to the family, it came too late for Joséphine. She died in April 1836 at the age of 50 from a "lingering and painful malady."[104]

The Favrot men continued to garner military and political titles during the 1830s. In 1835, Louis was appointed inspector of the Penitentiary House at Baton Rouge.[105] His younger brother Bouvier, who had married Marie-Aurore Villars in 1832, became captain of a volunteer company in the Louisiana Militia in 1836, and subsequently served in the Mexican-American War.[106] Then in October 1838, Louis's son Henri, not yet 12 years of age, joined the Chasseurs of East Baton Rouge—a military and social marching group—as a drummer.[107] Henri thus became the first member of the next generation of Favrots to enter military service. In 1841, he joined his father as one of the founding members of the Voltigeurs of West Baton Rouge, another marching group headed by his brother-in-law, William Reynaud.

On April 12, 1842, Marie-Françoise Favrot died at the age of 78, having outlived her beloved husband and seven of her 11 children. Born to a French Creole family in 1763, the same year that Louisiana was ceded to Spain in the aftermath of the French and Indian War, she was the last person in the immediate Favrot line with a direct link to the first French colonial period, and the last to have adult memories of the Spanish era. While her descendants would continue to speak French as their primary language for several generations to come, her death marked a milestone in the ongoing Americanization of the Favrot family.

CHAPTER 5

THE FRAGILE UNION

The spirit of national unity that surged in the wake of the War of 1812 soon began to fray as sectional differences—largely over the issue of slavery—intensified. When Missouri sought admission to the union as a slave state in 1819, Northerners worried that the delicate balance between slave and free states was at risk. To defuse the growing tensions between pro- and anti-slavery factions, Congress devised a two-part solution that came to be called the Missouri Compromise of 1820. One aspect of the plan entailed admitting Missouri as a slave state, while Maine, which was then a part of Massachusetts, would join the union as a free state. The second key element of the compromise was an agreement to divide the remaining Louisiana Purchase territory along an east-west line at latitude 36°30' North (aligning with the principal present-day border between Missouri and Arkansas). Slavery would be permitted in the territory south of that line, but prohibited north of it. While both Northerners and Southerners objected to aspects of these agreements, the result was a regional equilibrium—albeit a precarious one—that remained fundamentally intact for more than three decades.

Partisan politics contributed to the erosion of post-war solidarity. When none of the four major candidates in the presidential election of 1824 received a majority of votes in the Electoral College, John Quincy Adams (1767–1848) of Massachusetts was chosen by the U.S. House of Representatives under the provisions of the Twelfth Amendment to the Constitution. Andrew Jackson, who had won more electoral votes than Adams, decried the result as a "corrupt bargain" between Adams and Representative Henry Clay (1777–1852) of Kentucky, the speaker of the House at the time, who lobbied his colleagues for Adams's selection and then became secretary of state in the new administration. Soon thereafter, the long-dominant Democratic-Republican Party, which had produced four presidents in a row, disintegrated as Jackson's supporters broke off to form the new Democratic Party.

Jackson ran for president again in 1828, and this time he won. Regarded by many affluent and cultured voters as a crude, reactionary populist, he advocated the abolition of the Electoral College, opposed a national banking system, and embarked on wide-ranging campaigns to displace Native Americans from their traditional lands. After he was reelected in 1832, his opponents, led by Clay, established the Whig Party. The party's name, derived from the common term for anti-monarchical American colonists during the Revolutionary War, was a clear jab at Jackson, whose heavy-handed administration the party's founders considered "tyrannical." The Whigs advocated a relatively activist government, a central national bank, and substantial expenditures on infrastructure—stances that attracted many merchants, planters, and other moneyed interests across the country, despite significant differences of opinion within the party's ranks over the issue of slavery.

Louis Favrot and his son Henri Mortimer Favrot were both members of the Whig Party and became increasingly active in national and local campaigns in the 1840s. Henri was politically precocious. In September 1840, at the age of only 13, he delivered a speech in both French and English in support of William Henry Harrison (1773–1841), the Whig candidate for president of the United States. Harrison was a former U.S. representative and senator who, as governor of the Indiana Territory on the eve of the War of 1812, had led American troops in the defeat of Shawnee warriors during the Battle of Tippecanoe. He thus acquired the nickname "Old Tippecanoe," which in turn gave rise to the slogan "Tippecanoe and Tyler, too" during his campaign for the presidency with running mate John

Tyler (1790–1862). Henri's speech accused the administration of incumbent President Martin Van Buren (1782–1862), Jackson's anointed successor, of corruption and abuse of power. Warning that the American people were in danger of losing their "most Sacred privilidges [*sic*] and rights," Henri pledged that he and his fellow children would "Shed the very last drop of our blood to preserve our independence." The written version of his speech concluded with a rallying cry: "Success to Wm. H. Harrison. Death to Tyrants."[1] These were powerful words from an adolescent.

Harrison went on to win the election and was inaugurated on March 4, 1841. Sixty-eight years old and frail at the time he assumed office, he soon developed pneumonia and died just over a month later, making his tenure the shortest of any U.S. president. Vice-president Tyler, who succeeded to the presidency automatically, soon alienated his fellow Whigs by seeking to augment the power of the Executive Branch and vetoing legislation supported by the party. Widely derided as "His Accidency" because of his non-electoral route to the presidency, he was later stripped of his party membership and was not re-nominated in 1844.

Henri Favrot continued to promote the Whig cause after Harrison's death. For the 65th anniversary of American independence in 1841, he wrote a highly patriotic speech that described the political ascent of the United States in allegorical terms:

> A young stranger whose age seems near childhood, forehead encircled with a starry headband, came to sit one day among the old European civilizations. These asked themselves with shock who was this stranger who, under the emblem of youth, presents all of the strength and power of Alcides. . . .[§§] How is it that hardly having reached her dawn, she has grown so rapidly, and has raised herself up to the rank of the first nations through her astonishing industry, her enormous trade, and her ceaselessly

---

[§§] The published transcription of this document by Tulane University transcribed this name as "Aleide," but this author believes that is an error. Alcides was another name for the ancient Greek mythological hero Heracles (called Hercules by the Romans), known for his strength, which would make sense in this context.

growing population. . . ! Who indeed could have brought about
this Miracle. . . ! The stranger responds, this Miracle is the work
of Liberty. . . .[2]

Henri stated his hope that future generations would "learn from us to revere
the Fourth of July, 1776, eternal day of memory that made us rise to the rank of the
first nations, and made of an enslaved people a free people."[3] His reference to the
American colonists as "an enslaved people" may seem astonishingly ironic coming
from the son of a slaveholder, yet it was not unusual for white Americans in the
early 19th century to speak fervently of "freedom" even as they practiced, promoted, or at least tolerated the enslavement of Africans and African Americans. For
Southern whites in particular, living amidst the institution of slavery may have
amplified appreciation for their own civil liberties, even as they denied liberty to
others.

Rumors of slave revolts, imminent or actual, were rampant from the 1830s until the Civil War, feeding the fears of white Louisianians and stoking their growing
antipathy toward African Americans. In an account of a rumored uprising written
a few weeks after his Independence Day speech, Henri laid bare his views on racial
disparity. "For a very long time the Negroes of Louisiana have not revolted," he
wrote, "but several days ago, at a time when we did not suspect a thing, a plot was
discovered in West Feliciana by a steward, who, hidden in such a way as not to be
seen, listened to a number of Negroes in a shed, speaking in a mysterious tone of
voice, and exposing the means that they must employ to slit their masters' throats."
The next day, the steward reported what he had overheard to the authorities, and
some 30 slaves were arrested. Henri expressed his worry that some escaped con-
spirators might reach Baton Rouge, where the undefended garrison was full of
ammunition and weapons. "Perhaps this largely revolting race will manage to
butcher several people," he concluded, "but I think that Louisianians would not
demean themselves to this revolting and wretched population, and they would
prove anew that they have the right to be their masters."[4] While abolitionists disputed the last point, of course, such unabashedly racist views were widely shared
by white Americans of the period regardless of their stance on slavery.

Louis and Henri's loyalty to the Whigs was perhaps cemented by a familial connection to Henry Clay, the party's intellectual leader. Clay's brother, John, was married to Julie Duralde Clay, the great aunt of Henri's future wife, Célestine Dubroca Favrot.[5] Louis and Henri actively campaigned for Clay during the election to succeed John Tyler in 1844. In a speech possibly dating to September of that year, Louis argued that the country was in greater danger than it had been 30 years earlier, when the British burned Washington, D.C., and were about to lay siege to New Orleans. This time, he said, the menace was not a foreign power, but a domestic political party—i.e., the Democratic Party—which was "employing every means possible to reach its ambitious goals." He accused the Democrats of laying the groundwork for the dissolution of the country. "[C]ertainly one cannot think of the disunion of the States without foreseeing the disorganization of our government and of all of our fine institutions. And who does not shiver with horror at the idea of civil war?... Nature quakes in terror at the atrocious thought of seeing father against son, son against father, and brothers tearing each other apart!" He spoke explicitly against James K. Polk (1795–1849), the Democratic nominee, before concluding, "Fellow citizens, you who, like me, wish for the happiness of your country, renounce this vain title of Democrat which blinds you and recognize that true democracy consists of knowing to respect the Constitution and the laws."[6]

Henri followed up with two speeches in October and November 1844. "Henry Clay!!," he exclaimed, in the October speech. "Oh! Yes, I see all too well how [the name] reverberates to the very depths of your souls, how it makes all of the cords of your hearts vibrate, how much it reminds you of all that man has most dear in this world, Independence and Liberty." After praising Clay, he once again spared no rhetoric in lambasting Jacksonian Democrats, whom many Whigs blamed for the financial Panic of 1837 and subsequent depression of 1839–1841.*** "In 1840 the United States found themselves bankrupt, there was no more money in the Treasury, there was only an enormous debt left. Whose

---

*** In 1936, the Jackson Administration allowed the charter of the Second Bank of the United States—a troubled central bank modeled after its more successful predecessor, the First Bank of the United States (1791–1811)—to expire. The subsequent tightening of the money supply contributed to the financial panic that began the following year.

fault is it that affairs became so awful? Why, it is the two heroes of the Democrats, Jackson and Van Buren. Alas! One must be blind or of bad faith to support men who ruined their country, men who sewed the first seed of demoralization. As a true patriot, fellow citizens, I say that it would have been better in 1815 that New Orleans had been set to fire and blood, rather than being saved: since it is this glorious day that caused the decline of the Union. Without her, Jackson would never have escaped the profound void in which he was plunged, and never would the reins of the Presidency have been granted to him."[7] Henri's remarks reflect a dramatic shift from the Favrot family's adoration of Jackson after his victory in the Battle of New Orleans, when Henri's aunt Joséphine had written that Jackson's "name will forever be pronounced by us with veneration."

Henri's reputation for soaring oratory earned him an invitation to deliver a eulogy for Alexander Barrow (1801–1846), a U.S. senator from Louisiana and fellow Whig who died in office at the age of only 45. Speaking in English, Henri praised Barrow as an exemplary public servant:

> I rank myself among those who, though I am but little advanced in years, have greatly valued the virtues & talents of the one whose loss we deplore, and am obeying a natural impulse of my heart, in advising the young men of the present generation, to take as models of honor, courage, patriotism & bravery the actions of Alexander Barrow, whether in private or public life. . . . Never was a man better suited to maintain the laws & enforce the constitution of his country. Prompted by a pure conscience, he knew no deceit, had no ambition but that of an honest statesman, the prosperity & welfare of a free & independent people. How unblemished must have been his character through life, to have reached his last abode without a single enemy.[8]

In the 1844 presidential election, Polk narrowly defeated Clay in the popular vote, though he won the electoral vote handily. Once in office, he embarked on an expansionist agenda in keeping with the principle of "Manifest Destiny"—the belief that the United States was destined to possess territory spanning the entire width of the North American continent. In 1845, Polk orchestrated the annexation of Texas, which had declared its independence from Mexico in 1836. Then, in 1846, he used a minor border incursion by Mexican troops as a pretext for invading Mexico itself. American troops quickly occupied much of northern Mexico and, in the fall of 1847, captured the capital, Mexico City. The Mexican-American War ended in February 1848 with the signing of the Treaty of Guadalupe Hidalgo, under which Mexico ceded vast territory comprising much of what is now the southwestern United States, stretching from Texas to California.

The end of the Mexican-American War in early 1848 had profound implications for the upcoming presidential election that fall. When President Polk announced that he would not seek reelection, the Whigs took the surprising step of recruiting Zachary Taylor (1784–1850), a self-described political independent and a reluctant campaigner, as their nominee. An army general regarded as a hero for his leadership during the war, Taylor was also a slave owner from Louisiana, so in order to balance the ticket and appeal to Northern Whigs, the party nominated Millard Fillmore (1800–1874), a former U.S. representative from New York, for vice-president. Taylor and Fillmore won the election, though they earned less then 50 percent of the popular vote in a three-way race.

Taylor took office amid the increasingly bitter debate regarding the status of slavery in America's newly added territories. While he supported the admission of California and New Mexico as free states, he largely abdicated responsibility for any such decisions to Congress, which was at an impasse on the matter. In July 1850, just 16 months after becoming president, Taylor developed a serious stomach illness and a few days later became the second president to die in office. Vice-president Fillmore succeeded him, becoming the fourth—and final—Whig president.

In the fall of that year, Congress passed a series of bills drafted by Henry Clay, now a senator, and managed by Illinois Senator Stephen Douglas (1813–1861) that came to be known collectively as the Compromise of 1850. As a result, California was admitted as a free state, but the residents of the New Mexico Territory and the Utah Territory, which covered the rest of the land gained under the Treaty of Guadalupe Hidalgo, would be allowed to decide for themselves whether to permit slavery within their borders—a policy championed by Douglas and known as "popular sovereignty." In addition, Texas, which had already been admitted as a slave state in 1845, relinquished its claims on portions of the New Mexico Territory in exchange for federal assumption of much of the state's war debt. Meanwhile, a new Fugitive Slave Act strengthened an earlier law by compelling all citizens, whether in slave or free states, to cooperate in the return of runaway slaves to their owners or face severe penalties. Although each element of the compromise was met with fierce condemnation from different factions, both Southern and Northern politicians hoped that these actions, taken together, would help the nation avert violent conflict over the issue of slavery.

The fortunes of the Whig Party began to wane in the early 1850s as the tensions within the tenuous national coalition mounted. Nonetheless, the party initially remained relatively strong in Louisiana, thanks in part to its support for protective tariffs, which benefitted the sugar cane industry in the state's southernmost parishes, and its advocacy of a national banking system, which was heavily favored by business interests in New Orleans.[9] The Louisiana Whigs also attracted support by calling for a state constitutional convention, the goals of which included increasing expenditures for infrastructure and education, liberalizing banking laws, and providing financial aid to the commercial sector. While the Whig Party was not as popular in the Baton Rouge area, where tariffs and banking were not such vital issues,[10] the Favrots remained loyal members, perhaps because they believed that the party (which endorsed the Compromise of 1850) mirrored their own pro-slavery but pro-Union views.

By 1852, however, when Louis Favrot was serving as president of the West Baton Rouge Whig Club and Henri was its secretary,[11] the Louisiana Whig Party was on the verge of implosion. Expecting a boost from the success of the state constitutional convention that they had organized and dominated, the Whigs were caught off guard when the Democrats suddenly co-opted the main issues that the convention addressed, effectively removing many of the key distinctions between the two parties. The Democrats also exploited discontent over a minor provision of the proposed constitution regarding the apportionment of representatives to the state legislature. Voters ultimately approved the new constitution in November 1852, but the Whigs suffered significant defeats in the statewide elections the following month. Coupled with the resounding loss by the Whig candidate for president that same year, General Winfield Scott (1786–1866), the poor showing in the state races marked the beginning of the end for the Louisiana Whigs.[12]

The death knell for the national Whig Party came in 1854, when its leaders refused to take a clear stand on the Kansas-Nebraska Act. That act, by applying the doctrine of popular sovereignty articulated in the Compromise of 1850 and allowing white settlers in the would-be states of Kansas and Nebraska to determine through popular vote whether slavery would be permitted within those territories, negated a key provision of the Missouri Compromise of 1820. In response, anti-slavery Whigs, like their counterparts among the Democrats, bolted to help form the new Republican Party, which operated almost exclusively in the northern and western states. Southern Whigs tended to split between the Democratic Party and the rabidly anti-Catholic, anti-immigrant Know-Nothing Party. The Favrots apparently became Democrats, though any loyalty they felt for the party would not last long.

Sectional political differences were further inflamed in 1857 by the U.S. Supreme Court decision in the case of *Dred Scott v. Sandford*. The court ruled that African Americans, whether free or enslaved, were not American citizens, and therefore did not enjoy any of the rights of citizenship. Of more immediate political significance was the court's assertion that the federal government did not have Constitutional authority to regulate slavery in territories that lay beyond the nation's boundaries at the time of its founding. That aspect of the decision destroyed any possibility of further legislative compromises on the issue of slavery in new states and territories, which greatly alarmed Northerners who foresaw the balance of power tipping toward pro-slavery factions.

There is frustratingly little personal material in the Favrot Family Papers from the 1850s. The most significant development of the decade for the family was the construction of the main house on the Monte Vista plantation in West Baton Rouge, which still stands today. It was substantially completed in 1859, though finish work continued into 1860. The plantation and the house are discussed in more detail in the next section of the book.

At the very end of the decade, in December 1859, Henri and his brother-in-law, William Reynaud, received a land patent from the State of Louisiana for a roughly 280-acre plot in Iberville Parish, not far from West Baton Rouge.[13] The property, dubbed Swampfield, accommodated a sawmill, which Henri and William managed jointly and was operated in large part by slaves.[14] The mill was never as profitable as the pair hoped, however, and they sold it less than a year later.[15] Meanwhile, Henri, who had studied at the College of Baton Rouge, Jefferson College in Convent, Louisiana, and Transylvania College in Lexington, Kentucky, was also working as a lawyer. He served as parish attorney for West Baton Rouge while maintaining a private practice based in the parish courthouse. When the legislature was in session in Baton Rouge, which succeeded New Orleans as the state capital in 1849, he typically crossed the river every day for business or social meetings.[16]

The Election of 1860

The escalating sectional disputes that defined American politics in the 1850s came to a head in the lead-up to the presidential election of 1860. Illinois Senator Stephen A. Douglas, who had shepherded the Compromise of 1850 through Congress but was best known for his series of debates against former U.S. Representative Abraham Lincoln (1809–1865) in 1858, emerged as the likely nominee of the Democratic Party. It was Douglas who had promoted popular sovereignty—the right of voters in new territories to decide whether to permit slavery in those jurisdictions—and he continued to support the concept despite the Supreme Court's ruling in the Dred Scott case. Many Southern Democrats felt that he was, if not an outright foe of slavery, at least an unreliable advocate for the institution. Southerners began gravitating toward John C. Breckinridge (1821–1875), the sitting vice-president under Democratic President James Buchanan (1791–1868), as their preferred alternative.

In Louisiana, former U.S. Senator Pierre Soulé (1801–1870) led the faction of the state Democratic Party that favored Douglas, while sitting Senator John Slidell (1793–1871) led the Breckinridge wing.[17] Henri Favrot was at the State Capitol when the Louisiana Democratic Convention was meeting to choose delegates to the upcoming national party convention in Charleston, South Carolina.

He noted that the "Slidellists have a large majority,"[18] meaning that the state's Democrats were heavily leaning toward Breckinridge.

The national Democratic Party convened in Charleston from April 23 to May 3. As expected, Douglas quickly emerged as the front-runner, but over the course of some 57 votes, he never achieved the two-thirds majority required for the nomination. Meanwhile, dozens of Southern delegates walked out of the convention in protest when a pro-slavery plank they favored failed to make it into the party platform. Deadlocked, the remaining delegates agreed to reconvene in Baltimore in June.

As the internal dissension among Democrats festered, an entirely new party suddenly emerged, and quickly organized its own convention in Baltimore in May. The Constitutional Union Party was established by a group of former Whigs, mostly from the South, who opposed secession. They were joined by smaller numbers of anti-secession Democrats and Know-Nothings. The party's platform was simple: that the union must be preserved, and that a strict interpretation of the Constitution should guide all governmental policies and actions. The platform deliberately avoided a clear position on the status of slavery in states or territories, reflecting the party members' hopes that, by remaining neutral on the issue, they could somehow defuse the debates that were ripping the Democrats apart. The Constitutional Union Party convention was brief and harmonious, resulting in the nomination of John Bell (1796–1869), a former U.S. representative and senator from Tennessee, for president. Edward Everett (1794–1865), a former representative, senator, governor of Massachusetts, and president of Harvard University, received the vice-presidential nomination. Later in May, the Republican Party convened in Chicago, and nominated Abraham Lincoln for president.

When the Democrats reconvened as planned in Baltimore in June, most of the Southern delegates soon walked out once again. The remaining delegates, who were almost exclusively from the North and West, carried on and finally succeeded in nominating Douglas for president. The Southern delegates who had quit the convention formed a "rump" group, which nominated Breckinridge. The result was a definitive split of the Democratic Party into two bodies: the Northern Democrats and the Southern Democrats.

The Constitutional Union Party, with its anti-secession platform and its membership largely drawn from former Whigs, appealed to the Favrots. By July 1860, Henri had already declared his support for the Constitutional Union ticket, writing in his diary, "Politics interest me. Public affairs are in a sad state. Heaven knows how all of this will end. God grant that Bell and Everett are elected."[19] His father, Louis, chaired the Bell Committee in West Baton Rouge, and Henri became a "sub-elector," or alternate elector, for the Constitutional Union ticket.[20] He soon began campaigning actively for the candidates, giving speeches in Baton Rouge and Plaquemines, among other places.[21] In a speech at Bruslé Landing, a town along the Mississippi River, he "had to refute the charges of abolitionism made against the Bell and Everett ticket" by others, including Henry Watkins Allen (1820–1866), a close Favrot family friend who would later become governor of Louisiana under the Confederacy.

The election was held on November 6, 1860. Lincoln swept the North and West, winning 40 percent of the popular vote but a clear majority of the electoral vote—180 out of 303 total. Douglas ran second in the popular vote, but was a distant fourth in the electoral vote. Breckinridge, who had the second-highest electoral vote total, carried Louisiana and most of the South. Bell received less than 13 percent of the popular vote nationwide, but carried three states: Virginia, Kentucky, and Tennessee. Bell was a close second in Louisiana, however, and ran first in the Baton Rouge area, a strong showing for which Louis and Henri surely deserved some credit.

Henri went to Baton Rouge the day after the election to hear the nationwide results, which were being disseminated by telegraph. His diary entry for that day predicted the secession of Southern states that was now inevitable. "The news of the election was not favorable," he wrote. "Lincoln was elected . . . New Jersey was the only state in the North that went against Lincoln and in favor of the [Constitutional Union] ticket.[†††] A telegram from Charleston said that the majority of the [U.S.] Army from the South have already or are going to resign. They want to secede from the Union."[22]

[†††] Actually, Douglas barely carried the state of New Jersey, though the state's seven electors ultimately gave four votes to Lincoln and three to Douglas.

Over the next month, there were frantic efforts in Congress to concoct another legislative compromise that might ward off secession, but to no avail. In December, as predicted in the telegram that Henri had seen, the South Carolina legislature called a special state convention whose delegates voted unanimously to secede. Mississippi, Florida, Alabama, Georgia, and Louisiana all followed suit in January 1861, followed by Texas in February. Those seven states soon proclaimed themselves the Confederate States of America, with Jefferson Davis (1808–1889) as their provisional president and Montgomery, Alabama, as their temporary capital. Alexandre Etienne De Clouet (1812–1890), great-grandson of Louise Favrot De Clouet, Pierre-Joseph's sister, was one of Louisiana's representatives in the Confederate Congress and a signer of the Confederate Constitution, which drew very heavily from that of the United States, but with more explicit protections for the institution of slavery.

Immediately after Lincoln's election, Southern state militias began to prepare for war. In December 1860, Henri helped to form a new military company, later named the Delta Rifles, under the Louisiana Militia. He was immediately selected as the company's captain.[23] The appointment was confirmed in January by Louisiana Governor Thomas O. Moore (1804–1876).[24] Henri then spent the early months of 1861 assisting Lieutenant Colonel Henry Watkins Allen, the Favrot family friend and newly appointed commander of the Fourth Louisiana Regiment, with recruitment and organizational tasks.[25]

President Lincoln took office on March 4, pledging in his inaugural address that he had no plans "to interfere with the institution of slavery in the States where it exists," because he believed he did not have the Constitutional authority to do so. By then, however, the seven states that had seceded already considered themselves a separate nation. Lincoln declared the secessions illegal and refused to recognize the Confederacy as a legitimate government. Compromise of any kind was no longer possible.

The Onset of War

The Civil War broke out on April 12, 1861, when Confederate forces under the command of General P.G.T. Beauregard (1818–1893), a Louisianian, launched an attack on Union troops at Fort Sumter, which guarded the entrance to Charleston Harbor in South Carolina. The Union forces were vastly outgunned and surrendered two days later. When news of the attack reached Washington, President Lincoln issued an immediate call for volunteer soldiers. Recognizing that war had begun, the states of Virginia, Arkansas, North Carolina, and Tennessee, which had balked at secession, soon voted to join the Confederacy. With Virginia now in the fold, the Confederate government moved its capital to Richmond. Four slave states—Maryland, Delaware, Kentucky, and Missouri—remained loyal to the Union despite bitter dissent among their citizens.

Soon after the bombardment of Fort Sumter, Henri's regiment was ordered to the Gulf Coast to help defend against a possible attack by Union ships. He was stationed at several places along the coast until February 1862, when the regiment was ordered to Tennessee to join other Confederate troops in an effort to counter advancing Union forces under General Ulysses S. Grant (1822–1885). On April 6-8, Henri and his compatriots in the Fourth Louisiana Regiment were among the more than 100,000 Confederate and Union troops who participated in the brutal Battle of Shiloh, which took place in southwestern Tennessee about ten miles north of the Mississippi state line. The battle began when Confederate troops under General Albert Sidney Johnston (1803–1862) launched a surprise, early-morning assault on Union forces camped near the Tennessee River. On the first day of fighting, the Confederates advanced steadily as Union divisions retreated. General Johnston was mortally wounded, however, becoming the highest-ranking casualty on either side of the war. General Beauregard assumed command of the Confederate troops after Johnston's death.

Henri's troop, the Delta Rifles, took part in repeated assaults on the infamous "Hornet's Nest," an overgrown ravine overlooked by a Union position on a ridge.[26] A subsequent account by General Johnston's son, William Preston Johnston (1831–1899), a colonel in the Confederate Army who later became the first president of Tulane University, described the hellish fighting at the Hornet's Nest: "No figure of speech would be too strong to express the deadly peril of assault upon this natural fortress . . . whose infernal gates poured forth a murderous storm of shot & shell & musket fire which no living thing could quell or even withstand."[27]

Union troops rallied on the second day of fighting, and by April 8 succeeded in regaining lost territory. This time the Confederates were in retreat, leaving the Union with an important victory. On at least two occasions during the fighting at Shiloh, the troops from Louisiana were involved in episodes of friendly fire, first when Tennessee volunteers fired on them, and then later when they inadvertently exchanged fire with the First Arkansas division.[28] Henri was among those wounded at Shiloh, the bloodiest battle in American history to that date—though that tragic superlative would soon be surpassed multiple times.

While Henri was in Tennessee, the war reached the Gulf Coast. New Orleans, the largest city in the Confederacy and the gateway to the Mississippi River, was an obvious early target for Union troops. On April 18, 1862, Union naval vessels under the command of Captain David Farragut (1801–1870) began an assault on the Confederate garrisons at Fort Jackson (built near the site of the former Fort Bourbon) and Fort Saint Philip, where Henri's grandfather, Pierre-Joseph, had served as commandant 60 years earlier. The ships broke through the Confederate defenses on April 23, and two days later, Farragut reached New Orleans. Because the city's defenses had been stripped to reinforce Johnson's army on the eve of the Battle of Shiloh, Farragut and his troops landed with no shots fired (thus sparing New Orleans the destruction that befell other historic cities in the South during the war). On April 29, Farragut officially took possession of the city on behalf of the Union. A lengthy newspaper article from the Baton Rouge *Daily Gazette & Comet*, preserved in the Favrot Family Papers, announced the momentous event:

> Yesterday New Orleans was subjected to the most terrible humiliation and degradation which have ever fallen upon a brave and true people. After a valiant defense, by our forts below the city—after exhausting all our sources and skill—the greater resources on water of the enemy enabled them to pass our exterior fortifications with their large fleet, and they approached the city with a squadron of fifteen of their largest vessels, all steamships,

gunboats, or mortar vessels. . . .[Later, in New Orleans,] a boat came ashore with two officers, one Capt. Bayleis [Theodorus Bayley], second in command of the squadron, Capt. Farragut being a flag officer, and a lieutenant. These officers were greeted on touching the shore with the most uproarious huzzas for "Jeff Davis and the South," and with the most threatening demonstrations. . . .

The Mayor received the Federal officers in his office, with proper dignity. Capt. Bayleis stated the purport of the mission. He had been sent by Capt. Farragut to demand the surrender of the city and the elevation of the flag of the United States over the Custom House, the Post Office, the Mint, and the City Hall. The Mayor replied that he was not the military commander of the city, that he had no authority to surrender it, and would not do so, but that there was a military commander now in the city, and he would send for him, to receive and replay to the demand.

A messenger was dispatched for Gen. [Mansfield] Lovell. In the interval a number of citizens who were present, got into conversations with the U.S. naval officers. The Lieutenant seemed to be a courteous, well behaved gentleman, who bore testimony with apparent earnestness to the vigor and valor of our forts, and was quite communicative. The senior officer was more reserved, but still made large professions of peaceful intents. It was difficult, however, for him to conceal the bitter sectional hate of a Massachusetts man against a true Southern community . . ."[29]

Eventually, General Lovell (life dates unknown) arrived at the City Hall and informed Captain Bayley (1805–1877) that he had no intention of surrendering the city, and was prepared to fight Union troops on land "as long as he could muster a soldier." He explained that he had evacuated New Orleans in order to avoid a battle there, but that if the Union forces "desired to shell the town, destroying women and children, they could do so."[30]

Farragut chose to exercise restraint in responding to Lovell's defiance. After moving upriver to take out Confederate fortifications there, he returned to New Orleans and ordered his men to raise the U.S. flag over the City Hall. A few tense days later, Union General Benjamin Butler (1818–1893) arrived with a formidable force of some 5,000 troops and assumed control of the city as military governor. New Orleans remained in Union hands for the rest of the war.

The next goal for Union forces in Louisiana was capturing Baton Rouge. In early May, as Union ships were sailing up the Mississippi River toward the city, the Confederate state government fled to Opelousas, about 60 miles to the west, and established a temporary capital there. Union troops, encountering little resistance, quickly took possession of federal property in Baton Rouge, including an arsenal and military barracks. Later that month, after Confederate guerillas fired on Union sailors in a small boat, Commander Farragut ordered that the city be shelled. Several buildings were destroyed, and many were damaged, including the State Capitol. A large Union force arrived at the end of the month and fully occupied the city.

Henri Favrot was back in West Baton Rouge on leave by July 1862, having survived the Battle of Shiloh, a bout with typhoid fever, and a brief period as a prisoner of war. He was at home recuperating from an earache on August 5, when Confederate troops under the command of General John C. Breckinridge, the presidential nominee of the Southern Democrats in 1860, attempted to retake Baton Rouge.[31] Attacking from the north and east, the Confederate troops, including Henri's own Fourth Regiment, initially succeeded in pushing the Union troops back toward the river, along the city's western edge. Having done so, however, the Southern troops were then within range of Union gunboats. Under heavy fire, the Confederates retreated, and the Union forces retained control of the city.

Even as this major battle was being waged just across the river from the Favrot family's plantation, Henri apparently had his mind on personal matters beyond his own illness. He was in the throes of courting a woman named Félicie [or Félice] Célestine Dubroca[†††], usually called either Célestine or Titine, a member

---

[†††] Célestine Dubroca was adopted by her maternal aunt, Célestine Allain Soniat, and partially raised in Paris. Although Soniat was her legal surname, most documents in the Favrot Family Papers that mention her use Dubroca as her maiden name. This book follows that precedent.

of another prominent West Baton Rouge family and a distant cousin of Henri's. He proposed to her on August 10. Due to the exigencies of war, the local parish church in West Baton Rouge, which was cut off from communication with Catholic leaders in New Orleans, agreed to dispense with the reading of banns—the public announcement of upcoming nuptials, traditionally followed by a waiting period during which members of the public might express civil or religious objections to the marriage. Henri and Célestine were married just two days later.[32]

Henri soon returned to duty, once again helping to recruit men for a new company. As he traveled around the state, he became concerned about Célestine, who had remained at the family plantation in West Baton Rouge. The proximity of the Union troops just across the river in Baton Rouge, coupled with the ever-present possibility of renewed fighting in the area, convinced him to arrange for his wife to stay in Attakapas, near New Iberia in south central Louisiana, where the De Clouet family had lived for many years. Célestine returned to West Baton Rouge at least once during the war, however, for the birth of the couple's first child, Henry Louis Favrot, in July 1864. While the spellings "Henri" and "Henry" were often used interchangeably in 19th-century Louisiana, it is worth noting that Henry Louis seems to have been the first Favrot of that name to be given the English spelling at birth.[33] This may have been a tribute to the family friend, Henry Watkins Allen, though it is also possible that it was simply another milestone in the Americanization of the Favrot family.

Allen, at any rate, remained a close friend of the Favrots as he moved up the ranks in the Confederate army. After suffering crippling injuries in the battles of Shiloh and Baton Rouge, he was promoted to brigadier general in 1863. In September of that year, he appointed Henri, by then a major, to his personal staff as "Commissary of [his] Brigade" in Shreveport,[34] which became the temporary state capital after Opelousas.

Allen ran unopposed for the governorship of Confederate Louisiana in November. After taking office in January 1864, he issued a broadside addressed to the citizens of New Orleans, who had been living under Union occupation for nearly two years. The text demonized the occupying force as bullies and criminals, charges that had some justification given the notoriously petty and corrupt practices of General Butler, the initial military governor, but which ignored the significant improvements in public health and hygiene under his administration (Butler was relieved of command after less than eight months). The statement, with unwarranted optimism, also assured New Orleanians that the end of the war was near:

> I greet you as the Governor of Louisiana. Your trials and your troubles are well known, and your patriotic conduct fully appreciated by the Executive of your State. Do not be despondent. Do not despair; but rather let the fires of patriotism burn brightly at every fireside, for in a few short months you shall be free. You have been despoiled and robbed, and basely insulted. Every indignity that a brutal, unprincipled and vindictive foe could invent, has been heaped upon you. Bear your persecutions as did your fathers before you, and nerve your hearts for the coming hour. Our people are flocking to the army in every direction, and when the Spring campaign opens, half a million of gallant Confederate soldiers will strike for liberty and independence. Citizens of New Orleans! Be true to yourselves, and your State will be true to you. Spurn all propositions for compromises of any kind—spit upon the insulting proposal for a bastard [Union] State Government. . . ."[35]

In fact, by 1864, the prospects for a Confederate victory had already dimmed considerably. The previous summer, the Confederacy had suffered two critical losses in a row: On July 3, 1863, Union forces under Major General George Meade (1815–1872) defeated Confederate troops led by General Robert E. Lee (1807–1870) at Gettysburg, Pennsylvania, in the battle that was the subject of President Lincoln's famously eloquent address; the next day, Confederate troops at Vicksburg, Mississippi, surrendered to Major General Ulysses S. Grant after a nearly seven-week siege of the city. The Battle of Gettysburg marked the beginning of the end of Confederate penetration into Northern territory, while the surrender of Vicksburg isolated Confederate forces in Texas and the southwestern territories from sources of support in the East.

The final phase of the war arguably began in March 1864—the same month that Louisiana Unionists initiated the political Reconstruction of the state—when President Lincoln appointed Grant general-in-chief of all Union armies. Over the next year, Grant waged a relentless, multi-pronged campaign against Confederate forces. While the specific battles that ensued were often indecisive and in many cases even favored the Confederates, the Union succeeded in gradually degrading Southern infrastructure and supply lines, not to mention depleting the South's already short-handed armies. The widespread destruction of both private and public property throughout the South, coupled with the recruitment of freed African American slaves as soldiers in the Union armies, led many Southerners to believe that defeat was inevitable.

Henri Mortimer Favrot and the End of the War

In 1864, the Confederate Congress passed legislation authorizing each state to appoint a superintendent of army records, with the rank of colonel, charged with collecting and preserving documentation related to individual soldiers, military companies, battles, and other information deemed valuable for posterity. Governor Allen of Louisiana considered his friend Henri Favrot to be uniquely suited to the position. "[F]ew men are qualified to do this," the governor wrote to Henri. "I have selected you in preference to all others." He informed Henri that his duties, should he accept the appointment, would require travel to Virginia, Georgia, Tennessee, and "every other place where [Louisiana] troops are now stationed."[36] Henri, who had already been made a lieutenant colonel the previous February,[37] accepted the position and the promotion to full colonel.[38]

Henri wrote to his wife in October 1864 to inform her of his new appointment, which he realized marked a significant shift in the trajectory of his career. "You have accused me of having military ambition," he wrote in a teasing manner, "but you are mistaken because I am quitting the camps to take up the pen & give myself over to historical research." He noted that he had hoped the new position would allow him to reunite with Célestine and their infant child, at least for a while,[39] but he quickly received orders to report to Shreveport.[40] Shortly thereafter, Governor Allen ordered him to proceed to Richmond, Virginia, to collect information from the central records in the Confederate capital. In a letter to Henri, Allen wrote, "I desire you to spare no pains nor reasonable expense in obtaining all materials necessary for a full history of the part taken by Louisiana in this war & for a complete record of every [Louisiana] soldier living or dead."[41] This was a colossal assignment, given the tens of thousands of Louisianians who had served in the Confederate armies.

What followed was a taxing odyssey that took Henri through the battered South to Richmond in the last months of the war. The journey is well documented thanks to a series of letters he wrote to Célestine complemented by an incomplete journal written in English, most likely well after the fact. Taken together, these papers starkly depict Henri's personal experience of the final throes of the Confederacy.

Leaving from Shreveport apparently in late November, Henri first traveled on horseback to Alexandria, Louisiana, where he stayed for at least a few days[42] before moving on to Concordia Parish, on the western bank of the Mississippi River. He then engaged a guide named Thomas Jefferson Walker (life dates unknown), with whom he and a third man, Lallande Ferrière (life dates unknown), traveled through the woods—and swam through the bayous—to get to the river itself, which was heavily guarded by Union gunboats. For two days and two nights, the trio hid in the woods behind the riverfront plantations to avoid detection and capture. Finally, they sensed an opening, and successfully made the river crossing by night. "Our horses were nearly numbed with cold," Henri wrote in his journal. "Trembling in limb & body our first duty was to scrape the water off—This was soon done, for there was no time to spare—We saddled them in a hurry & rode off briskly; the exercise soon restored heat & circulation in the chilled bodies of our animals."[43]

Henri and Ferrière, with or without the guide, traversed southern Mississippi, spending one night in Woodville and then another in Liberty before arriving at Brookhaven, where they boarded a train for Jackson,[44] arriving on December 16.[45] Union forces had captured and withdrawn from Jackson several times since May 1863, and the city was in a shambles. Seeing the destruction, some of which was the work of troops under the command of Major General William Tecumseh

Sherman (1820–1891), Henri came to recognize that the Union general was a formidable foe. "Sherman will, I worry, take his path all the way to Georgia or South Carolina," Henri wrote to Céleste. "There are those who thought that we would have the time to bury him and destroy his army," he added. "I have many doubts."[46] Henri may or may not have known at the time that Sherman had already captured and burned Atlanta in September, and he had no way of knowing that just five days after the date of the letter, Sherman's army would capture Savannah in the culmination of his "March to the Sea," a scorched-earth campaign that left much of Georgia's infrastructure—along with a great deal of private property—in ruins.

Henri and Ferrière's next stop after Jackson was Meridian, in eastern Mississippi. From there, they had expected to travel by train to Mobile, but after learning of "interruptions in the railways, because of a raid made by the Yankees in Pollard [Alabama]," they changed plans. They instead made their way to Selma, Alabama, then to Montgomery, and then to Macon, Georgia. Once in Georgia, Henri saw first-hand the destruction wreaked by Sherman's troops. While rail service in Alabama had been "interrupted," in Georgia the railroad network had been virtually obliterated.[47] In his journal entry regarding that part of the journey, Henri expressed his revulsion at Sherman's methods, and what he regarded as the widespread barbaric practices of Union soldiers:

> Although my own Louisiana from Berwick's Bay to Alexandria bore the sad evidences of the ravages of war, I could not but be sadly impressed at the destruction of property in our sister state—The triumph of victory, the glory which attaches to the accomplishment of great deeds in the career of arms are great incentives to the ambition of men—But when the allurements of unrestrained power, leads [sic] the successful chieftan to the destruction of monuments reared under the auspices of peace, to the wanton sacking of towns & villages thronged with non-combatants, to the burning of homes, to the brutal assaults & outrages of a licentious soldiery upon unprotected women—and the complete annihilation of all the resources which are essential to the subsistence of the vanquished—the genius of civilization

shrinks from the appalling spectacles and instinctively crouches in the dark niche which history assigns to barbaric ages.[48]

The destruction of the railroads forced Henri, Ferrière, and a man identified as Colonel Keary, who had joined them at some point, to seek alternative transportation through Georgia. On December 22, they found a man who, for $150 per person, agreed to take them some 65 miles by cart. "We accepted," he wrote to Célestine, "paid in advance, and numbered six, not including the driver, embarked in a bad cart without benches or springs—pell-mell with baggage and feed for four mules, so thin that I can say that I did a study in mule anatomy during the 48 hours that they were in front of my eyes." The cart took them through Milledgeville and Sparta before dropping them in Mayfield, where they were able to catch a train. They reached Augusta, along the South Carolina border, in time for Christmas.[49]

Whether because of what he had seen on his journey thus far, or because of new reports of the war's progress, or both, Henri was becoming increasingly worried about the Confederacy's prospects for victory. In a Christmas Day letter to Célestine, he wrote, "Our country, our cause, our armies, have never been closer to succumbing than at this moment—We must not lose hope, God may come to our aid—We would need a miracle to save us. . ."[50]

Henri arrived in Richmond at the end of December 1864, and settled in for a lengthy stay.[51] He promptly visited the members of the Louisiana delegation to the Confederate Congress, who helped him gain access to the War Department, which maintained the records necessary for him to fulfill his mission. With paper supplies limited and restrictions on printing for non-essential purposes, he struggled to obtain an adequate number of blank forms on which he could enter information about individual soldiers.[52] Once he began his work in earnest, he found the routine rather monotonous. While his workdays were not especially long—typically lasting from 9:30 a.m. to 3:00 p.m.—he often spent much of that time on his feet, moving around frequently, which made him very tired.[53] He took a side trip to Petersburg, Virginia, in early February, to visit the Louisiana troops who had been helping to defend the long Confederate entrenchments against repeated Union attacks. In brutally cold weather, he witnessed the burials of several men who had been killed in action.[54]

Once in Richmond, Henri suddenly had access to much more timely—if not necessarily more accurate—information about the course of the war. His report in a January 9 letter to Célestine about the Battle of Nashville, for instance, downplayed its significance: "Our loss in dead and wounded is small," he wrote.[55] In fact, the mid-December battle decimated what was left of the Confederate Army of Tennessee, and ushered in the closing phase of the war's western theater. Even as rumors of the true scope of the confrontation circulated later in the month, Henri was able to put a positive spin on the news, telling Célestine, "We are assured that despite our losses, our number of soldiers has not diminished, thanks to the numerous recruits that we made during our time in Tennessee." Perhaps experiencing a resurgence of optimism, he suggested that the Confederacy could still emerge from the war, if not as an outright victor, then at least in a strong enough position to cement its independence: "My opinion is that if we can hold on six more months and win one or two great victories, we will dictate the terms of peace, as well as the clauses and conditions of the treaty recognizing our independence and the sovereignty of our government."[56]

In late January, Henri relayed news of two visits to Richmond by Francis P. Blair, Sr. (1791–1876), well known as an unofficial advisor to President Lincoln but also a friend of Jefferson Davis. "I believe," Henri wrote to Célestine, "that there is no doubt that he is the bringer of some message, or diplomatic note from Washington."[57] Indeed, Blair had taken it upon himself to approach Confederate authorities to discuss peace terms. His visits laid the groundwork for the unsuccessful Hampton Roads Peace Conference of February 3, 1865, during which President Lincoln and U.S. Secretary of State William H. Seward (1801–1872) met with Confederate Vice-President Alexander H. Stephens (1812–1883) and two other Confederate representatives. During the meeting, which took place on a steamboat in Hampton Roads, Virginia, Lincoln made it clear that any peace treaty would be predicated on the Confederacy's agreeing to lay down arms, rejoin the Union, and emancipate remaining slaves. The Southern representatives refused to consider any proposal that did not recognize their independence.

Henri's letters to his wife from Richmond also provide glimpses of daily life in the Confederate capital in the waning months of the war. The atmosphere in the city was generally tranquil when he arrived, but the high cost of living posed challenges for someone on a soldier's salary. A pair of boots at the time cost $350 to $400, butter ran $10 a pound, and apples that were "not pretty" were $1 apiece (the prices cited were in ruinously depreciated Confederate dollars). Henri managed to find sardonic humor in the poor quality and small portions of food served in his boarding house: "The old lady at whose house we board was saying yesterday that she had read in many a medicine book that to be healthy one must leave the table with some appetite—it is doubtless by concern for our health that each day she puts us in the position to put in practice the doctrines of these doctors that she has studied."[58]

The Confederate army was becoming increasingly desperate in early 1865, as casualties mounted and recruitment lagged. A letter from Henry Watkins Allen to Henri dated February 13, 1865, sheds light on a surprising proposal for augmenting the ranks of the Confederate military. He informed Henri of a "new & bold doctrine advanced in regard to the negroes, [which] at first astonished the people, but I believe all have agreed to it."[59] He was referring to a portion of his annual address to the state legislature, delivered the previous month, in which he put forth an initiative to recruit African American slaves to fight for the Confederacy in exchange for their emancipation. He argued that Louisiana plantations had, before the war, produced more food and cotton than the state needed, and given the reduction in the state's population due to casualties of war, plantation owners could afford to give up some of their slaves if those slaves would agree to fight. He went on to suggest an even more radical idea:

> This has now become a war of endurance, of heavy blows, and long, stout and determined resistance. Peace can never be made with Abraham Lincoln except by armed intervention. This blood-hound, like the "dark Mokanna,"[§§§] has deceived his people—will still deceive them until the terrible day of retribution comes. The time may come—is perhaps fast approaching—when we will have to give up the institution of domestic slavery

§§§ Mokanna, or Al-Muqanna, was a Persian who lived around the eighth century C.E. Dubbed the "Veiled Prophet," he was regarded as a heretic by most Muslims.

in order to secure our independence as a nation. The civilized world is opposed to the name of slavery—it prefers bondage under some other name. In Mexico they have Peons—in Russia Serfs—in England, France and Spain, Cooleys. The position of the slave in Louisiana is far superior to any of these; he is better clothed, better fed, better treated and cared for, and in every respect a much happier being. Still we cannot convince the world that they are wrong and that we are right. The public mind must be prepared for the change. Shall we continue to fight on, in a long protracted war with slavery, or shall we give it up and have peace and independence? Louisiana will rise en masse and say without hesitation, "We will abolish the institution—we will part with slavery without regret—if necessary to gain our independence."[60]

Allen assured Henri that "[t]here is not a dissenting voice in Louisiana" regarding the proposal. "They will all cheerfully give up slavery to gain our Independence."[61] In reality, many Southerners were steadfastly opposed to the idea, given that protection of a slave-based economy was unquestionably the South's principal reason for going to war in the first place. Nonetheless, the Confederate Congress reluctantly passed legislation in March 1865 allowing for the recruitment of African American troops, though it did not guarantee that slaves would be freed in exchange for military service. Perhaps a few thousand African Americans were convinced to fight on behalf of the Confederacy—not enough to yield any great strategic advantage at such a late stage of the war.

As Henri was wrapping up his work in Richmond and preparing to return to his family in Louisiana, he had no way of knowing that the Confederacy was entering its final days. On April 1, 1865, the same day Henri left Richmond,[62] Union forces defeated Confederate troops at Five Forks, a critical railroad juncture about 25 miles south of Richmond. On April 2, the Union army finally achieved a convincing victory at nearby Petersburg following a nearly ten-month-long siege. Confederate troops and government officials immediately began evacuating Richmond, which was occupied by Union troops on April 3. President Lincoln visited the former Confederate capital the next day, cheered by slaves and other Union sympathizers as he walked the streets.

General Lee and his troops fled westward, pursued by Union forces under General Grant. After a series of skirmishes along the way, Grant engaged the Confederate forces in a final battle near a small village called Appomattox Court House. Essentially surrounded, hungry, and cut off from supply lines, Lee's Army of Northern Virginia was finished. Lee surrendered to Grant on April 9.

Although Lee's surrender did not constitute a definitive end to the war—the Army of Northern Virginia was only one component of the Confederate military network—both Northerners and Southerners quickly recognized that the Confederacy was now doomed. A relieved President Lincoln and his cabinet had just begun the work of reunion when, on the evening of April 14, he and his wife attended a play at Ford's Theatre in downtown Washington. John Wilkes Booth (1838–1865), a prominent actor and Southern sympathizer who had previously plotted to kidnap the president and take him to Richmond, sneaked into Lincoln's private box and shot him in the back of the head. He then leapt to the stage, shouting "*Sic semper tyrannis*" (Latin for "Thus always to tyrants") and escaped. President Lincoln died the next day. The attempted simultaneous assassinations of Vice-President Andrew Johnson (1808–1875) and Secretary of State Seward, to be carried out by Booth's co-conspirators, failed. Johnson, a Southern Democrat who was Lincoln's running mate in the election of 1864 as part of the National Union ticket, succeeded to the presidency.

Lincoln's assassination, which Booth hoped would throw the federal government into disarray and give the Confederacy a last chance at survival, did not alter the finality of the Confederate military defeat. As news of Lee's surrender spread, other commanders across the South gradually followed suit. Jefferson Davis convened his cabinet for the last time on May 5 in the town of Washington, Georgia, after which the Confederate government was dissolved. Davis was captured by Union troops on May 10 and imprisoned.

A letter dated April 20 from Françoise Augustine Favrot Reynaud to her sister-in-law, Célestine, conveyed the news of Lincoln's murder. Françoise incorrectly reported that Seward, too, had been killed, when in fact he had survived knife wounds to his face and neck. She expressed the hope that the assassins were Copperheads—Northern Democrats who opposed the war—rather than Confederates. "In the current circumstances," she wrote, "this would not help our situation."[63]

Henri returned safely to Monte Vista, the family plantation, in the early summer of 1865. Numerous other Favrot family members of subsequent generations would serve in the military, but Henri appears to have been the last to make a full career of it. At least three of his first cousins, all sons of his Uncle Bouvier, also served in the Confederate army: Charles D. Favrot and Joseph Claude Favrot, who survived, and St. Clair Favrot, who was captured in battle and disappeared after his release.[64] As the survivors returned to civilian life, the Favrots, like all Louisianians, began adjusting to a new and extended period of political, economic, and cultural uncertainty.

The Aftermath

In late May 1865, President Johnson announced an initial amnesty program for most Confederate soldiers at the rank of colonel or below. Those who owned taxable property worth more than $20,000, however, were ineligible. Given that Monte Vista was still owned by Louis Favrot, Henri may or may not have owned enough property to disqualify him from this initial amnesty. Regardless, in September 1867 and again in December 1868, Johnson expanded the amnesty program to almost all former Confederate soldiers and officials. It is safe to assume that Henri was once again a U.S. citizen in good standing following the final amnesty announcement, if not before.

Henry Watkins Allen, the close Favrot family friend, was among those who were ineligible for the initial amnesty by virtue of his role as a "pretended" governor of one of the states in rebellion as well as his final rank as a brigadier general in the Confederate army. Threatened with arrest and possible execution, he delivered a farewell address to the people of Louisiana on June 2, 1865. He urged them to accept the Confederate defeat and begin repairing their property and their lives. "Let us not talk of despair," he said, "nor whine about our misfortunes, but with strong arms and stout hearts adapt ourselves to the circumstances that surround us."[65] He soon fled to Mexico City, where he went on to become editor of an English-language newspaper there. Henri, along with other Louisianians, personally provided financial support to Allen while he was in exile.[66]

Allen died in Mexico City in 1866. His remains were exhumed and returned to New Orleans the next year. In 1878, the town center of West Baton Rouge, a few miles south of the Favrot plantation, was renamed Port Allen in his honor. His remains were moved again in 1885, this time to the Capitol grounds in Baton Rouge. On that occasion, Henri Favrot, then 58 years old, delivered a lengthy eulogy on behalf of his friend. The speech recalled the oratorical skills that he had first exhibited as a teenager. "It was with no feelings of vanity that I accepted the honor conferred upon me," he said, "and my greatest regret is that neither my pen nor my voice will do justice to the subject. If, however, there is eloquence in sincerity, warmth in friendship & veneration to the memory of those who were bound to us by its sacred ties, I yield to no one the deep & solemn impressions which these feelings inspire on an occasion like this."[67]

The Thirteenth Amendment to the U.S. Constitution, ratified in December 1865, abolished slavery throughout the country, completing the process begun by President Lincoln with the Emancipation Proclamation of 1863, which had freed only those slaves held in areas then "in rebellion." President Johnson formally declared the "insurrection in certain Southern states" to be ended in April 1866, but the reintegration of the seceded states was only just beginning. The nation was already in the throes of Reconstruction, the name applied to the highly contentious era lasting from the end of the war until 1877, as federal officials instituted a variety of policies and procedures related to the readmission of Confederate states to the Union. All of those states except Tennessee, which had been occupied by Union troops for much of the war, were placed under federal military rule.

During the Reconstruction Era, white Southerners repeatedly sought to restrict the rights of newly freed African American slaves. In 1865 and 1866, Southern states enacted an array of laws known as the "Black Codes," including broad "vagrancy" laws under which unemployed or self-employed African Americans could be arrested and forced to perform involuntary labor once again. The Black Codes also abridged former slaves' property rights and freedom of movement.

Louisiana, which was readmitted to the Union in 1868, witnessed a number of violent incidents during Reconstruction. In July 1866, a white mob attacked a group of more than 100 African Americans marching toward the site of a Louisiana Constitutional Convention. More than 250 people, including both white and African American delegates to the convention, were killed or wounded in what came to be called the New Orleans Riot of 1866. During the presidential election of 1868, won by General Ulysses S. Grant, white Louisianians again resorted to violence and fraud to suppress the African American vote. In 1874, several thousand members of a white supremacist organization known as the Crescent City White League, who had demanded the resignation of Louisiana's Republican governor, William Pitt Kellogg (1830–1918), overpowered New Orleans police and occupied the city's key public buildings. They then proclaimed the establishment of a new state government. The attempted insurrection was quelled several days later when federal troops arrived and forced the White League to stand down.

The Black Codes and persistent violence directed against African Americans helped to spur the adoption of the Fourteenth Amendment to the U.S. Constitution, ratified in 1868, which extended citizenship rights to former slaves and protected all citizens from being deprived of "life, liberty, or property, without due process of law," among other provisions. The Fifteenth Amendment followed in 1870, and guaranteed that no male citizen would be denied the right to vote "on account of race, color, or previous condition of servitude."

Louis Favrot died in June 1876, a year before the end of the Reconstruction Era, at the impressive age of 88. He had outlived nine of his ten siblings, including Pulchérie, who died in 1846, just before her 43rd birthday, and Octavine, who died in 1868, aged 73. The last surviving child of Pierre-Joseph and Marie-Françoise was Bouvier, who died in 1881 at the age of 82.

After leaving the military, Henri returned to his legal practice and was later appointed judge of West Baton Rouge Parish, following in the footsteps of his father and his Uncle Philogène.[68] He served as superintendent of education for West Baton Rouge and as a member the Board of Supervisors of Louisiana State University.[69] He died in 1887 following a stroke suffered during a meeting of that body,[70] during which he was advocating the establishment of a campus laboratory for sugar research.[71]

In 1879, Henri had formally turned over all the Louisiana army records he had collected to General P.G.T. Beauregard.[72] He had retained them personally through the end of the war and the upheaval of Reconstruction in order to ensure their preservation. The records provided valuable information about the individuals who served in the Louisiana militia during the Civil War. Like his grandfather, Pierre-Joseph, who established the Favrot tradition of preserving the family's personal papers, Henri proved to be an important steward of a vital documentary history.

FAMILY LIFE &
CIVIC INVOLVEMENT

CHAPTER 6

PIERRE-JOSEPH FAVROT'S EDUCATION MANUAL FOR HIS SONS

The Favrot Family Papers contain few documents of a personal nature from before the 19th century. There is one such item dating to 1798, however, that is among the most engaging pieces in the entire collection. It is a detailed yet compact pamphlet composed by Pierre-Joseph Favrot as an academic and ethical guide for his two sons: Louis, about ten years old at the time, and Philogène, then about seven. Bouvier was not born until the following year, and Pierre-Joseph apparently did not think the material was relevant to the education of his daughter Joséphine or other daughters to come.

Pierre-Joseph wrote the manual while he and his family were living at Fort Saint Philip, the isolated post surrounded by the pestilential swamps of Plaquemines near the mouth of the Mississippi River. Bereft of a school, a church, or any regular cultural or recreational activities, Fort Saint Philip was a challenging place to raise a family. Pierre-Joseph's wife, Marie-Françoise, took responsibility for teaching all of her children to read and write, but otherwise, there seems to have been no formal instruction available to them.

In that context, Pierre-Joseph created a booklet that could serve not only as a primer for his sons on a variety of subjects, but also as a reference that they might consult regularly as they grew. Although he himself did not have the benefit of a formal education, Pierre-Joseph was well read, and as a third-generation military officer under the French and Spanish crowns, he and his family enjoyed high social status in colonial Louisiana. The manual he composed was as much an essay on the proper behavior of a late 18th-century gentleman as a textbook of basic knowledge.

The content and organization of the manual reflect prevailing educational theories in post-Enlightenment France, which in turn were influenced by classical and medieval academic models. Ancient Greek and Roman children typically began their studies by learning linguistic and critical thinking skills such as grammar and dialectical reasoning, followed by the study of such mathematical and scientific subjects as arithmetic and astronomy. Music, by virtue of the mathematical basis of its pitches and harmonies, was included in the latter group of subjects. In the early Middle Ages, Saint Augustine (354–430 C.E.), the highly influential Christian philosopher, formally grouped these areas of basic knowledge under the heading of the Seven Liberal Arts, typically organized into two subgroups: the Trivium, consisting of grammar, logic, and rhetoric, and the Quadrivium, comprising arithmetic, geometry, music, and astronomy. Augustine argued that proficiency in these subjects was necessary for a complete understanding of scripture.

The Enlightenment, a 17th- and 18th-century movement that challenged the authority of hierarchical institutions such as the Roman Catholic Church and monarchical government, emphasized individual intellectual development based on reason, analytical inquiry, and empirical investigation. Seminal treatises by scientists and philosophers such as René Descartes (1596–1650), Sir Isaac Newton (1642–1747), and Jean-Jacques Rousseau (1712–1778) upended centuries of collective wisdom regarding the natural world and the nature of humanity. Rousseau, in particular, promoted the concept of education as preparation for informed, responsible citizenship. The Enlightenment reached a political climax in the French Revolution, which overturned not only the *ancien régime*, but also long-held assumptions about social class and the relationship between the individual and society.

The post-revolutionary period was marked by a resurgent interest in the role of intuition and emotion in the arts, literature, and education. A reaction to both the rationalist epistemology of the Enlightenment and the rapid urbanization that accompanied the Industrial Revolution, this movement, which came to be called Romanticism, idealized nature and the purity of thought that it might inspire. One influential figure in French educational philosophy of the period was Stéphanie-Félicité, Madame de Genlis (1746–1830), a prolific author who wrote novels, children's books, and essays on religion and other subjects. A devout Catholic closely associated with the Bourbons—she had tutored Louis Philippe, Duc d'Orléans, whom Pierre-Joseph Favrot entertained at Plaquemines in 1798— she also advocated experiential learning, such as nature walks led by botanists. Her teaching techniques emphasized ethical development through a series of morality plays.

Pierre-Joseph was acquainted with Madame de Genlis through her husband, Charles-Alexis Brûlart, Comte de Genlis (1737–1793), who had been helpful to him when he was living in Paris in the 1770s. While it is impossible to gauge the explicit influence of her writing on his educational philosophy, it is noteworthy that in 1802 he asked a friend to send him several volumes of Madame de Genlis's works.[1] Although this request came several years after he wrote the education manual for his sons, the content and tone of his booklet are certainly consistent with the spirit of Genlis's theories.

The manual's title page included an inscription addressed initially to Pierre-Joseph's son Louis: "My dear son, remember what your affectionate father asks of you, which is to apply yourself and to learn by heart the contents of this little book. Be polite so as to make yourself be loved by everyone. Wherever you are, follow the dictates set forth in this book." A separate note indicated that the booklet was prepared for Louis and for his younger brother, Philogène, "if he wishes to make use of it."[2]

The manual was organized primarily as a series of questions and answers grouped together under seven headings, which overlapped with, but did not exactly correspond to, Augustine's Seven Liberal Arts. The headings were: "Arithmetic Table," "Grammar," "The Languages," "The Arts," "Physical Sciences," "Geography," and "History." These were complemented by a set of guidelines on "The Conduct of a Wise Man." There was also a brief overview of basic fencing technique titled "First Fencing Lesson."

The manual took little for granted. In the section titled "Arithmetic Table," for instance, it began not with lists of numbers or multiplication tables, but with the fundamental question, "What is arithmetic?" The answer: "It is the art of calculating well and with ease." The section went on to define each of the four basic arithmetical operations—addition, subtraction, multiplication, and division—and to answer questions about the applications of arithmetic in daily life, advanced mathematical calculations, and the values of various monetary units.[3] Similarly, the section on "Grammar" began with questions and answers regarding the necessity of studying the subject, followed by explanations of punctuation and diacritical marks. It then defined both prose and poetry, describing the various ways in which each might be used.[4]

The section on "The Languages" began by citing the Tower of Babel as "the origin of the number and diversity of languages." It purported to list the ten "most popular and most widely spoken languages in the world" at the time, including Persian but notably omitting any East Asian tongues (though it later noted that Chinese was the most difficult language). A relatively lengthy discussion of diphthongs—essential to spoken French—concluded that section.[5]

The exploration of "The Arts" began with a single question and answer regarding the definition of engraving. It then moved on to music. The manual's answer to the question "By whom was Music perfected?" is curious: "It is believed that the Hebrews were responsible, but today their music is not as brilliant or as imaginative. Today, the music of the Haitians surpasses that of all other nations."**** The final art addressed in the manual was dance, which had long been a popular activity in southern Louisiana. Perhaps responding to, or anticipating, attacks on dance as a licentious endeavor, Pierre-Joseph emphasized its moral acceptability: "As [dance] is in itself innocent, it was used in sacred ceremonies by the Israelites. See Judges 21:19." Explaining the value of dance, he wrote: "It is good in that it imparts to all movements of the body a certain pleasure and joy. It produces a relaxed and free air, which is evident in the gait and in the position of the chin, and which is most pleasing in young people."[6]

"Physical Sciences" were addressed in a section that included optics, mechan-

---

**** Pierre-Joseph's use of the term "Haitians" suggests that the manual, while dated 1798, may have been revised after 1804, when the Republic of Haiti was formed.

ics, statics, and astronomy, the last of which received the most extensive treatment of any specific subject area in the booklet.[7] The section on "Geography" described the Earth as being divided into four continents—Europe, Asia, Africa, and America—and described the "discovery" of the New World. It also listed major capital cities and the "main rivers of Europe."[8] The "History" section separated "sacred history" from "secular history" before defining three types of government: monarchy, aristocracy, and democracy. Interestingly, in listing examples of democratic societies, Pierre-Joseph said it was "found in several Swiss cantons, in the province of Groningen [in the Netherlands], and in several imperial cities." He did not include the United States.[9]

The core of the manual was surely the essay on "The Conduct of a Wise Man." It consisted of 35 brief statements, each comprising one, two, or three sentences, addressing points of ethics, etiquette, and religious faith. These included:

> My Son, love always without selfishness; forgive without weakness.
>
> If you must submit, do so without servility.
>
> Always be sympathetic to the misfortune of others. Be tolerant of the faults of your peers, and always be a loyal friend.
>
> My Son, speak little, think nobly, and cheat no one.
>
> Do not be curious about the affairs of others and, without affectation, always keep your own hidden.
>
> My Son, never betray a confidence.
>
> Be boastful of nothing.
>
> Keep silent and do not stoop to idle gossip.
>
> Do not criticize through ostentation.
>
> My Son, always be fair and always consider the profession of flatterer as a vile and evil one.

Do not try to appear more intelligent than you are.

Do not commit yourself indiscriminately and honor your
word invariably.[10]

The present-day reader who is familiar with the full biographies of Louis and
Philogène cannot help but speculate as to the influence of their father's educational manual on their character and behavior. Both served as officers in the military of
the young United States, earning praise and significant promotions. Both went on
to practice law and were appointed, in tandem, to the same judgeship. Both even
dabbled in the amateur practice of medicine—Philogène while serving in the military, and Louis on an ongoing basis throughout his adult life.[11] Yet personal documents in the Favrot Family Papers suggest that the two brothers were different
in key respects. Louis seems to have maintained a rather serious demeanor, while
Philogène was a prankster who often made flippant remarks in letters to his family.
Philogène was more hot-headed and occasionally found himself at odds with his
superior officers in the army, a trait that once led to his arrest for insubordination.
And while both brothers valued "honor" above almost all else, Louis eventually
peacefully settled the family's long-simmering feud with Sébastien Hiriart, whereas Philogène died on the dueling field over the original slight that led to the feud.

While it is, of course, impossible to establish the precise impact of
Pierre-Joseph's educational manual on each of his sons' character development,
the two brothers' clear reverence for their father, evident in numerous letters,
suggests that they valued his guidance on moral and intellectual matters. Each,
perhaps, heeded his father's instructions to "follow the dictates set forth in this
book" as much as possible given his own unique personality. Equally important,
the manual contributes significantly to the understanding of educational and social traditions that informed the Favrot family history over the ensuing centuries.

CHAPTER 7

DOMESTIC & SOCIAL LIFE IN THE 19TH CENTURY

The content and tone of the personal correspondence in the Favrot Family Papers dating to the 19th century suggest that family members felt genuine and deep affection for their parents, siblings, and children—and often for more distant relatives and even friends. Many letters were filled with terms of endearment, and those written by children to their parents frequently concluded with expressions of respect and devotion. A letter from Philogène to his mother, written while he was stationed at La Balize during the War of 1812, included a valedictory passage that covered the entire family at home in West Baton Rouge: "As a good son and a good brother, I embrace Papa, Phine [Joséphine] the dreamer, the *modest* Favrot [Louis], Tavine [Octavine] the sweet girl, Bouvier the lover and the sensitive Toutou [Pulchérie]."[1]

Family members who were away for extended periods eagerly awaited letters from home, and vice versa. They sometimes became anxious, sad, and even angry when letters did not arrive in a regular fashion. Unfortunately, given the unreliability of mail service in the early and mid-1800s, such disappointment was common. There was also evidence that mail was occasionally read illicitly by the deliverers or intercepted by nosy parties. In response, the family took to using code names for certain people. "Do not mention Britannicus under this name or under the name of the above-mentioned nymph in your letters," wrote Marie-Françoise to her daughter Joséphine in an 1810 letter. "I am bound to show them to Sir George and Sans-Chagrin when they ask me for them, and those nicknames have been guessed and disapproved of by the latter. In the future, if you have something to say about them, use the words rain, wind, or moss."[2]

Some family members were not as diligent about writing as their relatives and friends would have liked. Henri Mortimer Favrot, in 1850, resorted to writing a satirical poem to his cousin Guy Duplantier (life dates unknown) to chide him for not writing more often. The poem, as translated from the original French, began:

> That the flames crowned by my thunderous chime
> And the measured beat of my arrogant rhyme
> Come to my aid, offer me their refrain
> To pursue here below, with hate and disdain
> The friend who so readily swore,
> Not to dance the gavotte, not to his friend ignore
> But to speak a few times, aided by paper and pen
> Which today is sold in a notebook, by ten
> Tremble before me, oh! Drunken traitor,
> And tell me if you can, hiding behind something greater,
> Of lacking time, that which is so often quoted
> By people like you, who are far from devoted.[3]

Much of the personal correspondence centered around updates on family members' health, recent visitors, and other family news. The tone was typically rather serious. From time to time, however, the correspondents would share lighter stories, discuss social activities, or reminisce about occasions when the family was together.

Financial difficulties sometimes prevented the Favrots from enjoying social events. During the War of 1812, Marie-Françoise wrote to Philogène: "Your father came back only last night from the other bank [of the Mississippi River, i.e., Baton Rouge] where he had gone on Tuesday for a ball given by the officers of the fort for the Claiborne ladies, the Governor's wife, and the General's wife, who arrived a few days ago. Everyone here was invited, but nobody cared to go. None of the ladies on this bank of the river went, although they had been invited. When one is in our position, balls are not very tempting and I believe that we are not the only ones who feel that way."[4]

Such social occasions could be fraught. At one ball given later that year, which the Favrot siblings attended, Louis asked a Mrs. Valerian to dance, and she accepted. Her husband then intervened, leading to an argument between the husband and wife. Afterwards, rumors began circulating that Louis had challenged the husband to a duel. Louis denied it, and the situation was eventually defused, but the event was ruined for all of the guests. "Everyone agrees that Mr. and Mrs. Valerian's conduct deserves reproach," wrote Marie-Françoise in a letter to Philogène, "and they have all expressed opinions to that effect."[5]

Henri provided a vivid account of a Mardi Gras ball in Baton Rouge in February 1842. He described the guests' varied costumes, which included men dressed as an Italian bandit and a Knight Templar, and a woman with dark eyes dressed as an "Andalusian," which Henri noted matched her Mediterranean features. There was one guest, however, whose surprising attire delighted the crowd:

> While ten gentlemen without costumes were warming themselves a female costume came and entered into the room which had been designated for those of this sex. All eyes were trained on this last person who was recognized as male but not personally; then a young lady very politely said to him: Madam, come close to the fire, you must be cold; but in responding to the politeness shown, he slightly uncovered a face half-hidden by a fan . . . the young lady, laughing, said to him, I recognize you, you are a gentleman of my acquaintance; so she pronounced his name and all of those present recognized him. . . . He was made to dance and he resembled a dowager ready to get married for the third or fourth time.[6]

The pressure to write frequently sometimes led to poorly conceived attempts to keep correspondence entertaining. Philogène played a practical joke on his family in 1817, for instance, that backfired terribly. In a letter to his mother that is now lost, the unmarried Philogène claimed that he had fathered a child, and apparently asked his mother to adopt the baby in order give the impression that it was "legitimate." Having a child out of wedlock, while not uncommon, was extremely scandalous in early 19th-century Louisiana. Philogène's mother initially reacted to the story with horror and dismay: "Could I hear without the strongest emotion that my son, without a home or money of his own, was a father and perhaps could only have become so by bringing dishonor and despair to a family or at least to an unfortunate woman who perhaps had regarded him as a means of support for her and for her child?" Marie-Françoise went on to state that she had considered adopting the child, but decided that she could not do so for fear of damaging her other children's reputations. She simultaneously decried and defended the social mores that would inevitably lead to such a child's ostracization: "While protesting the prejudice that plunges your child into oblivion, you cannot help respecting it and admitting that it is useful in curbing vice and that it is beneficial that laws uphold this prejudice."[7]

Philogène's tale was quite convincing. After learning through Louis that the entire story was intended as a joke, Marie-Françoise chastised Philogène for bringing her anguish. "Must I imagine that my son used all of his rhetoric and his pathetic style only to amuse himself and that it was a game for him to make me cry and to move me to the extent that it did?"[8] Philogène's siblings were equally outraged. "One would have to be possessed by the Devil, as you are, to choose the subject you selected to play such a trick on Mama," wrote Louis. Philogène soon wrote back to seek his family's forgiveness: "I must have been out of my mind not to see the trouble that that cursed letter of February 1 would cause you. This impulse is among the ones that often seize me; I don't know why." He went on to blame "uncertainty over what I was going to write about," and pledged never to play such a trick again.[9]

While Philogène's tale proved to be a fabrication, there is evidence of extramarital sexual activity on the part of at least one family member. Just before the onset of the Civil War, Henri was in his early thirties and not yet married. His diaries from that period included a number of cryptic mentions of visits to "V.," sometimes spelled out as "Venus." On several occasions, he used a more extensive phrase, such as "Visit to Venus and sacrifice."[10] The term *"un sacrifice à Venus"* ("a sacrifice to Venus") was common 19th-century French slang for sexual intercourse.[11] These diary entries suggest that Henri was involved in a continuing sexual relationship with an unknown woman (the fact that he also noted when "V." was ill or traveling indicates that the code name applied to one specific woman). It is surprising that Henri would have so freely used this term in a diary, which, though perhaps private at the time, was likely to be read by subsequent generations in a family known for retaining personal papers.

The reach of the Favrot name had remained rather limited over the course of the family's first century in Louisiana: Claude-Joseph had only one son—Pierre-Joseph—to survive into adulthood, marry, and reproduce; Pierre-Joseph, in turn, had only two sons—Louis and Bouvier—who lived long enough to marry and have children; and Louis had only one son—Henri Mortimer—who survived past childhood. The family tree began to grow more rapidly, however, in the 1830s as Bouvier and his wife Marie-Aurore Villars had five children, including four sons who went on to establish their own branches of the family. Meanwhile, beginning in the 1860s, Henri and his wife Célestine had a total of seven children. Their first, Henry Louis Favrot, born in 1864, was followed by Charles Allen Favrot, born in 1866, who went on to become an architect and is the principal subject of the first chapter in the third section of this book. Their other children were Edgar Dubroca Favrot, William Reynaud Favrot, Leopold (Leo) Mortimer Favrot, Louise Alzire Favrot, and finally Corinne Augustine Favrot, born in 1880, when her father was 54 and her mother 39.

In 1889, Henry Louis Favrot became involved in a scandal that harked back to Philogène's disastrous practical joke of seven decades earlier. Henry's young cousin Lilie Dubroca became pregnant, and when coerced by her parents to identify the father, she named Henry. He vigorously denied it, claiming that the two had been nothing more than friends, but in order "to save the honor of her family," he agreed to marry her. The marriage was short-lived. In June of that year, while Lilie was staying in a boarding house in St. Louis, she committed suicide by drinking poison. She left a note addressed "To the public," in which she stated that Henry was not in fact the father of the unborn child: "I assert that the man bearing the name of my husband is not guilty of that of which he is accused. His character in this case has been blackened for my own selfish motives, and they must be known while it is yet in my power to make them. I have nothing more to leave behind me but this proof of my husband's innocence."[12] The suicide—and Lilie's dramatic, exculpatory note—made headlines in newspapers across the country. Lilie never revealed the name of the actual father.

French remained the Favrots' primary language through most of the 19th century, though each successive generation became more comfortable speaking and writing English. While he was away in Richmond during the Civil War, Henri, writing to his wife in French, encouraged her to practice English with some of the Anglophone women then residing with her in the Attakapas region. "[G]o often in their room," he advised, "speak with them, and ask them on my part to correct you when you make errors of grammar, of language as much as of pronunciation."[13] Henri and Célestine's children, however, increasingly spoke English, sometimes as their primary language. In a letter possibly dating to 1891, Célestine felt the need to encourage her son Charles to practice his French, and possibly even to take formal French lessons.[14] This represents a remarkable linguistic shift from one generation to the next.

By the end of the 19th century, the Favrot family was also in the early stages of another profound cultural transformation. Henri and Célestine's sons Henry and Charles both decided to pursue careers and make their home in New Orleans. Two of their siblings soon joined them on a temporary basis. The family's center of gravity, long in the Baton Rouge area, was beginning to shift toward the state's largest city.

The Monte Vista Plantation

The Favrot family moved many times during the colonial period, as Claude-Joseph and then Pierre-Joseph accepted successive military assignments throughout Louisiana. During Pierre-Joseph's brief posting at Baton Rouge from 1799 to 1800, however, he made a decision that would ultimately root the family in that area for more than a century. In July 1800, he bought a plantation just across the Mississippi River from Baton Rouge, in what would come to be known as West Baton Rouge. The property, later dubbed Monte Vista, was rather small as plantations went, measuring 18 *arpents* (or about 3,450 feet) along the river by 40 *arpents* (about 7,673 feet) deep, for a total area of about 600 acres.[15] The plantation's primary product at the time was indigo dye.[16]

After Pierre-Joseph was reassigned to the Plaquemines post in the fall of 1800, he relied on a slave named Sam and an elderly tenant named Cardine to manage the plantation.[17] His wife's brother-in-law, Armand Allard Duplantier, lived in Baton Rouge and frequently checked in on the property. Profits were elusive, and Pierre-Joseph soon wondered whether buying the plantation had been a good idea. In August 1802, Armand wrote to him: "In your first letter, you spoke about selling the property. In your last one you said nothing about that. Let me know positively your intentions and my [sister-in-law's]. I could sell it easily. Land is in demand and is selling at a good price."[18] Pierre-Joseph had envisioned the plantation as a key element of his retirement plan, however, and given the political changes that were then looming for the Louisiana colony, he seems to have decided that keeping it was still the best option.

The Favrots finally moved to the plantation for good in 1804 following Pierre-Joseph's retirement and the transfer of Louisiana to the United States. By 1805, the family had amassed a trio of properties with a total of 43 *arpents* of river frontage and a standard depth of 40 *arpents*, comprising more than 1,400 acres. The primary Favrot plantation included a main house, a storehouse, a kitchen, six fenced-in slaves' cabins, and "a yard, garden, and orchard." Next to that plot was an apparently undeveloped property five *arpents* wide owned by Pierre-Joseph's daughter Joséphine, who received it as a gift from her uncle Armand Duplantier. In addition, Pierre-Joseph controlled a concession—essentially a land grant—with a width of 20 *arpents* near Devil's Cypress Grove (also known as Devil's Swamp), north of Baton Rouge.[19] Pierre-Joseph sold the concession at Devil's Swamp in June 1806.[20] The fate of Joséphine's property is unclear, but it was not mentioned in Pierre-Joseph's next will dating to 1809.[21]

The family continued to struggle to make a profit from the plantation.[22] As early as 1812, Pierre-Joseph had considered a "lottery" or "raffle" to sell the property,[23] but that effort was unsuccessful. Coupled with his ongoing difficulty in obtaining back retirement pay from the Spanish government for himself and his sons, as the king had promised to all retired Spanish soldiers during the retrocession of Louisiana to France, the precarious finances of the plantation caused frequent anxiety for Pierre-Joseph. (Of course, perceptions of financial well-being are always somewhat subjective—the Favrots continued to own slaves, occasionally bought luxury items, and never lacked food, clothing, or medical care, such as it was in that era.) The family's financial problems were exacerbated by bad weather and other challenges. "What can we do to compensate for a lost crop?" asked Marie-Françoise in a letter to her son Philogène in 1813. "Everything in Nature seems to rail against us. We cannot prosper in anything."[24]

Pierre-Joseph was still actively trying to sell the plantation in the fall of 1818 when he received a business proposition from his nephew Brognier De Clouet. Brognier had left Louisiana early in the War of 1812, initially settling in Philadelphia and then Bordeaux, France. From there he went to Spain, where he obtained a military commission and was offered the governorship of the territory of Matanzas on the northern coast of Cuba, about 50 miles east of Havana. In preparation, he had sold his rum distillery in New Orleans to his sons-in-law, who then decided to put it up for auction. Brognier encouraged Pierre-Joseph to buy the business, which he claimed would bring in "three times the profit of [Favrot's] plantation." Brognier offered favorable financing terms out of familial devotion, but noted that he would extend a similar deal to his own nephew if Pierre-Joseph did not accept. "You have the first choice," he wrote, "because you have less money and more family."[25]

Pierre-Joseph took the proposal seriously, dispatching Philogène, who was living in New Orleans at the time, to visit the distillery and assess its business potential.[26] Philogène dutifully did so and sent a thorough report back via his mother. He found the facility generally in good condition, and noted that some of the slaves who would be sold with the property were "very skilled."[27] Pierre-Joseph, who was then actively entertaining offers on the plantation,[28] wrote a follow-up letter to his son, peppering him with questions about the potential output and possible sale price of the distillery. Interestingly, all prices were still cited as being in *piastres*, the name of the old Spanish currency, rather than U.S. dollars.[††††][29]

---

†††† Creoles often used the terms "piastre" and "dollar" interchangeably for many years after the transfer of Louisiana to the United States.

Even as Pierre-Joseph was carefully weighing the distillery purchase, Brognier began suggesting to his uncle that if he decided not to buy the distillery, he should move his family to Cuba instead. "Here are my reasons," Brognier wrote, "which are based on my experience. The price of one Negro at home will buy you two here with some money left over. The work of these two [slaves], because of the fertility of the soil, will produce that of four in Louisiana. In this new colony you can obtain land at low prices. . . . We have fish and game in abundance."[30]

By February 1819, Brognier informed Pierre-Joseph that he was venturing into the interior of Cuba to select the site for an entirely new colony.[31] The selection came quickly: the next month, he reported that the colony was to be established at the Bay of Jagua along the island's south central coast.[32] In June, he wrote to Pierre-Joseph again with a detailed sales pitch, outlining the numerous incentives that the Spanish government was offering to families who settled in the colony, which was then called Fernandina de Jagua. The incentives included a substantial grant of arable land, an additional plot of land in the town that was to be built on the bay, and exemptions from duties on agricultural equipment and food supplies. "In conclusion," Brognier wrote, "every honest and industrious man cannot fail to prosper in this country; the man who is not accustomed to manual labor must necessarily have the means to purchase some Negroes. Settlers who come with large sums of capital are assured of making large fortunes within a few years, barring unforeseen circumstances."[33] The letter's promotional tone serves as a reminder that hucksterism in real estate ventures is hardly a new phenomenon.

None of the financial schemes that Brognier proposed to his uncle ever came to anything. The planned auction of the distillery was delayed and in fact may never have taken place because of "a few envious persons who [were] scheming over" the property, according to Brognier.[34] Meanwhile, Pierre-Joseph cited his declining health as an impediment to moving to Cuba.[35] Interestingly, however, the colony that Brognier established at the Bay of Jagua went on to become the city of Cienfuegos, once the third and now the 13th most populous city in Cuba.[36] Its well-preserved Spanish colonial town center is a UNESCO World Heritage Site.[37] A plaque on Brognier's former house, now the Cienfuegos tourist office, credits him—under the name Don Luis DeClouet—as the city's founder.[38]

By the late 1850s, the Favrot family's finances had stabilized to the point that they could build a new main house on the Monte Vista plantation. The house was built between December 1857 and May 1859 under Louis's supervision, using heart cypress wood and bricks made by the Favrots' slaves. Other materials were generally delivered by steamboat, but were often of poor quality and had to be returned.[39] The house was originally sited about 800 feet from the Mississippi River levee, and was approached via an allée of live oaks. Over time, however, the river inevitably shifted and the levee was moved, greatly reducing the area of land between the house and the riverbank.[40]

The design of the house is emblematic of antebellum Louisiana plantation architecture. The principal façade, facing the river, is a perfectly symmetrical composition of five structural bays with porches (or "galleries") running the full length of the house on the first and second floors, capped by a steeply pitched roof with two dormer windows. The galleries are supported by simple square pillars that are relatively robust on the lower level and noticeably slenderer on the upper level.

The abolition of slavery in the wake of the Civil War, of course, completely changed the plantation economy of the American South. The Favrots strained to adjust to new economic realities, which were complicated by the continuing upheaval of Reconstruction. Nonetheless, they managed to acquire other properties during that time, the largest of which was a plantation called Monte Sano, almost directly across the river from Monte Vista, which they rented to sharecroppers.[41] By the late 1800s, the family was making money by selling various commodities including pecans,[42] corn, and sugar cane.[43]

Following Henri's death in 1887, Célestine took the lead in managing the family's properties. By the late 19th century, she owned or co-owned several properties besides Monte Vista, including at least two houses in New Orleans that she may have inherited through the Dubroca family: one on Rampart Street and one on Customhouse Street, which was renamed Iberville Street in 1904. Ownership of the Rampart Street house was split three ways, between Célestine and two of her sisters.[44]

The rental income from these properties was sometimes disappointing. In a letter to her son Charles dating to around 1886, Célestine complained, "I am furious with our city properties. Can you believe it, the Rampart Street one paid in only $18.26 for 6 months, which gives us each $6.00. The Customhouse Street house leaves us in debt $47.00. I feel like burning them, it is better to know you have nothing, then you expect nothing."[45] Célestine's other properties included one at Pointe Coupée that she apparently inherited from the Soniat branch of her family.[46]

The gradual shift of the family's epicenter from West Baton Rouge to New Orleans began in the mid-1880s when Charles moved to the city to join the architectural practice of his cousin James Freret.[47] He initially lived with Freret's family in their house on Constance Street. Charles's brother Henry moved to New Orleans in 1888 to study law at Tulane, living in a room rented from his cousins, the Duplantiers.[48] In the 1890s, Henry and Charles's brother Leo also moved to New Orleans to study at Tulane. While there, he lived with Charles and his new wife Beatrice Freret Favrot, James Freret's daughter.[49] Another brother, William (usually called Willie), also stayed for a time in Charles and Beatrice's guest room.[50]

With several of her children now living in New Orleans, Célestine soon followed suit, moving to a house at 1571 Henry Clay Avenue in New Orleans with her two youngest children, Louise and Corinne. The family retained ownership of Monte Vista, however, and Willie later returned to West Baton Rouge to manage the plantation. Célestine and the young girls regularly spent summers there for years, and other family members would occasionally join them to escape the heat of the city.[51]

Célestine finally sold Monte Vista around 1920. The buyer was Horace Wilkinson, Jr. (1888–1966), a descendant of Louisiana's first governor, a prominent state legislator, and owner of the Poplar Grove plantation just downriver from Monte Vista. Following the catastrophic Mississippi River Flood of 1927, the U.S. Army Corps of Engineers proposed realigning the levee and building a new river road that would have required the demolition of both properties. After surveyors staked out the path of the proposed new road, Wilkinson's father, Horace Wilkinson, Sr. (1854–1941), who had also served in the state legislature, invited the project engineers over for a sumptuous dinner, accompanied, of course, by ample libations. Afterwards, the group took a walk around the property, which drew compliments from the engineers. Wilkinson then pointed to the stakes and noted what a shame it would be if the properties were razed for a road. The gambit worked: the engineers arranged for the road to be rerouted, and the houses were spared.[52] The result is still readily visible on contemporary maps: River Road, which runs along the West Bank of the Mississippi, swerves inland twice a few miles north of Port Allen, once for Poplar Grove and once for Monte Vista, which is now just a few dozen yards from the levee.

Monte Vista remained in the Wilkinson family for several generations, but is now owned by another family. The main house was added to the National Register of Historic Places in 1980. Although the house is private, the current owners occasionally rent out the property for weddings and other special events. Recent online photographs and comments from people who have been married there indicate that the venerable structure is in excellent condition.

Slavery and Servants

The earliest explicit reference to slave ownership within the Favrot family appears in the 1761 marriage contract of Louise Favrot, Pierre-Joseph's sister, and Alexandre De Clouet. The contract recorded a "gift" of a mulatto slave girl to Louise from her maternal grandmother, Marthe Frémont Bruslé. The document also noted that the future husband would be bringing into the new household two African and two Native American slaves.[53] Claude-Joseph Favrot and his wife Louise also must have owned slaves, since Pierre-Joseph inherited an unspecified number of African slaves from his mother upon her death in 1773.[54]

The Favrot Family Papers contain numerous records of slave purchases by the family during the 18th and 19th centuries, but few records of sales or deaths, so it is not always possible to know precisely how many slaves they owned at a given time. Pierre-Joseph's will from May 1805, however, provided an accounting of his property as of that date. He reported owning 30 slaves, including two infants and nine other children under the age of 18. With a few exceptions, the roster briefly noted each adult or adolescent slave's duties—the list included ten adult men and women who primarily served as field workers or woodcutters, along with two laundresses, two barbers, a seamstress, a tailor, a shoemaker, a carpenter, a cook, and several general servants. The roster also noted each slave's racial make-up, whether "Negro," "mulatto" (a person with one white and one African or African American parent), "quadroon" (a person who is one-quarter African or African American), or "griffe" (a person who is three-quarters African or African American). Interestingly, several of the children were identified as being one step "whiter" than their mothers—the identities of their fathers, who may or may not have been members of the extended Favrot family, are unknown.[55]

By the time Pierre-Joseph made a new will in 1809, the total number of slaves he owned remained the same at 30. Several slaves listed in 1805 did not appear in the new roster, but they had been replaced by new slaves or additional children of existing slaves.[56] According to the Louisiana Census Index of 1810, there were only nine slaves living at the Favrot plantation by then, suggesting that the family may have sold some of their slaves or had not replaced some who died.[57]

There is evidence that the Favrots were well aware of, and fundamentally understood, growing abolitionist sentiment not just in the United States, but around the world. In the 1830s, Louis Favrot wrote a letter to the editor of an unnamed newspaper on the subject of raising and educating children. In criticizing the use of corporal punishment in schools, the letter included a telling reference to the abolitionist movement: "Is it not a shame that in the 19th century, when in all the despotic countries one sees the former regime's old prejudices being abolished and one hears the cries against slavery everywhere in the world, that the punishment of whipping was adopted in a Louisiana school, thus making our children similar to slaves? How horrible!"[58] Taken at face value, that passage might suggest that it was written by someone who objected to slavery on moral grounds, but there is no evidence that Louis or any other members of his family ever seriously questioned the legitimacy of slavery until near the end of the Civil War.

Overall, personal details regarding the Favrots' slaves are rare in the family's papers, so it is difficult to form a complete sense of how the slaves were treated. There are occasional references, however, to violent physical punishment even for minor infractions. In a diary entry in November 1860, for instance, Henri noted, "I gave Sylvain [a slave] a thrashing to teach him to get up earlier."[59]

The Emancipation Proclamation issued by President Abraham Lincoln on January 1, 1863, declared that all slaves in areas that were still in rebellion against the United States were thenceforth free. Of course, the constituent states of the Confederacy at the time considered themselves to be part of an independent nation no longer subject to U.S. law, so the immediate impact of the proclamation was limited. Moreover, the proclamation did not apply to areas within the Confederacy that were then under Union control, including the state of Tennessee and the southeastern portion of Louisiana. Nonetheless, the presidential order provided freedom—and some protection—to all slaves who managed to escape their owners and reach safe harbor in the North.

By the spring of 1865, many white Southerners were coming to realize that the war was nearing its end, and slavery with it. Some slaves dared to leave on their own; some were freed by their owners, albeit reluctantly. It seems that at least a couple of the Favrots' slaves chose to leave Monte Vista during that time. While the family did not intervene in their departure, correspondence reveals that the Favrots and their relatives, like many slave owners, were bewildered by events that were upending their racial worldview. In a March 1865 letter to her aunt Célestine Dubroca Favrot, who was still staying with relatives in Attakapas, Amélie Reynaud recounted the decision by a slave named Adine to leave the plantation with her children, commenting, "I find Adine rather ungrateful, and I am sure that she will regret leaving us more than once." She added: "[W]e learned from the other servants that Adine's goal in leaving was to find an education for her children. Would you have suspected Adine of this ambition? I admit that I thought her very innocent, this is the last motive to which I would have attributed her conduct."[60]

A little more than a month after Lee's surrender to Grant at Appomattox, Amélie wrote to her aunt again. The Confederate loss was sinking in, and she expressed concern about the future:

> May God have pity on us, for I truly do not know what will become of us, the future seems dark, I already see separation, misery, and vexation of all kinds. . . . I cannot help but feel sad in thinking of all the suffering that our brave soldiers have endured with heroic courage, of all of the blood that was shed, of so many unfortunates crippled for nothing, without results, for us to be a hundred times worse off, to have fewer rights than when we left

the Union over a few differences that could have been resolved by mutual concessions. Cursed slavery! Why did we not abolish it ourselves?"[61]

The Favrots kept paid servants at Monte Vista in the late 1800s, including a housemaid named Roselia, who was of Native American and African heritage;[62] an Acadian "yard man" named Felix; his mother, Madame Leonard, who cooked for the family; and a young African American named Louis de Bardeaux.[63] The household also included Mary Sampson, known as "Aunt May," whose parents had been killed in a train accident when she was 12. After railroad officials were unable to find any of the child's family members at either the point of origin or the destination, Charles and his wife Beatrice, who had been traveling to New York by train, effectively adopted her and brought her back to Louisiana. She thenceforth helped with sewing and childcare, straddling the line between servant and family member. When Célestine and her two young daughters moved from Monte Vista to New Orleans, both Aunt May and Roselia moved with them.[64]

Half a century later, Aunt May was told of a newspaper ad placed by someone seeking to know the whereabouts of a Mary Sampson whose parents had been killed in a train wreck. She answered the ad, and went to visit her blood relatives in Canada. After a while, however, she declared, "The Favrots are my family," and returned to New Orleans and continued to live in Favrot households for the rest of her life. Her remains are interred in the Favrot family tomb at Metairie Cemetery.[65]

Illness

Illness and death were near-constant themes in early 19th-century Favrot correspondence. Fevers were common and their origins little understood, making effective treatment difficult. Stomach ailments were endemic, and were typically treated by administering syrup of ipecac to induce vomiting,[66] which could lead to dehydration and exhaustion. Skin diseases and unexplained aches might be treated with poultices and other folk remedies, some of which had scientific bases, many of which did not. Infants and young children were particularly vulnerable to infections and other maladies, as evidenced by the premature deaths of five of Pierre-Joseph and Marie-Françoise's 11 children.

The Favrot family's letters were often remarkably candid in their discussion of potentially embarrassing afflictions. While the family was stationed at Plaquemines in 1801, Philogène, then only ten years old, developed urinary problems, which may have been caused by a kidney stone or a urinary tract infection. Pierre-Joseph reported his son's pain and discomfort to various relatives, who replied with sympathy and advice. Armand Duplantier wrote: "I was sorry to hear of Philogène's indisposition. It is unusual in a child of his age and deserves all your attention. . . . His health should improve quickly with refreshing food, but, if his condition is caused by stones or some evil humor, which would be quite extraordinary at his age, it requires the care of an experienced practitioner."[67] The term "evil humor," while suggestive of a sexually transmitted disease, was also sometimes used more generically to explain otherwise mysterious bodily discharges. At any rate, the problem had cleared up by July 1801 without the need for surgery or catheterization.[68]

Mosquitoes, which often carried infectious agents, plagued the Favrots while Pierre-Joseph was stationed at Plaquemines. Joséphine, in a letter of September 1801 to her friend Hélène de Grand-Pré, complained about the tiny winged terrors: "There must be a thousand around me if there is one. I cannot form a single letter without having to jump up, waving my arms. Noise, nothing frightens them. They are fearless." She mentioned Philogène's illness before reporting on the ailments of her youngest brother: "If you could see the poor little Bouvier, you would pity him. He has been tortured by abscesses and boils, especially on the face and head. They had to cut his beautiful curly hair, which had been so becoming to him."[69]

When Pierre-Joseph developed a lesion on one of his buttocks in 1809, he was as forthright in discussing the ailment with his family as he had been with Philogène's urinary troubles. He described a pus-filled wound, which, upon examination, the doctor discovered to be the opening to an abnormal channel running between the rectum and the surface of the skin. Based on the description, it is highly likely that Pierre-Joseph was suffering from a fistula, a common but little-discussed condition even today. He went away to Bayou des Écores for surgery, after which he wrote to his wife: "[The wound] is as long as a finger and is close to the anus. I have to wait a month before thinking of going home."[70] The surgery, which probably involved a painful cut to lay open the channel to the surface of the skin—a procedure that is still used to treat a fistula in the present day—appears to have been a success.

Physical maladies were not the only medical problems that afflicted the Favrot family. Both Marie-Françoise and Joséphine seem to have suffered from what would now be considered anxiety disorders. Marie-Françoise, in particular, was often nearly incapacitated by worry about her family, especially when her sons were on active duty during the War of 1812. Philogène wrote to her while he was stationed at Fort Saint Philip: "Your dark forebodings about your family's fate are always exaggerated by your prompt imagination, which is naturally inclined to see the worst." In the same letter, he wrote, "[Joséphine] worries me. She is like a sea—stormy below and calm on the surface. Everything seems very volcanic . . . "[71] When tragedy did strike, both mother and daughter had difficulty pursuing their normal lives. After Philogène's death in the duel, Octavine later wrote, "my mother's health was nothing more than a long series of sufferings. She didn't leave her room, for more than a year she was bedridden, grieving every day for the loss of this beloved child."[72]

Louis, like Philogène, had studied medicine informally and became a highly respected amateur doctor. Initially ministering to his own family and slaves, he soon developed a reputation within the broader community. According to his obituary, "When Dr. Doussan, a very successful physician of [West Baton Rouge] parish, left for Europe in 1831 or '32, there being no regular practitioner here, he advised his patients all to send for his friend, Favrot, whenever his services were needed. . . . During the great cholera epidemic of 1831–32, the medical attention of Mr. Favrot was the means of saving many valuable lives during the continuance of that terrible scourge, and it was a marked feature of his generous nature that he treated the poor without cost or charge."[73]

Louis Favrot wrote a detailed and wrenching account of the illness and death of his infant daughter Octavie (not to be confused with his sister Octavine) in early 1829. Louis carefully documented the child's symptoms and treatment over the course of three months. The ailment began with a stiff neck and swelling along the spine, followed by intestinal difficulties. After several weeks, Louis noticed that her eyes would cross as she tried to focus on an object. Louis prescribed various emetics and oils to try to regularize her digestion, but to little avail. Eventually, the child's eyes began to appear sunken. Late one night, Louis noticed that her pulse and breathing had weakened, her skin was pale, and her extremities began to feel cool to the touch. He placed the baby it a hot bath, "and, after several minutes, a final effort by nature was made to open her eyes to me but she no longer saw, for some instants afterwards she was no more."[74]

While Louis was respected as a medical amateur, trained doctors were sometimes regarded with almost mystical admiration at the time. Over the course of four months beginning in October 1837, Octavine Favrot kept a journal in which she described the frequent visits of Dr. Albert A. Siemiontkosky [possibly Siemiontkowski] (1810–1838) to the Favrot household. Siemiontkosky made alternating medical and social calls to check in on Marie-Françoise and her children.[75] The family's adoration for the doctor was such that, on the occasion of his feast-day—the day associated with his patron saint—both Octavine and her then-pre-teenage nephew, Henri, composed and presented poems dedicated to him.[76] The family was shocked when Siemiontkosky died in an accident of some kind at the age of only 28.[77]

Siemiontkosky's successor as the Favrots' physician was Dr. Thomas Jefferson Peniston (1806–1882), for whom Peniston Street in New Orleans was named later. Peniston was married to Amélie Duplantier (1821–1845), half-sister of Augustine Duplantier Favrot and the namesake of Amelia Street in the same city. As Marie-Françoise's health declined further in 1842, Octavine began another journal describing her mother's last days. The journal was addressed, but never delivered, to Dr. Peniston, who Octavine believed had been sent by divine providence to continue the tender care that her mother had received from Siemiontkosky.[78]

Religion

The Favrots, like most French Creole families, had deep Roman Catholic roots. Favrot weddings and baptisms were virtually always performed in the Catholic Church through the early 19th century, and numerous documents attest to early family members' religious faith and acceptance of Catholic doctrine. In his last will and testament of May 1805, for instance, Pierre-Joseph wrote: "Enjoying a perfect health of all my mental faculties, believing firmly in the ineffable mystery of the Holy Trinity, Father, Son, and Holy Spirit, three separate persons and one True Being, and in the Incarnation of the Divine Word, made man to redeem us in the pure womb of the Virgin Mary, Mother of God, our Lady . . . we want to make our testament which I am writing in my own hand."[79]

In February 1810, Pierre-Joseph took his daughters Joséphine, then 24 years old, and Octavine, who was 14, to New Orleans. The primary purpose of the trip was for Octavine to prepare for her first Holy Communion by studying with the nuns at the Ursuline Convent. Pierre-Joseph was also eager to give both of his daughters the opportunity to attend theatrical performances and Mardi Gras balls after Octavine completed her studies,[80] but his wife did not approve of her engaging in frivolous activities so soon "after such a solemn act." She would have preferred that Octavine "remain in the convent for three days [after her first communion] to express her thanksgiving."[81] Pierre-Joseph apparently ignored his wife's admonition, however, and the trio went on to take advantage of the cultural and social events of the Carnival season.[82]

Not all Favrot family members have been practicing Catholics. Louis, for instance, was alternately identified as a Deist or more generically as a "Theist." An astonishing letter from the 1830s sheds light on his nontraditional religious views. The impetus for the correspondence is unknown, but apparently after expressing his beliefs to a Catholic priest, the priest called him an atheist, which offended Louis. In a lengthy response, Louis wrote, "Is it in the nature of a Catholic priest to accuse all those who do not think as you do of atheism? Might it be a consequence of their profession to deceive men and to let them remain ignorant in order to make it easier to force them to submit to their despotic rule?"

The letter went on to criticize the Catholic Church for certain rituals that Louis likened to sorcery. "Please, what is a baptism, if not an exorcism? Do you not say during this ceremony, 'Child, I am exorcising you?' You say it in Latin and with good reason. Everyone says . . . 'Oh, how beautiful this [language] is; I don't understand anything.'"

Louis continued:

> I shall tell you that having been reared in the Christian religion, I followed its virtues until I was 22 by doing what I thought you were doing: believing blindly. . . . I read Father [Charles] Rollin's *Ancient History*, written for youth in order to propagate the Christian religion. When I came up to the Sacred History, I saw that God was given all the same passions as men. I saw a miserable creature being debased, sinking down like the worst scoundrel of that time, even ordering the massacre of a whole nation: men, women, and children, even the ones still in their mothers' wombs. At that point, my indignation was such that I threw away the book and did not want to touch it again, saying, 'I am no longer a Christian; such a God is not mine. . . .'" Therefore, I became a Theist, which is the finest of all religions and the basis of all others.

Addressing the priest as a "miserable creature" and a "contemptible reptile," Louis denied such central tenets of the Catholic faith as the Holy Trinity, "where one sees a virgin conceive and give birth while still keeping her virginity and chastity," and the moral authority of the Pope. He argued that Christians had been responsible for untold violence through religious wars, the Crusades, the Inquisition, and numerous massacres of nonbelievers. He concluded the letter: "May the future cleanse you of your past sins. So be it . . ."[83]

Although he did not consider himself a Christian, Louis was a member of a Masonic Lodge, whose leaders seem to have believed that all of its members were Christians. Some of the lodge's rituals and religious foundations are illuminated in Louis's copy of a Masonic notebook preserved among the Favrot Family Papers.

The notebook began with "Observations and Dispositions," which described the decoration of the lodge and the positions of key participants during the ceremony to induct new members. For the occasion, a copy of the lodge's constitution was placed on the altar, along with a Bible open to St. Peter's Second Epistle, which urged the faithful to pursue virtue and knowledge and to beware of "false teachers." The document also contained a complete and detailed script for the conduct of the ceremony, consisting primarily of questions posed to the candidates and their required answers. Excerpts from the script, with questions read by the master of ceremonies, follow:

> The First Warden makes the candidate known on the door. The First Officer is warned that someone is knocking on the door. The Master is notified.
>
> The Master: "My brothers, a note tells me that a profane person is at the door."
>
> Q: "How does he pretend to be admitted?"
>
> A: "Because he is a free man with good morals."
>
> Q: "Ask for his surname and first name, his birth place, his age, his home address, his state and his religion."
>
> The questions are asked, one after the other, giving time to the Secretary to write the answers.
>
> The entrance is opened with great noise and the candidate is firmly pushed inside. There is a pistol shot close to him and the Master of ceremonies touches his left breast with the point of a dagger.
>
> Q: "Profane one, what do you see and what do you feel?"
>
> The Candidate [blindfolded]: "I see nothing but I feel the point of a weapon pricking me."

The Master: "Profane one, learn that the blindness in which is symbolized the blindness of a man who does not follow the way of virtue and justice and that the point you feel reminds you that our swords are always ready to punish you. If you become enlightened about your duties toward the Society you want to join, is it of your own volition, without influence or suggestion that you have decided to be a Mason? If curiosity leads you here and is your only guide, if your motives are not praiseworthy, tremble, Sir, as you will not escape from the eyes of men accustomed to reading the most hidden parts of hearts. Public contempt, Masons' hatred and divine revenge would reach you wherever you go, but if your intentions are pure, if love of virtue guides you, you have nothing to fear. Masons praise themselves as being Christian, religious, and they undertake nothing that is contrary to the feelings of devotion toward God, to the obedience of laws, to the submission toward superiors. Decide whether you want to risk the dangers and trials you have to expect."

One waits for the answer.

[The Master:] "Be careful, after you give your approval, you are on your own."

The candidate answers.

[The Master:] "Since it is so, you will be conducted to the altar."[84]

Louis's religious views caused friction within the family. His cousin Brognier De Clouet apparently wrote Louis a letter in which he referred to him as an atheist, and Louis again took umbrage, responding, "As I am not a Christian, you accuse me of Atheism. I find that Atheism is a monstrosity and I doubt that it exists." In a notation inserted between lines, he added, "You should read the Quran a bit."[85]

Louis, whose obituary referred to him as a Deist,[86] raised his children in accordance with his religious beliefs, though it appears that most if not all of them primarily identified as Catholics in adulthood. Henri, for one, married in the

Catholic Church and attended Catholic services. He was not above criticizing the church's rituals, however. In describing a Catholic service he attended while in Richmond in 1865, he wrote: "The bishop [John] McGill preached, but I was too far from the pulpit to understand the sermon—I greatly regretted this, since it is said that he says wonderful things, speaks with good judgment, good sense, and of things that are relevant to all levels of intelligence—the default of most Catholic priests is to speak only of mysteries that they cannot explain—which leaves them incomprehensible to themselves and to their listeners."[87]

Henri's son Charles was not a practicing Catholic in early adulthood, but when he fell in love with Beatrice Freret, who was a devout Catholic, he agreed to convert to her religion. A substantial majority of Favrot family members in the 20th and 21st centuries have identified as Catholics.

CHAPTER 8

CIVIC ENGAGEMENT & DOMESTIC LIFE IN THE EARLY 20TH CENTURY

There is very little material from the 20th century in the Favrot Family Papers. The advent of the telephone may have been partially responsible for a decline in the volume of personal correspondence beginning in the late 19th century. Then the invention of the automobile made it easier for family members to visit one another—Charles Favrot bought the family's first car in 1905[1]—further reducing the need to write letters. Moreover, by the early 1900s, many family members—at least those in the line that is the primary subject of this book—were concentrated in New Orleans, and with the exception of a brief period during World War I, military service rarely separated young Favrot men from their parents, siblings, and spouses for extended periods—circumstances that had inspired many letters over the preceding centuries.

Fortunately, several key sources provide useful information about the Favrot family's activities and experiences in the first few decades of the 20th century. These include *Pops: A Memoir*, a biographical sketch of Charles A. Favrot (whose nickname later in life was "Pops"), written by his daughter-in-law Helen Parkhurst Favrot. Helen's husband was Charles' son Henri Mortimer Favrot, Sr., known as "Morty," who was, of course, named after his grandfather who served in the Confederate army. Another memoir titled *All My Loves: Letters and Memorabilia from the 1920s*, written by Helen and her daughter Claire Favrot Killeen, provides additional insights into the family history. The lives and careers of Charles, Morty, and Morty's son H. Mortimer Favrot, Jr., known as "Tim," are the focus of the last section of this book.

Charles and Beatrice Favrot had five children, all born in the 1890s: Olga (pronounced ALL-guh), who went on to marry Clarence B. Read; Carmen (pronounced car-MEN), who remained single; Morty; Gervais (pronounced zhair-VAY), who founded a major contracting company and married Mabel Cooper; and Clifford ("Cliff"), who became a prominent real estate developer and manager and married Agnes Marsh Guthrie. After Mabel Cooper Favrot died in 1936, Gervais married Charlotte Felder.

Charles was already well established in his career by the early 20th century. The same was true for most of his siblings. Henry, having been cleared of impropriety in the suicide note left by his first wife in 1889, married Marie Richmond, of Savannah, Georgia, in 1902. They soon had two children: Henry Richmond Favrot and Allain Declouet Favrot. The senior Henry was a successful attorney in New Orleans and served three terms in the Louisiana State Senate between 1904 and 1916. As senator, he opposed legal gambling and was credited with shaping legislation that led to the conversion of thousands of acres of swampland into usable agricultural land. Henry died prematurely in 1918,[2] and his widow, Marie, died the next year.

As for Charles's other siblings, William Reynaud Favrot, known as Willie, married Elise Williams in 1897. The couple later moved to New Mexico, where Willie worked as a merchant. Edgar Dubroca Favrot, who remained in West Baton Rouge as a planter, married Estelle Banner in 1905. Leo Mortimer Favrot married Rosie Harrison in 1899. His career as an educational administrator and reformer is discussed later in this chapter. Corinne Augustine Favrot married Henry Tardy Hart in 1906. Louise Alzire Favrot never married. She became an organist and a music teacher.[3]

Other branches of the Favrot family tree also grew rapidly in the late 19th and early 20th centuries. Bouvier, Louis's brother and the only other child of Pierre-Joseph and Marie-Françoise to reproduce, had eight children. Among his grandchildren was Joseph St. Clair Favrot, who was appointed or elected to several state governmental posts in the 20th century, in addition to serving briefly as the consular agent of France in Baton Rouge from 1916 to 1917.[4] His son Joseph St. Clair, Jr., was a well-known Louisiana historian. He served as a judge and district attorney, and was president of the National District Attorneys Association in 1959. He was also instrumental in saving the Magnolia Mound plantation house in Baton Rouge, once the home of Favrot cousin Armand Duplantier.[5]

Another of Bouvier's grandchildren was George Kent Favrot, who reached the highest political office of any member of the Favrot family. After receiving an undergraduate degree from Louisiana State University and a law degree from Tulane, George entered law practice in 1890 in Baton Rouge. He went on to serve as district attorney and a district judge before being elected to the U.S. House of Representatives in 1906.[6]

On November 7, 1906, after he was elected to Congress, but before he took office, George shot and killed his longtime friend Dr. Robert H. Aldrich (1867–1906),[7] who had allegedly made insulting comments about George's wife. George turned himself in to local authorities and was jailed for five months. A grand jury indicted him for murder in February 1907, but the indictment was thrown out on a technicality. After a second grand jury declined to indict him in April of that year—allegedly citing an unwritten "higher law" that a husband was justified in killing someone who had impugned his wife's reputation—he was set free.[8] He subsequently took his seat in Congress. Upon failing to win reelection in 1908, he returned to law practice and served in the state legislature from 1912 to 1916. George was then reelected to the U.S. House of Representatives in 1920, serving two terms. He was elected to a district judgeship in 1926 and held that post until his death in 1934.[9]

Célestine Dubroca Favrot died in 1921 at age 79 at her home at 1571 Henry Clay Avenue.[10] By then, the Monte Vista plantation had been sold. The new hub for her branch of the family was Richmond Place, an enclave in Uptown New Orleans developed in the early 1900s by a group of investors including her sons Charles and Henry, both of whom built houses there. In addition, the family was in the early stages of amassing a series of adjacent properties in Covington, just across Lake Pontchartrain from New Orleans, which would soon become a private compound unofficially known as Favrotville.

Long after English had become the Favrots' primary language, French—and France—still held a certain interest for a number of family members. Morty and Tim each spent a summer at the architecture school at Fontainebleau, France. French remained the preferred language of Morty's aunts Louise and Corinne even after their move to New Orleans.[11] As late as 2014, Tim still used the French word *tante* when referring to either of his great aunts.

Leo M. Favrot and the Reform of "Negro" Education

The rapid cultural changes that reshaped the American South in general and the Favrot family in particular after the Civil War are evident in the remarkable career of Leopold (Leo) M. Favrot, the fifth of seven children of Henri Mortimer Favrot and Célestine Dubroca Favrot. A son of a slaveholder, Leo became a prominent advocate for the improvement of public education for African Americans in Louisiana and Arkansas. He went on to work for an influential national educational philanthropy and later played key roles in various international educational commissions and conferences.

Born in 1874, Leo attended Tulane University, graduating with a bachelor's degree in 1894. He served for three years as principal of the Port Allen School, near the Favrot family plantation in West Baton Rouge Parish, followed by two years as principal at the Poydras Academy, one of the "Poydras Schools" established with the financial support of Julien Poydras (1740–1824), a Creole planter and politician from Pointe Coupée Parish, and the namesake of Poydras Street in New Orleans, where he also once owned property. After serving as principal of a third school in Leesville, Leo became superintendent of schools for West Baton Rouge Parish and later for St. Martin Parish.[12] He was the Louisiana state high school supervisor from 1910 to 1912 before moving to Little Rock, Arkansas, where he became the state agent for "Negro" schools. He returned to Louisiana in 1916 to accept a similar position, serving for seven years. While working for the state, he also managed to earn a master's degree from George Peabody College for Teachers in Nashville, awarded in 1922.[13]

Leo gave lectures and wrote numerous articles on the topic of African American education. In 1918, he issued a pamphlet titled "Aims and Needs in Negro Public Education in Louisiana," in which he catalogued the many challenges facing schools for African Americans and suggested means for addressing those problems. Especially noteworthy, given the state of race relations in the South at the time, was his simple but eloquent plea for recognition of universal human dignity: "For all the arguments in favor of an education for the Negro on the grounds of material gain, are as nothing in comparison with the simple argument that he is a human being, with the desires and hopes of other human beings; that under the influence of civilization he is ambitious to do and have what other human beings do and have." *The Southern Workman*, a journal published by the historically black Hampton Institute, praised Leo's pamphlet for "show[ing] the critical reader how wisely and how sympathetically the problem of inadequate schools for Negroes in Louisiana is being studied by Southern white educators."[14]

Leo's article "A Study of County Training Schools for Negroes in the South," published in *The Journal of Social Forces* in 1923, carried an introduction by James H. Dillard (1856–1940), a former professor at Tulane University, director of the Negro Rural School Fund, and later the namesake of Dillard University. The study covered some 142 schools established to teach African Americans "right principles of living and some skill in the arts of the home and the farm," in addition to basic academic instruction. The article criticized common problems such as inadequate teacher compensation, unequal teaching loads, and "over-crowded" curricula that included too much irrelevant coursework.[15]

One of the milestones in Leo's career was his invitation to address a meeting of the National Association for the Advancement of Colored People (NAACP) in Cleveland, Ohio, in June 1919. His speech was both a candid assessment of "some problems" in the education of African Americans in the South and an optimistic, forward-looking manifesto for positive change. It was also notable for its advocacy of mutual understanding among whites and African Americans. "I think the most intelligent of us," Leo said, "whether of the white race or the colored race, realize that it is for us, members of the two races, to learn to live together in a democracy in peace and harmony." In an era in which even relatively liberal whites often harbored highly patronizing attitudes toward African Americans, Leo seems to have sincerely sought input from the audience he was addressing: "I am glad to have the opportunity of meeting the members of your society and to get their viewpoint on matters relating to colored people and the adjustment of race differences."[16]

Leo's progressive views, not surprisingly, were unpopular in many quarters of Louisiana and the rest of the South. His speech to the NAACP, coupled with a series of similar speeches he gave at Southern University the following year, drew a backlash from Louisiana state school superintendent T.H. Harris (1869–1942), who wrote to him: "The time [is] not right for public utterances of this kind." After a suspicious fire destroyed the training school in Jackson Parish, a worried Leo began to grow more cautious in his work and words.[17]

In 1923, Leo became the Southern field agent for the General Education Board (GEB), which was based in New York. Established by John D. Rockefeller, Sr. (1839–1937), and incorporated in 1903, the GEB was dedicated to "the promotion of education within the United States of America, without distinction of race, sex, or creed." Its programmatic priorities included the improvement of public education for both whites and African Americans in the South, and the expansion of educational opportunity in rural areas. The GEB was also instrumental in revamping medical education throughout the United States under the leadership of the organization's secretary, Abraham Flexner (1866–1959), who later founded the Institute for Advanced Study in Princeton, New Jersey.[18]

The GEB, while relatively progressive in its dedication to improving educational opportunities for African Americans, was by no means radical. It built alliances with African American leaders who accepted the realities of the Jim Crow South, eschewing the more vocal advocates of true racial equality. The organization also helped to form the Commission on Interracial Cooperation, conceived as a more moderate counterpart to the sometimes "confrontational" NAACP. Leo Favrot, while working with the GEB, once warned: "Any indication of a radical tendency on the part of a trusted Negro leader, or a bold and outspoken insistence on equal rights and privileges in public education or in anything else, would temporarily check, in many communities, the advance of Negro public education." It seems that both the GEB and Leo himself, shaken by the angry and even violent reactions to his earlier statements, were prepared to push for slow, evolutionary change at best.[19]

In 1929, New Mexico officials approached the GEB to request assistance in reforming elementary and secondary education in their state, with an emphasis on improving opportunities for the state's large—and generally low-income—Hispanic population. Leo and his fellow GEB field agent Jackson T. Davis (1882–1947) traveled to New Mexico in early 1930 to review specific proposals by educators there, including the creation of a demonstration school—similar to those funded by the GEB for African Americans in the South—in which specially trained teachers would be given flexibility to develop curricula geared toward the unique needs of Spanish-speaking students. On the field agents' recommendation, the GEB agreed to provide funding for the experimental San Jose Technical School, and Leo became the organization's chief liaison to New Mexico, visiting the state often in the 1930s. After students in the demonstration school showed modest but significant progress in intelligence and achievement test scores, the program was gradually extended to rural schools throughout the state.[20]

Having earned a national reputation for his work, in 1930 Leo was appointed by U.S. President Herbert Hoover (1874–1964) to serve on a commission charged with studying the educational system in Haiti and making recommendations for its improvement.[21] The commission was chaired by Robert R. Moton (1867–1940), an African American who had succeeded Booker T. Washington (1856–1915) as the head of the Tuskegee Institute in 1915. While visiting Haiti in July 1930, Leo narrowly escaped death when his airplane went down on "a lonely beach." The plane was finally found after a four-hour search, and Leo and his fellow passengers were discovered to be unharmed. The brush with disaster was the subject of a front-page article in an issue of *The Afro-American*, a Baltimore-based newspaper with wide circulation. The placement of the article in such a prominent publication serves as testimony to the high esteem in which African Americans across the country held Leo Favrot.[22]

Leo participated in conferences addressing education in Pacific countries and other topics in the mid-to-late 1930s. After retiring from the GEB in 1939, he lectured on a part-time basis at Louisiana State University. He died in 1949.[23]

Favrotville

Favrotville, the enclave of Favrot family-owned properties in Covington, Louisiana, owes its origins to illness. In 1899, Charles's wife Beatrice was stricken with tuberculosis. In search of purer air, Beatrice and their children temporarily moved to the Covington area, north of Lake Pontchartrain, for 13 months while she recovered. They stayed at Claiborne Cottage, a resort built around the former St. Tammany Parish courthouse and renowned for its mineral springs. Charles visited every weekend and often went up mid-week for one night. The whole family returned to New Orleans in the fall of 1900, but Charles and Beatrice always remembered their time at Covington fondly, despite her poor health at the time.[24]

Returning from a summer vacation in North Carolina in 1905, Charles, Beatrice, and their children were stopped in Chattanooga, Tennessee, due to an outbreak of yellow fever in New Orleans, which turned out to be the final epidemic of the disease in the United States. Knowing they would be prohibited from reentering the city until the epidemic had subsided, they decided to divert to Covington and stay at Claiborne Cottage again. They were not alone in their choice of refuge: in fact, the Covington area experienced relatively rapid growth in the late 19th and early 20th centuries thanks to a stream of New Orleanians seeking sanctuary from yellow fever outbreaks.[25] (This surge began, of course, before it was widely understood that the disease was spread by mosquitoes, which were ubiquitous in Covington just as they were in New Orleans.) The family returned to New Orleans once the danger of infection appeared to have passed.

Another illness drew the family back to Covington more than a decade later. In 1916, Morty and his brother Gervais had enlisted in the army and were stationed along the Mexican border. Morty soon developed tuberculosis, however, and was sent to an army hospital at Fort Bayard in New Mexico, where he spent six months regaining his health. He was honorably discharged in November 1916, before the U.S. became involved in World War I. Gervais went on to receive an officer's commission and served in France briefly in 1918. Cliff also received a military commission but remained in the U.S. as an instructor at the University of Minnesota.[26]

Morty's doctors at Fort Bayard recommended that he continue his recuperation in the "Ozone Belt"—a term derived from the false belief that the abundance of trees in the area north of Lake Pontchartrain produced large quantities of ozone, which was also incorrectly thought to have salutary effects on those suffering from infections. Based on that advice, Morty and his mother Beatrice rented a house in Covington at the corner of South America Street and 16th Avenue, where they stayed for nine months.[27]

This third major sojourn in Covington inspired the family's first real estate purchase in the area. In 1919, Charles bought the house next door to where Beatrice and Morty had lived during his recovery. From that foothold, a compound of family-owned properties gradually developed as Charles's siblings and then his children bought or built their own houses nearby.[28] Before long, the enclave earned the informal moniker "Favrotville."

One of the prominent properties in the immediate vicinity was a boarding house called The Oaks, which occupied a full block running from America Street to what is now South New Hampshire Street. The large house had been owned by a member of the Allain family, to whom the Favrots were distantly related. Gervais bought that house and demolished part of it, salvaging the lumber and some plumbing fixtures and setting them aside for Morty's use in a new house he had designed for his own family on America Street. By the time Morty began building his new house in 1937, however, the lumber had rotted, leaving only old bathtubs to be reused.[29] In 1952, Morty bought a cottage that had been the home of the proprietor of the Oaks at the end of America Street and renovated it for his family's use.[30]

By then, Favrot family members collectively owned a large swath of contiguous property between South New Hampshire Street and a bend of the Bogue Falaya, a tributary of the Tchefuncte River. The roads between New Orleans and Covington were poor at the time, so family members typically commuted to and from Favrotville by boat. In 1921, Charles bought a boat that had been used as a tender at the Louisiana State Penitentiary at Angola[31] and rechristened it the *Jane Audrey*, after his and Beatrice's first granddaughter.[32] He later sold that and designed his own boat, called the *Jane Audrey II*. There were also commercial vessels, such as the *Camellia*, which connected New Orleans with Mandeville several times a day. The *Camellia* had a live band and refreshments. From Mandeville, passengers took a train the rest of the way to Covington.[33]

Summers at Favrotville became ritualized for many family members. As early as the 1920s, Morty's wife, Helen, and Gervais's wife, Mabel, would head there each year by April with their children. Their husbands would come up for the weekends and Wednesday nights.[34] Entertainment at Favrotville included tennis, bowling, and swimming by day, and house parties, dances, singing, and card games in the evenings. The river itself provided numerous opportunities for recreation— the children would often rent skiffs and paddles at a nearby park and row to the mouth of the river or up to White Sulfur Springs.[35]

The family even published its own intramural newsletters covering goings-on at Favrotville and back in New Orleans, including *The Bogue Falaya Baloney*, *The Lowe-Downe Gossippe*, and *The Weekly Weekly Wasp*, whose title alluded to an earlier "handwritten little gazette" that Leo Favrot had produced as a child living at Monte Vista.[36] The publications included family news, gossip, and inside jokes, including this teasing faux advertisement:

> Before building your home consult Charles A. Favrot, the leading architect of the city. A competent assistant, graduate of the Boston Tech, will be sent upon request to talk prospective builders into doing what they don't want to do.[37]

Remarkably, since Charles bought the Favrots' first house in Covington nearly a century ago, all of the properties in the Favrotville compound have remained in the family. Current generations of family members still fondly recall summers spent there during childhood. "Favrotville is different from any place I've ever been before or since," said Kathleen Van Horn, one of Tim and Kay Favrot's daughters. "Between the last paved street and the river it was just a big, huge parcel of land that was never subdivided by a street. Within the property there were only shell-covered roads, more like paths. It was our own little world."[38]

Several family members now live at Favrotville full-time. The enclave remains dear to the extended family, including those whose branches never owned property there. In 2015, it was the site of a Favrot family reunion that drew more than 200 participants.

The Favrots and Tulane University

The Favrot family has a long history of association with Tulane University and Newcomb College, the affiliated women's college that is now fully integrated into the university. It is not clear who was the first family member to attend the university or its predecessor, the Medical College of Louisiana, but by the early 20th century, at least a half-dozen Favrots had studied there, including brothers Henry, Charles, and Leo and several of their children. Charles's daughter Carmen attended Newcomb, where she was involved with the famous Newcomb Pottery enterprise. Carmen specialized in metalworking—a less well-known but integral component of the program—producing a range of intricate silver jewelry.[39]

Four family members bearing the Favrot surname have served on the university's Board of Administrators, now called the Board of Tulane: Charles Favrot (from 1932 to 1939), Cliff Favrot (1951 to 1968), Sybil M. Favrot (1981 to 1996), and Tim Favrot (1986 to 2000). Both Sybil and Tim also served on the President's Council, a separate advisory body. Leo M. Favrot received an honorary degree from the university, as did Cliff, who was also honored as the "University Distinguished Alumnus" in 1973. Tim Favrot was recognized as the outstanding alumnus of the School of Architecture in 1985.[40]

Cliff's tenure on the Board of Administrators coincided with a period of protracted debates among university leaders regarding racial desegregation. In 1951, when he joined the board, Tulane was, like most prominent, private southern universities, a whites-only institution. Tulane's president at the time, Rufus Harris (1896–1988), a dynamic and progressive administrator, had been working for several years to convince the board to accept the inevitability of desegregation. Initially emphasizing pragmatic and pedagogical concerns, such as growing pressure from governmental agencies and other outside groups that were important sources of funding, Harris seems to have become increasingly committed to desegregation as a moral imperative. While the board in the early 1950s appeared open to at least token desegregation initiatives, most members remained chary of sweeping changes, citing among other concerns the provisions in the original bequests of both Paul Tulane (a Northerner, it should be remembered) and

Josephine Louise Newcomb dictating that their money should be used only for the education of white students.[41]

It was Cliff Favrot who, in 1952, suggested that President Harris confer with leaders of other private southern universities such as Duke, Emory, Vanderbilt, and Rice to discuss prospects for desegregation. Harris recognized that, if a group of prestigious universities were to announce a simultaneous decision to desegregate, the backlash against any one school might be diminished. Soon thereafter, he sent a letter to Vanderbilt's chancellor, Harvie Branscomb (1894–1998), proposing such a joint move by the two universities. Branscomb reacted favorably, but the proposal was thwarted by a negative vote of Vanderbilt's trustees.[42] Despite growing support for desegregation among Tulane faculty members and students, as evidenced by a May 1954 editorial in the university's newspaper, the *Hullabaloo*, arguing that the institution should admit "Negro" students "freely and graciously, as early as possible,"[43] the university ultimately did not enroll its first African American students until 1963.

In addition to holding numerous volunteer leadership positions, the Favrots have been generous financial supporters of Tulane. McAlister Auditorium, the university's primary performance hall, completed in 1940, was financed, designed, and built by members of the extended Favrot family (the design and construction of the auditorium are discussed in the last section of this book). The Favrot Field House, an intramural sports facility dedicated in 1958, was built by Gervais Favrot's contracting company and named in honor of his brother Cliff, its principal benefactor.[44]

The family's philanthropic legacy at Tulane includes the Charles A. and Leo M. Favrot Professorship of Human Relations, which dates to 1953, making it among the earliest endowed chairs in the social sciences in the United States.[45] In 1996, Tim Favrot and his wife Kay endowed the Charles A. and H. Mortimer Favrot Chair in Architecture, in honor of Tim's father and grandfather.[46] As of 2015, Tim and Kay had endowed several professorships in the School of Architecture, and the Favrot name now graces the lobby of the school's venerable building, Richardson Memorial Hall.

ARCHITECTURE & DEVELOPMENT

CHAPTER 9

LOUISIANA IN THE GILDED AGE

The education and career of Charles Favrot signaled a profound shift in the culture of the Favrot family. Descended from a long line of soldiers, several of whom had also practiced law and held public office, Charles instead was drawn to the arts, and in particular, architecture (though he also became a talented amateur violinist and painter). There being no professional schools of architecture in Louisiana in the early 1880s, however, he enrolled in the mechanical engineering program at Louisiana State University, earning his bachelor's degree in 1884.[1] Charles left the family plantation in West Baton Rouge the following year to become a draftsman in the New Orleans office of James Freret, whose wife, Aline Allain, was Charles's distant cousin.

Charles's entry into the profession came at a time when American architecture was finally coming into its own. Before the Civil War, most civic, institutional, and upper-class residential buildings in the United States drew almost exclusively on European architectural precedents, often with only very subtle adaptations to the local climate and culture. After the war, however, several uniquely American modes of architectural expression began to appear. These included what architectural historian Vincent Scully later dubbed the Stick Style, characterized by ornamental wood strips that mimicked the underlying structural frame, and the Shingle Style, associated with often-rambling assemblages of boldly geometric forms clad in wood shingles. Louisiana native Henry Hobson Richardson (1838–1886) lent his name to the Richardsonian Romanesque style, which alluded to early medieval European architecture but was infused with a robust sculptural quality that gave it a distinctly American flavor. In the wake of the Chicago Fire of 1871, the skyscraper emerged as the quintessential American building type and an armature for unprecedented architectural experimentation.

The architecture of New Orleans developed in several distinct phases during the 19th century. The city, which had been composed almost entirely of modest vernacular buildings during the colonial period, began to attract the interest of prominent out-of-town architects soon after the Louisiana Purchase of 1803. Benjamin Henry Latrobe (1764–1820), a British-born architect whom President Jefferson appointed "surveyor of public buildings of the United States" and who served as the second architect of the U.S. Capitol, designed New Orleans' first U.S. Custom House, which was completed in 1807 but later demolished. He moved to New Orleans in 1818 to oversee construction of the city's waterworks. Before his death from yellow fever in 1820, Latrobe also designed the elegant Louisiana State Bank, which still stands at the corner of Royal and Conti streets. The bank building now houses a special event space named Latrobe's in honor of the architect.

In the 1830s, several talented architects with established reputations in New York moved their practices to New Orleans, which was enjoying a booming economy at the time. These included James Gallier, Sr. (1798–1866), a native of Ireland (who had changed his surname from Gallagher), and New York-born Charles B. Dakin (1811–1839). Gallier and Dakin formed a firm and in 1835 won the commission for the huge St. Charles Hotel, occupying a full block on St. Charles Avenue between Common and Gravier streets. The grand structure was capped by a soaring dome, and became a social hub of the area upriver of Canal Street—the center of the city's English-speaking population—before it burned down in 1851. Gallier also designed the Municipal Hall for the Anglo-American community at 545 St. Charles Avenue, completed that same year. The imposing neoclassical structure, which served as the New Orleans City Hall from 1852 until 1957, is now a multipurpose facility known as Gallier Hall.

Charles Dakin's brother and fellow architect, James H. Dakin (1806–1852), also moved from New York to New Orleans in the 1830s. He went on to design several local landmarks including the Arsenal, a sturdy Greek Revival building at 615 St. Peter Street completed in 1839. Gallier's son, James Gallier, Jr. (1827–1868), also became a prominent New Orleans architect, designing the Leeds Iron Foundry of 1852 (now the headquarters of the Preservation Resource Center at 923 Tchoupitoulas Street), and his own residence at 1132 Royal Street, built in 1857 and now a popular historic house museum.

The architecture profession in New Orleans grew more sophisticated after the Civil War as its first generation of exceptional native-born practitioners reached maturity. James Freret and his older cousin William A. ("Will") Freret (1833–1911) were among the most prominent and talented local architects of the era. Will was the son of a former mayor of New Orleans (who was the namesake of Freret Street), while James was the son of the mayor's brother, a wealthy cotton-press owner. Will went on to enjoy nationwide influence when he served as head of the Office of the Supervising Architect of the U.S. Treasury Department— the federal government's chief architect—from 1887 to 1889. In that capacity, he oversaw the design of post offices, custom houses, and other federal buildings across the country.[2]

James Freret attended Spring Hill College in Mobile, Alabama, before heading to Paris in 1860 to study architecture at the famed École des Beaux-Arts. After the Civil War broke out in 1861, he sailed back to Louisiana, successfully penetrating the Union's naval blockade of the South.[3] He was commissioned as an officer in the Confederate Army's engineering corps, was wounded in battle, taken prisoner, and later released.[4] He established his architectural practice before the war ended.

Much of James's early professional work was done for the Roman Catholic Church. His first significant commission was the gilded-bronze, Moorish-inspired altar for the Immaculate Conception Jesuit Church at 130 Baronne Street. Designed in 1867 and built in Lyons, France, the altar was displayed at the Paris Exposition that opened that year, and was awarded first prize in its category.[5] The altar was shipped to New Orleans and installed in 1873.[6] He also designed the Administration Building at his alma mater, the Jesuit-run Spring Hill College, as well as a chapel at the historic St. Louis Cemetery No. 1 back in New Orleans. James went on to design dozens of institutional, commercial, and residential buildings in New Orleans and in several smaller Louisiana cities.[7]

One of James's greatest works—and one of relatively few of his commercial projects still standing—is the former Produce Exchange at 316 Magazine Street, completed in 1883, which is now part of the New Orleans Board of Trade complex. An elegant Renaissance Revival building with hints of Baroque flair, it testifies to the architect's affiliation with the École des Beaux-Arts. The original exchange hall, now restored for use as an event space, is capped by a glass-paned dome that was later covered in painted murals.

James was entering the most successful phase of his career when he hired Charles Favrot as a draftsman in 1885. The distinguished architect was a second father figure to his young cousin, who also lived with James and Aline in their house at 2340 Constance Street. The other residents of the house were the Frerets' children: Beatrice, Nette, Nana, Livie, Pauline, René, Allain, and Walter.[8] Charles and Beatrice, known as Bat, soon began a lengthy courtship that eventually led to their marriage.

Charles apparently became restless in the progress of his career before long. In the fall of 1886 he returned to Louisiana State University for further study. Beatrice teased him for spending time away from New Orleans, which by then was the cultural center of the deep south: "[P]lease don't look too much like a hoosier when you come back to the city," she wrote in a letter to him.[9] In late October, Beatrice's sister Nette wrote to Charles pleading with him to return to New Orleans as a favor to her father, who had become ill. She even suggested that Charles might take over James's role in the office if he did not recover soon.[10] In a letter written the next day, however, James himself encouraged Charles to continue his studies.[11]

James recovered, but Charles returned to work for him anyway. By the summer of 1887, however, he was exploring other professional possibilities. In a diary entry from June of that year, he wrote, "I am corresponding with several architects trying to better my position and chances by going West. I do not meet with much encouragement."[12] Indeed, the response he received from an architect in Burlington, Iowa, that same month included a refrain that would be familiar to many architects even today: "[O]ur work here is cyclical . . . Considering this I think it rather up hill [*sic*] business to pay men big wages for eight hours work and extra prices for extra hours, and then keep them in idleness in the winter . . ."[13]

In December 1887, a friend and former colleague from James Freret's office named Abner Haydel (1868–1941) wrote to Charles about his architectural studies at Cornell University. "We will have the Romanesque style all next term," he wrote. "It is the coming style in the United States. They make a specialty of that study here."[14] Charles may have been inspired by his friend's experiences at Cornell, because he himself enrolled in the school's graduate architecture program the next fall. He was admitted as a "special" student,[15] and managed to complete what was typically a two-year academic program in just 11 months.[16] Charles's study at Cornell was financed by James Freret, his former boss and future father-in-law.[17]

Charles returned to New Orleans in July 1889, and once again went to work in James's office while also living at the Frerets' house.[18] He left his cousin's firm in 1890, however, to form a professional partnership with Southron R. Duval (1862–?). That partnership was dissolved in 1892. The dissolution agreement stipulated that neither partner would practice architecture for a period of two years, so Charles went into contracting to earn a living.[19] Charles built the house for his mother at 1571 Henry Clay Avenue during that time.[20]

Charles and Beatrice finally got married on January 8, 1891, some six years after the beginning of their courtship, at the church of Notre Dame de Bon Secours on Jackson Avenue. The wedding reception was held at the Freret family home on Constance Street.[21] The couple's first child, Olga, was born in late September of that same year.

Early Professional Success

The most momentous decision of Charles's career came in 1895, when he entered into a second professional partnership, this time with Louis Adolphe Livaudais (1870–1932). "L.A.," as he was commonly called, had also worked in James Freret's office, and when James died in 1897, Charles and L.A. inherited a number of their mentor's clients, providing a solid foundation for their new business.[22] Favrot & Livaudais went on to become one of the leading architecture firms in Louisiana, working on a wide variety of building types spanning a broad range of styles.

One of the firm's earliest commissions was for the Natchitoches Parish Courthouse in the city of Natchitoches (pronounced NACK-uh-dish by locals), in northwestern Louisiana. Built in 1896, it is a heavy, simple, Romanesque Revival structure in dark red brick, accented by a clock tower. The design appears rather stodgy in comparison to the firm's later work, but that may be due in part to alterations made after a fire in 1933, including reductions in the height of the clock tower and that of the stair tower on the corner. The building still stands, but now houses a genealogical library.[23]

A significant milestone in the firm's early years was the completion in 1900 of a mansion for Simon Steinhardt (1857–1914), a commodities exporter and president of a steamship company.[24] The house occupies a highly visible site on the downriver corner of St. Charles Avenue, the premier street in Uptown New Orleans, and Rosa Park, a "residential park" centered around a common greensward. The St. Charles Avenue façade draws heavily on the Queen Anne style with its asymmetrical composition, round-ended porch, and tall, projecting gable. The Rosa Park façade is more sedate, but introduces a hint of the Renaissance Revival with its triple-arch portico beneath a stained-glass window bay. When finished, such a prominent and elegant house must have served as an effective advertisement for the young architects' talents.

In 1904, just nine years after the firm's founding, Favrot & Livaudais realized its most impressive residential project—and arguably the most magnificent of all the houses on St. Charles Avenue. The William Perry Brown House, at 4717 St. Charles, was designed for a merchant known as the "Cotton King" of New Orleans.[25] Brown (ca. 1861–1914) also founded the Southern Trust and Banking Company, which later merged with Hibernia National Bank to form the largest financial institution in the South.[26] The mammoth house is in the Richardsonian Romanesque style—the burlier, richer cousin to the Romanesque Revival of the Natchitoches Parish Courthouse—clad in rough-hewn, brownish limestone, and made all the more imposing by the artificial mound on which it is perched. White-and-grey marble steps, laid so that their alternating grains create a zigzag pattern as they rise, lead to a deep porch defined by a series of immense arches and squat, cylindrical columns. Above, a central bay soars upward to a steeply pitched gable. The central gable and flanking dormers bristle with stone finials that lend an almost ecclesiastical air to the structure.

Favrot & Livaudais ultimately designed at least a dozen buildings on St. Charles Avenue in diverse styles. Among the others are the house at 6020 St. Charles, which was built for Judah Seidenbach (1850–1903?), a cashier at A. Lehmann & Co., an importer and exporter of dry goods, in 1903. Its relatively plain Tudor Revival exterior belies its ornate interiors, including extensive, paneled wood wainscoting and a rather eccentric Moorish arch over the living room fireplace.[27] The exterior of another house at 6110 St. Charles, completed in 1905,[28] evokes a large Swiss chalet, with its characteristic wood tracery bands and scalloped fascia panels under the broad gables.

The Isaacs House at 5120 St. Charles, finished in 1907,[29] is a sprawling Mediterranean-style villa with a broad porch and robust brackets supporting a red-tile roof. The house was later converted—with remarkably few architectural changes—into the Milton H. Latter Memorial Library, a branch of the New Orleans Public Library. Similar in architectural spirit is the house at 1 Audubon Place, a private, gated street just upriver from the Tulane University campus. The house, which stands next to the entry gate on St. Charles, was designed for William S. Penick (life dates unknown), a prominent attorney and businessman, and completed in 1911.[30] Favrot & Livaudais also designed the houses at 3 and 7 Audubon Place.

With the growing success of the firm in those early years came long hours for the partners. Charles routinely worked six full days a week plus partial days on Sundays. On his way home each Sunday, he would pick up some sweets and the "funny papers" for the family. An avid exerciser, he then would often spend Sunday afternoons bicycling through Audubon Park with a few of his children. Charles was also a member of the St. John Rowing Club, and frequently went sculling in the morning before going to the office.[31]

A Foray Into Real Estate Development

Within a few years of establishing their firm, both Charles and L.A. apparently became interested in investment opportunities to supplement their professional income. In 1902, they jointly purchased a property called Shadow Plantation, in the Baton Rouge area not far from Monte Sano—the plantation across the river from Monte Vista—which was still in the Favrot family at the time. Charles's brother Edgar managed the new plantation, whose principal product was cotton. The Shadow Plantation is now the site of Southern University at Scotlandville.[32]

A more consequential real estate opportunity arose in July 1905, when the owner of a parcel of land between Lasalle and Freret streets and between the Nashville Canal (now Nashville Avenue) and State Street in Uptown New Orleans subdivided the property and offered eight individual lots for sale. Charles, his older brother Henry, and L.A.'s brother Alfred Fortune Livaudais (1869–1918?)[33] were among the seven people who bought the lots (Henry bought two). The owners agreed to develop the land as a private "residential park" in the manner of nearby Rosa Park, but with a simple street down the middle instead of a shared greensward. [34] They further agreed to name the street Richmond Place in honor of Henry's older son, Henry Richmond Favrot, whose middle name was also his mother's maiden name.[35] The scope of the development grew over the next two years, as two adjacent parcels were integrated with the first one. In the end, Richmond Place ran all the way from Freret Street to Loyola Avenue with no cross streets within the private enclave.[36]

Charles designed and built a house for his own family at 18 Richmond Place, completed in 1906. He did much of the mechanical, electrical, and plumbing work himself.[37] It is an understated, wood-frame Colonial Revival structure with a broad dormer at the third-floor attic above the front door. The house soon became a hub of Favrot family life, assuming the role that Monte Vista had played in the 19th century. The extended family would often come for Sunday dinners or "musical evenings," during which Charles typically played the violin.[38] The house's "upstairs back hall" served as his painting studio while doubling as a home barbershop—Charles cut his sons' hair himself until each turned 15.[39]

Charles also designed his brother Henry's house at 17 Richmond Place, across the street, completed in 1906.[40] It is the grander of the two residences, with a deep porch supported by four tall, unfluted Doric columns and a Palladian window over the front door. It is raised on a brick plinth and approached by broad brick steps with curving railings. It was in this house that Henry died in 1918 of asphyxiation when he accidentally knocked a natural gas line loose in the bathroom.[41] After Henry's wife Marie Richmond Favrot also died the next year, Charles and Beatrice welcomed Henry and Marie's orphaned son Richmond, then about 12 years old, into their own home.[42] Charles's sister Louise took in Richmond's younger brother, Allain.[43]

Tragedy struck the family again on Thanksgiving Day in 1922 when Beatrice died following an automobile accident. She had been driving back to New Orleans after attending the annual Tulane-LSU football game. According to contemporary accounts, Beatrice's body showed no signs of injury—it was believed that she died from shock. Her daughter Olga, who was also in the car, was unhurt, while Olga's husband, Clarence, suffered only a minor injury. After the incident, Olga, Clarence, and their children moved into 18 Richmond Place with Charles, and Olga assumed the domestic roles that her mother had previously played.[44]

Growing Professional Prominence

Favrot & Livaudais enjoyed an abundance of work in the very early 1900s, but the period was not without its disappointments for the architects. Charles was devastated when, in 1907, they failed to win a design competition for the headquarters of the Whitney Bank and Trust Company, to be built at the corner of St. Charles Avenue and Gravier Street in New Orleans' Central Business District. Charles had hired an artist and draftsman from Paris to work with him on the project and then, convinced that the design was destined for success, he went to the extra expense of producing a six-foot-tall plaster model of the proposal in hopes of sealing the deal. Unfortunately, the bank instead chose a scheme by the New York firm of Clinton and Russell, in association with local architect Emile Weil (1878–1945). The proposal by Favrot & Livaudais was awarded second prize, but that was scant consolation for Charles, who felt that the firm had missed its chance for a breakthrough into very large-scale work.[45]

Despite that setback, Favrot & Livaudais received other significant commercial commissions in New Orleans in the early 1900s. The ten-story office building at 305 Baronne Street, completed in 1907,[46] was considered a "skyscraper" in its day. Narrow in plan, the tower is notable for the pronounced horizontal striations that add interest to the otherwise largely unadorned shaft. One of the firm's most intriguing commercial projects of the period was a showroom and office building for the Otis Elevator Company at 856 Carondelet Street, finished in 1912.[47] The design is fundamentally Italianate with its heavily bracketed eaves and campanile-like tower, which, logically, housed the demonstration elevator. It also bears distinct traces of Frank Lloyd Wright's "Prairie School" aesthetic, however, most obviously in the pier at one corner of the building that is crowned by a stone sphere. The building was recently converted to residential use.

The firm also rapidly expanded its portfolio of civic, institutional, and commercial projects outside New Orleans in the 1910s. The Citizens Bank of Lafourche, at 413 W. 4th in the city of Thibodaux, is a one-story Beaux-Arts gem completed in 1910.[48] The building still stands, though it has been marred by an unsympathetic addition over one of its wings. Several commissions for courthouses soon followed, including the De Soto Parish Courthouse of 1911, in Mansfield, in northwestern Louisiana.[49] It is an exceptionally refined, two-story Beaux-Arts structure in buff brick and stone, with a rusticated base and tall, arched windows lining the upper level. The most distinctive feature is a shallow balcony over the main entrance, supported by two pairs of stout brackets. The building clearly served as the model for the Allen Parish Courthouse, in Oberlin, which was finished three years later[50] and would be almost indistinguishable from its predecessor if not for a pair of rickety canopies added later on either side of the main entrance.

The most significant concentration of Favrot & Livaudais projects outside of New Orleans is in Lake Charles, in southwestern Louisiana. After a major fire destroyed the city's downtown in 1910, several public and private clients independently called on Favrot & Livaudais—by then one of the most prominent architecture firms in the state—to design new buildings for them. The first to be completed, in July 1912,[51] was the Calcasieu Parish Courthouse, an imposing Beaux-Arts structure with a cruciform plan and a shallow, octagonal dome over the main courtroom at the center. A grand portico with four fluted Doric columns announces the main entrance. Convex bays at the corners of the crossing add a hint of the Baroque. Sadly, a mundane modern addition now obscures the original rear façade.

Directly across the street is the Lake Charles City Hall, which opened in August 1912[52] (though local tradition still has it that the building was completed in 1911) and was designed by Favrot & Livaudais in association with local architect Ira C. Carter (life dates unknown).[53] In contrast to the stately, somewhat reserved courthouse, the city hall is an exuberant building that incorporates a variety of Renaissance Revival motifs—its soaring clock tower, for instance, is decorated with cartouches that would be at home in early 20th-century Paris, but is capped by an open pavilion with a decidedly Italian feel. The dark red brick façades are encrusted with creamy terra cotta accents including slightly over-scaled quoins and shallow arches over the second floor windows. Original drawings in the possession of Mathes Brierre Architects, the present-day firm that is the successor to Favrot & Livaudais, show that the architects designed not only the building and its interiors, but also custom desks, tables, chairs, coatracks, filing cabinets, and a wide range of light fixtures for the project.[54] The building was renovated in the early 2000s and reopened in 2004 as an arts and cultural center.[55]

The third major Favrot & Livaudais project to be built in Lake Charles was the Church (now Cathedral) of the Immaculate Conception, situated across a side street from the City Hall. Dedicated in December 1913,[56] it was executed in a rather sober Italian Romanesque Revival style that contrasts with both the city hall and the courthouse. The red brick building is greatly enlivened, however, by belt courses that veritably leap over each of the structure's many arched windows before continuing on their horizontal paths.

A decade and a half later, in 1928, Favrot & Livaudais completed another major project in Lake Charles. The Calcasieu Marine National Bank Building is a restrained Neoclassical commercial structure sited a block from the courthouse.[57] Decoration on the building is relatively minimal, but includes columns and pilasters with papyrus-inspired capitals around the entrance and a spread-winged eagle perched atop the parapet over the main façade. A slender chamfered corner where the two street façades meet is a subtle but elegant touch. Other commissions in Lake Charles followed, including four schools, a dormitory for the State Normal School, and even a jail.[58]

By the mid-1910s, Favrot & Livaudais was expanding its reach internationally, working on projects in Central America, including several in La Ceiba, Honduras, an important port on the country's Caribbean coast. The first of these, designed in 1914, was a bank for the Vaccaro brothers,[59] two Italian-Americans who, along with their brother-in-law Salvador D'Antoni (1874–?), founded the Standard Fruit Company, one of the major banana exporters in the region. Favrot & Livaudais's next major project in La Ceiba was the Custom House, completed in 1917.[60] The original construction drawings for the project, which bear notes and titles in both English and Spanish, depict a modest yet elegant Spanish Colonial Revival structure with a two-story block facing the water and a one-story wing at the rear. On the waterside elevation, a large canopy is cantilevered over the adjacent roadway, providing shelter for trucks loading or unloading goods. Broad, shallow arches protect a porch on the second floor running the entire length of the façade.[61] It appears from online amateur photographs that the building is still standing, but has been heavily altered and is in poor condition. Favrot & Livaudais later designed a brewery in La Ceiba,[62] as well as the Vicente D'Antoni Hospital and Clinic, named after Salvador D'Antoni's brother, which opened in 1924.[63] The hospital, originally a simple brick building with a tile roof, is still operating out of the same facility, though it has been remodeled and expanded many times.

Favrot & Livaudais also designed the Cathedral of Our Lady of the Rosary in Bluefields, Nicaragua,[64] a small city on the Caribbean coast that got its name from a Dutch pirate who prowled the area in the 1600s. The exact date of the project is uncertain. Online photographs suggest that the structure was replaced by a more modern church in the mid-to-late 20th century.[65]

Back in New Orleans, in 1921, the firm completed two of its most prominent projects, both at the intersection of Carondelet and Gravier streets. The New Orleans Cotton Exchange, which replaced that organization's previous facility on the same site,[66] is an elegant, eight-story Renaissance Revival structure with a chamfered corner marked by the members' entrance at the ground level. Above

the rusticated base, two-story arches spanning the second and third floors correspond to the location of the original trading floor within. Another row of arched
windows distinguishes the top floor, above which is a heavy copper cornice. The
original elevation drawings of the project reveal the building's exemplary propor-
tions and composition.[67] The building now houses commercial offices.

With the Hibernia National Bank Building, directly across Gravier Street
from the Cotton Exchange, Favrot & Livaudais finally had the chance to design
the headquarters for a major financial institution, perhaps making up for the loss
of the Whitney Bank competition years earlier. At 355 feet, it was the tallest
building in New Orleans from its completion in 1921 until 1965.[68] The building
is symmetrically composed about the main entrance on Carondelet Street, which
is defined by majestic Corinthian columns. Above the tall base, the main shaft of
the tower is U-shaped in plan, with a slender tower emerging from the central portion and rising the last few stories. The building is crowned by a gleaming white
lantern—reminiscent of an Italian Renaissance *tempietto*—that once housed a
working navigational beacon serving ships on the Mississippi River.[69] The lantern
is now illuminated in different colors for special occasions.

In the early 1920s, Favrot & Livaudais undertook the first large-scale restoration of multiple historic buildings in the Vieux Carré—a French term meaning "Old Square" used by many locals to describe what is now commonly called
the French Quarter. The client for this initiative was William Ratcliffe Irby
(1860–1926), an entrepreneur, philanthropist, and member of the Tulane Board
of Administrators who bought deteriorating landmarks including the Lower
Pontalba Building facing Jackson Square and paid for their renovation. Favrot
& Livaudais also worked on repairs to St. Louis Cathedral made possible by a
then-anonymous donation by Irby.[70]

Another Irby-financed restoration project was that of the late 18th-century
building at 417 Royal Street, which at the time housed a restaurant called the
Patio Royal. Irby later bequeathed the building to Tulane University—the primary beneficiary of his substantial estate. In the mid 1950s, Cliff Favrot, as a member of the Tulane board's Real Estate Committee, met with restaurateur Owen
Brennan (1910–1955), who was interested in leasing the property. In preparing
for the meeting, Cliff discovered that the original act of donation by Irby had been

written out longhand by Charles Favrot himself. The Brennan family ultimately leased and later bought the property, which is now the world-famous Brennan's restaurant.[71]

Favrot & Livaudais produced yet another grand mansion with the completion of 6145 St. Charles Avenue in 1924. A lavish Mediterranean villa that initially had 16 large rooms, it is covered in rough-hewn stone and has a magnificent green-tile roof.[72] It may be the only residence on the avenue that can compete with the firm's earlier William Perry Brown House for sheer Gilded Age grandeur. In the same year, Favrot & Livaudais completed the Odenheimer Aquarium at the Audubon Zoo,[73] which is extant but no longer used for its original purpose. A large house for merchant Irwin Isaacs (life dates unknown), at 84 Audubon Boulevard, was built in 1928 in a French Colonial style.[74]

One of the firm's last great projects was the Municipal Auditorium, a huge event and exhibition facility situated lakeside of the Vieux Carré that officially opened in January 1930.[75] With seating for 6,000[76]—and the capacity to hold even more for some events—the auditorium was a popular venue for Mardi Gras balls, concerts, and expositions for decades until its closure following Hurricane Katrina. Although designed before the stock market crash of 1929, the building's architecture anticipated the more severe yet still elegant style that became popular for institutional buildings during the Great Depression.

Civic and Professional Engagement

Charles developed an active interest in civic affairs as early as the mid-1910s, when he became involved in the Progressive Union, later known as the Association of Commerce, which in turn was a predecessor of the New Orleans Chamber of Commerce. Serving on the board of the Association of Commerce continuously from 1914 onward, he later accepted the chairmanship of the group's City Plan Committee. In 1918, he represented New Orleans at the National Conference on City Planning in St. Louis.[77]

The City Plan Committee advocated the establishment of a municipal planning commission and the preparation of a comprehensive plan for the city's future development. To support its work, the committee collected data and prepared maps of New Orleans's current physical form. The most elaborate research initiative was an aerial survey conducted in 1921, in which airplane-mounted cameras took overlapping photos of the city that were later stitched together to form a 40-foot-square map—an impressive feat for the era. Presumably due to a lack of government or institutional funding at the time, Charles financed the aerial survey personally.[78]

Meanwhile, Charles was also active in his profession. He became a member of the American Institute of Architects (AIA) in 1911,[79] and the following year he was serving as acting chairman of the Executive Committee of the Louisiana Chapter of the AIA when the Tulane University administration announced its intention to eliminate the school's architecture department, which had been established in 1894. The decision, while apparently based purely on financial considerations, was nonetheless surprising, given that Tulane's architecture program had been gaining a reputation as "the greatest in the South."[80] Charles was one of the signatories of a letter decrying the decision to shut down the program, stating, "[W]e feel that your Board is doing serious injustice to the people of this City and State, and before any decided action is taken by you in this direction, we urge a conference with you to more fully discuss this matter." The pressure from the AIA Louisiana Chapter—coupled with an offer by the chapter to fund a scholarship in the architecture department—helped convince the Tulane board to retain the program.[81] When a similar threat to the program arose in 1919 after enrollment declined during World War I and the influenza epidemic of that year, Charles and his colleagues at the chapter again sprang into action by providing certain financial guarantees for the coming term. Once again, with the chapter's help, the school survived the period of fiscal uncertainty.[82]

Charles served as president of the Louisiana Chapter of the AIA from 1913 to 1916,[83] and was a member of the national AIA board for an extended period, including three terms as first vice-president from 1918 to 1920.[84] He reportedly declined offers to assume the presidency of the national organization.[85] He was elected to Fellowship in the AIA in 1923.[86]

The City Plan Committee's advocacy efforts finally bore fruit that same year, when New Orleans established the City Planning and Zoning Commission (later split into separate bodies). In the commission's first meeting, Charles was elected chairman by acclamation. With that election, he went from being a private-sector advocate to a public official. Oddly, however, the municipal government failed to appropriate any money for the commission's operations in its early years, so once again, Charles voluntarily covered the necessary costs from personal funds. Between 1923 and 1925, he donated a total of $1,985 to the commission's coffers.[87]

Charles was reelected annually as chairman of the City Planning and Zoning Commission for 16 years, a run that was interrupted only by his death.[88] His long tenure was remembered fondly by his colleagues and constituents. Commission staff member C. Mildred Horner (life dates unknown) once recalled: "He was the finest, most considerate and kindest man I have had the good fortune to work under. I was never conscious of the fact that he was the boss; rather, I always felt that he was more like a relative—perhaps an uncle."[89]

Charles was also instrumental in the formation in 1930 of the New Orleans Civic Affairs League, later renamed the Bureau of Governmental Research.[90] Officially conceived as a non-partisan organization "devoted to the study of Public Affairs" in the Crescent City, it clearly grew out of his and others' growing alarm over the heavy-handed administration of Louisiana Governor Huey Long (1893–1935), as well as concern about the impact of the rapidly worsening Great Depression and the lack of "independent leadership within the community." In a speech at the initial meeting of the organization, Charles criticized the increasing political power of those "whose only theory is to debauch and endeavor to enrich themselves and their friends at the expense of the public funds."[91] Perhaps predictably, Charles was elected as the group's first president. He remained on the organization's board until his death.[92]

Upon L.A. Livaudais's death in 1932, Favrot & Livaudais officially disbanded. The successor firm was Favrot & Reed, with Morty Favrot—who had worked in the office for some time—as one of the principals. Charles, who was in his late 60s at the time, effectively retired from architectural practice, though he continued to serve as a frequent advisor to his son's firm. He remained active, however, with the City Planning and Zoning Commission, the Board of Governmental Research, and the New Orleans Chapter of the Red Cross, on whose board he also served.

Charles was also an enthusiastic participant in the city's annual Carnival celebration. Initially a member of the Krewe of Proteus, the second-oldest Mardi Gras parade organization, he later joined the Krewe of Atlanteans, with which he was affiliated for more than 40 years. According to Helen Parkhurst Favrot's biography of Charles, "Until the year before his death, he was always one of the revered triumvirate which included St. Denis Villere (1874–1938) and Warren Kearney (life dates unknown), who annually escorted the queen and maids of Atlanteans to the royal box" during the Atlanteans Ball.[93] Villere was a prominent New Orleans stockbroker, and Kearney was an attorney.

In 1934, Charles was awarded the Loving Cup, presented annually since 1901 by the *Times-Picayune* newspaper to a New Orleans resident who has made outstanding contributions to the community. The formal award ceremony, however, did not take place until 1936. In his acceptance speech, Charles said, "My hope is that by persistence and perseverance the people will eventually see the right [*sic*] and will insist that public service be placed in the same category with American industry, which has built its success upon the solid foundation of efficiency and economy."[94]

On March 10, 1939, after attending a meeting of the Tulane Board of Administrators, Charles suffered a fatal heart attack. An obituary editorial in the *New Orleans States* newspaper printed the next day lauded him as a man who "belonged to the band of stalwarts who lifted New Orleans out of the mud, who redesigned its machinery, and who put civic progress on the broad highway, which has no ending, to greater prosperity . . ."[95] When Helen Parkhurst Favrot wrote the tribute to her father-in-law titled *Pops: A Memoir* in 1964, she noted that even then, a quarter-century after his death, people who had worked under Charles Favrot at the City Planning and Zoning Commission still referred to him affectionately, respectfully, and universally as "the chairman."[96]

CHAPTER 10

THE EMERGENCE OF
THE MODERN ERA

H. Mortimer Favrot, Sr., who was commonly called Morty, was born in 1894 in the New Orleans house of his grandmother, Célestine Dubroca Favrot, at 1571 Henry Clay Avenue.[1] He never knew his grandfather and namesake, who had died seven years earlier. Morty was the middle of Charles and Beatrice Favrot's five children, and the first boy.

Like his father, Morty had an artistic temperament. He had a natural flair for freehand drawing and learned to play several musical instruments. One peculiar talent he had was the ability to write with both hands simultaneously, starting at the center of a page and writing forward with one hand and backward with the other, creating mirror-image text[2]—a rare skill, but one that he shared with the great Finnish-American architect Eero Saarinen (1910–1961).[3]

Given that his father was already a highly successful architect, Morty seemed predestined for a career in architecture himself. He enrolled in the architecture department at Tulane, probably beginning his studies in the fall of 1911, just as Stanley Thomas Hall—the new building for the College of Technology that would also house the architecture program—was nearing completion. It was during his time as a student that the Department of Architecture was first threatened with closure for financial reasons, but saved in part through the efforts of his father and other prominent members of the local chapter of the AIA.[4]

Having narrowly survived its brush with elimination, the architecture department soon became more firmly established with the appointment of Nathaniel Cortlandt Curtis, Sr. (1881–1953), as professor and program head in 1912. Under his leadership, the department began producing a yearbook featuring student and faculty work. Morty's cross-sectional drawing of a domed, neoclassical interior space was included in the 1916 yearbook (published after he graduated). Other architecture faculty members during Morty's time at Tulane included the stalwart William Woodward (1859–1939), an artist who had been instrumental in the founding of the department in 1894, and Samuel S. Labouisse (1879–1918), a nephew of Henry Hobson Richardson who died during the influenza epidemic of 1918. Curtis resigned in 1917 to accept a position at the University of Illinois, but later returned to New Orleans to practice and teach.[5] His son, Nathaniel Cortlandt Curtis, Jr. (1917–1997), studied architecture at Tulane and went on to co-found the well-regarded New Orleans architecture firm of Curtis & Davis.

Morty's social life while in architecture school centered around the Delta Kappa Epsilon fraternity, whose members were commonly known as "Dekes." He took pride in the fraternity's origins at Yale University in 1844[††††] and its many prominent alumni, including President Theodore Roosevelt (1858–1919), Admiral Robert E. Peary (1856–1920), and Senator Henry Cabot Lodge (1850–1924). Morty remained an enthusiastic member of the organization in his post-collegiate life—among his more active roles was helping to lead a fund raising campaign in the early 1920s to buy a house for the Tulane chapter.[6]

Morty graduated from Tulane in 1915. Although the university had offered the Bachelor of Architecture degree since 1910, his degree was a Bachelor of Engineering in architectural engineering.[7] (Coincidentally, one of the signatures on the degree was that of the president of the Board of Administrators at the time, Robert M. Walmsley (1833–1919), whose great-great-granddaughter, Kay

---

[††††] The Delta Kappa Epsilon chapter at Yale received a five-year suspension in 2011 following a public incident in which chapter members chanted obscene slogans that "threatened and intimidated others," according to an article in the *New York Times* dated May 17, 2011.

Gibbons, would later marry Morty's son Tim.)[8] Morty then spent a year of graduate study at the Massachusetts Institute of Technology (MIT).[9] It was after his return from MIT that he and his brother Gervais enlisted in the army and served along the Mexican border until Morty contracted tuberculosis and was honorably discharged.[10] Following his convalescence, Morty went to work full-time with his father at Favrot & Livaudais.[11]

An Auspicious Vacation Acquaintance

There is a long tradition of well-to-do New Orleans families leaving the city for all or part of the hot, humid summer. The mountains of North Carolina were a popular destination for such families in the early 20th century. The Favrots, in particular, were fond of the Piedmont Inn, located in Waynesville at the foot of Eaglenest (or Eagles Nest) Mountain. Morty arrived there in August 1922 with his friend Stanley Morris (life dates unknown).[12] It is unclear whether any family members were with him on that trip.

Also vacationing at the Piedmont Inn that month were Mabel Parkhurst (1871–1951), of Indianapolis, Indiana, and her 22-year-old daughter, Helen. One evening, as the Parkhursts were preparing to leave for home the next morning, Helen's friends informed her that two "handsome and eligible young men" had just arrived from New Orleans, and encouraged her to meet them. Helen initially resisted, saying that she was hot and tired after a day of horseback riding, but finally gave in. After bathing, she went to greet the young men—Stanley and Morty. Before long, Morty and Helen were dancing the Tango and the Fox Trot, followed by a moonlit stroll together. The next morning, just before Helen's departure, Morty took her to a shooting range and taught her how to fire a rifle.[13] They then said their good-byes.

Helen, like Morty, came from a storied family. Her grandfather, John W. Dittemore (1843–1902), was a Union soldier in the Civil War who was wounded in one leg and left for dead during the Battle of the Wilderness on May 5, 1864, in northern Virginia. He was eventually found alive and taken to a hospital in his home state of Indiana. His wounded leg was amputated, and he endured a grueling recovery under the care of the Sisters of Providence, a Catholic order of nuns. Dittemore, despite his own fiercely anti-Catholic religious views, vowed during his convalescence that if he should survive and ever have a daughter, she would be educated at a school run by the order. True to his pledge, he sent his daughter Mabel—later Helen's mother—to St. Mary-of-the-Woods College, near Terre Haute, Indiana, which had been founded by the Sisters of Providence in 1840. In 1912, after Dittemore's death, both Mabel and Helen, then 12 years old, converted to Catholicism.[14]

Helen followed in her mother's footsteps academically, going off to St. Mary-of-the-Woods College in 1918. Gregarious and ambitious from an early age, she was elected class president each of her four years there. She began to develop an interest in journalism at college, where she edited the biweekly newspaper.[15] She also had a penchant for promotion: before she and other women from her senior class embarked on a trip to Washington, D.C., in April 1922, she wrote to both the *Indianapolis Star* and the *Washington Post* to inform them of the group's upcoming visit, providing a detailed itinerary. As it happened, her letters managed to reach a man named Everett C. Watkins (1883–1955), who was a correspondent for both newspapers. Watkins subsequently interviewed Helen while the group was in Washington. She generally found the experience enjoyable, despite being taken aback when Watkins asked her if she believed the women in her group were as "good-looking as last year's class."[16] She must not have been overly offended by the patronizing question, however, as she regularly exchanged letters with him over the next several years. Watkins clearly had a romantic interest in Helen, which she may or may not have requited; regardless, his journalistic connections proved valuable to her as she embarked on her own career in that field.

Meanwhile, a few weeks after their brief encounter in North Carolina, it was already clear that Morty, too, was smitten with Helen, despite the rather embarrassing fact that she was not quite certain of his given name. She had apparently insisted on calling him "Monty" during the short time they spent together, and he must have been too nervous or timid to correct her at the time. In a letter written after his return to New Orleans, he gently pointed out that "[f]olks usually call me 'Morty' (not Monty)—but I answer to the name of Henri—or will if it's one of the prerequisites to being dreamed about." He enclosed with the letter a newspaper clipping about the new Hibernia National Bank Building by Favrot & Livaudais, for which he was a member of the design team.[17]

Helen soon responded with a letter of her own, describing her experiences as a new teacher of Latin, English, and literature at the high school in Mount Comfort, Indiana.[18] The casual tone of her letter—written in an era in which formality was the norm even in personal correspondence—suggests that she had become remarkably relaxed around Morty during their brief time together in North Carolina. The letter was peppered with witty lines, such as: "I'll send you the latest bulletins of Mt. Comfort—if a Comforter won't prove a wet-blanket." She signed the letter, "Pedagogically, Helen."[19]

Thus began a three-and-a-half year correspondence between Helen and Morty, punctuated by several unsuccessful attempts to see each other again, which would ultimately—and improbably—lead to their marriage.

Early Career at Favrot & Livaudais

Morty began working in the office of Favrot & Livaudais during the summer after his junior year of college. One of the first drawings he did for the firm was of the bank project in La Ceiba, Honduras, in 1914. He had the opportunity to see the finished project in person in 1922, when he traveled to La Ceiba to inspect the work on the Favrot & Livaudais-designed hospital then under construction there. Upon arrival in Honduras, he was impressed by how fast plants grew in a true tropical environment: "A fellow built a fence near the hospital about 18 months ago," he wrote to Helen, "[and] now it is a grove of trees." His letter included a wry commentary on the role of women in Honduran society: "They have *women's rights* in Honduras—i.e., the women are granted full rights to work—while the men lay up and snooze in a hammock."[20]

Morty soon found his "niche" in the office. "As the only one of the junior members of the firm that is a native of Louisiana," he wrote to Helen, "it is becoming more and more apparent that the 'glad hand stuff,' the lining up of friends, the building up of a clientele is going to fall mostly on me." While he expressed disappointment that this emerging role kept him from drawing as much as he would have liked, he accepted that his primary contribution, at least in the near term, would lie in drumming up business for the firm. "I like it all right—I can still make little sketches occasionally, talk to clients and work out their ideas, in fact be the go-between—betwixt the drafting room and the client. Salesmanship, in a way—but in a dignified, indirect matter—without blatant 'advertising' so repugnant to a professional man."[21] Such views were common among architects of the day—indeed, the ethical code of the AIA at the time expressly prohibited outright advertising or other "unprofessional" business development activities.

In 1923, Morty took a sabbatical—apparently at the urging of the firm—to pursue a three-month course at the new Conservatoire Américain de Fontainebleau, a school based in the famed Château de Fontainebleau, about 30 miles southeast of Paris. Founded in 1921 as a music conservatory, the school added short-term curricula in architecture, painting, and sculpture two years later. Morty must have been among the school's earliest students in the architecture division. He left New York aboard the ocean liner *Mauretania* in mid-June,[22] stayed at Fontainebleau until October, then traveled to Belgium, Switzerland, Italy, the South of France, and Spain before returning home in December.[23] Only later did he learn that, on his way to New York to catch the ship to Europe, he had been in Washington, D.C., at the same time as Helen, but they did not run into each other there.

Following his return to the office, Morty was the lead architect for the Metairie Country Club, for which he designed "everything except the floor plans." The clubhouse, combining French and Spanish Colonial motifs, was sheathed in integrally colored stucco in graduated shades, mimicking the effect of differential changes over time and thus making the building appear older than it was. The basic form of the building may have owed a debt to sketches of French farmhouses Morty had made while on his European sojourn.[24]

Morty worked on the various restoration projects in the Vieux Carré sponsored or supported by William Ratcliffe Irby, including those at the St. Louis Cathedral, the Lower Pontalba Building, and the Patio Royal. He also was involved in the renovation of the New Orleans Board of Trade Building, originally designed by his grandfather James Freret.[25] Although the firm was not large—and it is possible that everyone in the office had a connection to some or all of these projects—the fact that Morty was associated with so many of the office's most prominent jobs suggests that he was already being groomed for a future leadership position.

Long-Distance Courtship

Morty and Helen continued to write each other regularly, though thanks to Helen's frequent moves and unexpected travels over the next couple of years, a number of Morty's letters were delayed or never received. Helen's family already owned property in Miami, and at some point in 1923 she moved there and began writing for the *Miami Herald*. Morty suddenly became very interested in her adopted state. He had heard rumors of great fortunes to be made there in real estate. In a letter to Helen written in May of that year, he asked, "Do you suppose an enterprising young architect, 'flying squadron' for an old and well respected firm, could drop in, grab off a million or two in jobs and write the home office to grind out the plans?"[26] The flippant tone of the question belied Morty's serious consideration of a possible move to be with the woman he barely knew, but with whom he was already in love.

By 1924, Helen was a bylined reporter for the *Herald*, a noteworthy achievement in an era in which women journalists were typically relegated to supporting roles if they could find relevant work at all. Her beat was Miami history—of which there was not much at the time, given that the city had been officially incorporated less than three decades earlier. The city had grown quickly, however, and she found plenty of material to support articles about the construction of key landmarks, social history, and the origins of local churches. She also wrote a gossip column called "Wave Whispers." The column was perhaps atypical of its genre, however, incorporating mythological and literary allusions that revealed the author's depth of knowledge and verbal skill.[27] Her assignments became more diverse over time, and in December 1924, she wrote a nationally syndicated article about sports and recreation in Miami.[28]

Helen's parents moved into a new house in Coral Gables in 1925, amid the continuing South Florida real estate boom.[29] Morty, still pining for Helen, realized he had the perfect excuse to come visit her: Favrot & Livaudais was continuing to expand its sphere of work, and in those days architectural offices in Florida could not keep up with the demand for new buildings, so Morty would travel to Florida to explore business opportunities there. In the summer of 1925, he wrote to tell Helen of his plans, and she replied eagerly that she would be happy to see him, though the specific dates of his trip were not yet settled.[30] In September, he finally reached Miami only to discover that Helen was out of town—she had not received his most recent letter confirming the date of his arrival.[31] She apparently returned on his final day there, just in time for him to see her for the first time in three-and-a-half years, though they ended up spending most of their day together visiting with Helen's family. Morty learned that day that Helen's ailing mother was far from committed to staying in Miami—a revelation that might complicate his plans for more direct courtship.[32]

The brief visit emboldened the rather shy Morty to state his feelings more directly in a letter written after his return to New Orleans. "Helen, sweetheart, I do not know what is in store for us. Is it going to be necessary that I come and live in Miami in order to get you? From the way your mother spoke I have no assurance that you all wouldn't move somewhere else." He then suggested that the Parkhursts consider moving to New Orleans, before continuing, "Life has such a different aspect with you involved—it takes on a new meaning . . ."[33]

Morty must have assumed that the Parkhursts were unlikely to accept his suggestion that they move to New Orleans, because he was still actively exploring the prospects for moving to Florida under the auspices of Favrot & Livaudais. He soon made a formal proposal to his father and L.A. Livaudais that the firm open an office in Miami. Despite the continuing boom in South Florida, the partners were unconvinced of the long-term business prospects there, but L.A. offered Morty a choice between two options: first, that he travel to Miami at the firm's expense "to exploit the thing for whatever might be in it," or second, that he take a leave of absence to explore the professional possibilities there on his own, with the option of returning to the firm at the end of that period. Charles gave his consent to both of these offers.[34]

Morty's decision was quick. By the end of September, he had arranged to enter into a partnership with Walter Ferguson (life dates unknown)—a distant cousin by marriage to a member of the Freret family—and to set up an architecture and real estate development company in Miami. He excitedly wrote to Helen with the news, boasting that he and Ferguson "confidently expect to make at least $25,000 apiece," presumably over their first year in business. Because he did not believe he could be a member of two architecture firms at once, Morty resigned from Favrot & Livaudais and sold his stock in the firm (though he did so with the agreement that he could buy it back after a year—an arrangement that proved to be fortunate).[35] He might not have made such bold and impetuous career decisions had he known that Helen had been corresponding with several other men over the previous few years who were equally interested in her affections.

The exact date of Morty's arrival in Miami is uncertain, but there is evidence that he was living there and had already established a business address by early December 1925.[36] Suddenly, Morty and Helen's excruciatingly slow, postal courtship of the past several years turned into a whirlwind. Their engagement was announced in the *Miami Herald* on January 28, 1926. They were married four days later, on February 1, at the Gesu Catholic Church in downtown Miami. The engagement announcement explained the haste of the wedding by saying that it had been "advanced to participate in the New Orleans Mardi Gras," where the couple would spend their honeymoon.[37] For Morty, it seems, even a wedding ceremony that he had eagerly anticipated for more than three years could not take a back seat to such an important New Orleans tradition.

A Burst Bubble and the Return to New Orleans

Helen and Morty returned from their honeymoon just as Miami was on the brink of economic disaster. The real estate boom that had fueled the region's astonishingly rapid growth had begun to sour. Following a classic pattern, sales slowed, prices declined, borrowers defaulted on loans, and banks became shaky. The effects quickly hit home for the Parkhursts when some now-unknown problem arose regarding the title to the new house they had built in Coral Gables. They were forced to move back to their previous house in Miami proper, where Helen and Morty were also living at the time.[38] Morty suddenly found himself in close quarters with his new in-laws.

This overly cozy living arrangement did not last long, however. With the collapse of Miami real estate, Morty's business prospects there dried up. By the summer of 1926, he had returned to New Orleans and to his former job at Favrot & Livaudais. Helen stayed behind to pack up their belongings in preparation for leaving her parents and joining her new husband in a city she had visited only once. A letter to Morty written during this time expressed her mixed feelings:

> In the first place, I am eager to leave—I long to be with you; but I dread going to New Orleans more than I ever did anything and sometimes I'm overcome with an almost uncontrollable bad-little-girl impulse to run away and hide—in a corner. It's a ridiculous feeling and I'm ashamed of it. Suppose [*sic*] it is natural, though, for New Orleans will mean the complete surrender of my past—not a lurid one, but a completely delightful and interesting past.
>
> I've been a thoroughly spoiled only child, I've been superbly independent about everything—work, play, friends. *Don't think for a moment that I regret having to surrender my independence for you. I glory in it and I'd do it a thousand times over.*
>
> What I'm getting to is this: when I first reach New Orleans, I want to crowd the first few weeks with hustle and bustle so that I won't have time to remember that I'm an alien.[39]

The financial collapse of Miami real estate was soon exacerbated by physical catastrophe as two hurricanes—one in July and one in September of 1926—devastated South Florida. Morty's losses from his brief venture in Miami totaled $19,000.[40] Fortunately, he and Helen had a place to live waiting for them in New Orleans—a duplex at 1917 Joseph Street owned by Morty's father—and Morty had already returned to secure employment at Favrot & Livaudais. He was once again working on projects in Central America, and Helen accompanied him on several trips there.[41] They also frequently visited Covington, where Favrotville was still in its infancy—at that point, Morty and his siblings were taking turns using the house that Charles owned there. The family's additional properties would come later.

The stock market crash of 1929 hit while Charles Favrot, his daughters, and his daughters-in-law were on vacation in New York City. Amazingly, they remained blissfully unaware of the crash until they got home to New Orleans and caught up on the news.[42] At the time, of course, few people had any inkling of how deep and how long the financial crisis would be.

For the Favrots, the ominous economic developments of late 1929 were tempered by the recent announcement that Helen was pregnant. She gave birth to Tim in April 1930. Tim's sister Claire Parkhurst Favrot followed in November 1931, and their brother James Freret Favrot was born in 1934.

Favrot & Livaudais continued to earn commissions—albeit at a slower pace—in the early years of the Great Depression. One residential project completed in 1931 grew out of the Favrots' deep roots in West Baton Rouge. William Von Phul (1871–1949), owner of a plantation near Monte Vista and a distant cousin of Morty's by marriage, hired the firm to replicate his family's historic plantation house, which had fallen into disrepair, on a site at 1530 Calhoun Street in New Orleans. Morty led the effort to measure the existing house, number and salvage some elements of the structure, and incorporate them into the new building.[43] Other projects of the early 1930s included a French vernacular-style mansion at 444 Broadway, built for Joseph E. Blum (life dates unknown), co-founder of the venerable real estate firm of Latter & Blum.[44]

A Generational Shift

Following L.A. Livaudais's death in 1932 and Charles Favrot's retirement from active practice in 1934, Favrot & Livaudais was reconstituted as Favrot & Reed, with Morty and Alan C. Reed (?–1950) as the principals.[45] The transformation marked not only a generational change in the firm's leadership, but also a major shift in design philosophy. Whereas Favrot & Livaudais had produced an eclectic body of work drawing on a wide variety of historical styles, the successor firm's work in the 1930s and '40s reflected the gradual emergence of Modernism as the dominant movement in architecture. Most of Favrot & Reed's projects could be grouped into three major categories: first, Art Moderne, with its stripped-down aesthetic that was especially popular for commercial projects; second, a simplified Colonial Revival style, commonly used for schools and other public buildings of the New Deal era; and finally, unabashed International Style Modernism, characterized by abstract forms and geometrical purity, as seen in many of the firm's civic and institutional projects.

The former City Hall in Lafayette, Louisiana, completed in 1939 under the auspices of the Public Works Administration (PWA), is a textbook example of the hybrid Art Moderne/Neoclassical style. It was designed by Favrot & Reed in association with architect Frederick J. Nehrbass (ca. 1900–?).[46] The building is a symmetrical composition of rectangular volumes, with subsidiary bays that step away from the central block in both plan and elevation. Quirky decorative motifs, including a shallow, scalloped cornice and subtle, vestigial scrolls at the tops of the two large piers flanking the entrance, merely hint at the more elaborate sculptural elements found in similar spots in classical architecture. The building now houses the Lafayette Downtown Development Authority.[47]

Favrot & Reed worked in association with Weiss, Dreyfous & Seiferth Architects on a dozen buildings financed by the PWA at the Southwestern Louisiana Institute, now the University of Louisiana at Lafayette. These projects, completed in 1940, were designed in a Colonial Revival style that related to the older buildings on the campus.[48] All told, Favrot & Reed was involved in at least 35 PWA projects built throughout Louisiana between 1935 and 1940.[49]

A milestone for Favrot & Reed—and for the Favrot family—during this period was the construction of McAlister Auditorium, a landmark of the Tulane campus. The genesis of the project dates to a visit to New Orleans in the late 1930s by Amelie McAlister Upshur (1885?–1952), a great-granddaughter of Louis Favrot's and distant cousin of Morty's. At the time, Amelie was contemplating a substantial donation to an as-yet undecided institution to support construction of a building memorializing her mother, Armentine Reynaud McAlister (life dates unknown). The building would also provide a venue for installing two historic portraits in her possession: one of Marie-Augustine Gérard Duplantier and one of Augustine-Eulalie Duplantier Favrot, Louis Favrot's mother-in-law and wife, respectively.

During Amelie's visit, Charles Favrot urged her to consider Tulane as the site for the memorial building. Meanwhile, Charles's nephew Richmond, who by then controlled the largest collection of the family's documents, broached the idea of combining his and Amelie's related holdings and depositing them in a secure room in the same building. Amelie, who had been leaning toward Duke University as the venue for the memorial, remained noncommittal as she left New Orleans. To stoke her interest in a single repository for the family papers, Morty began sending her sample translations of Favrot documents from the French and Spanish colonial periods, along with other material about the family's history. The strategy worked, and ultimately Amelie decided to make her gift to Tulane.

Morty was instrumental in negotiating the details of the donation between his cousin and the university. Amelie proposed that her gift go toward a large auditorium building to be named for her mother, which would include a "Memorial Room" where the Favrot family documents and portraits might be preserved, assuming their various owners agreed. Morty presented her proposal to Tulane's attorneys, who requested only minor revisions.[50] Once the basic agreement was in place, Amelie directed that Morty's architecture firm design the building and that Gervais's contracting firm build it, both terms that the university accepted.[51] Charles, who was on the Tulane Board of Administrators at the time, was named chair of the building committee.

With the donation agreement done, Morty and his firm set to work on designing the project. The result is one of the most distinctive Depression-era buildings in Louisiana. In plan, McAlister Auditorium is reminiscent of the ancient Roman Pantheon, but with several additional appendages. The core of the building is a large cylinder—analogous to the Pantheon's rotunda—housing the main auditorium space. The cylinder is capped by a shallow, concrete dome measuring 110 feet in diameter but only three inches thick at its apex. It was the largest concrete dome in the country at the time of its completion.[52]

At the front of the building is an entrance portico evoking that of the Pantheon except that it is bracketed by semicircular, apse-like bays on either side of the lobby. It was one of those semicircular bays that originally housed the Memorial Room devoted to the storage of the Favrot Family Papers.[53] To the rear of the auditorium is a rectangular block that accommodates the stage and support facilities. Rectangular bays at the sides of the rotunda provide spaces for balcony seating.

The decorative program of the building is consistent with the pared-down aesthetic of Art Moderne, incorporating abstracted versions of Classical forms and motifs. The exterior surfaces are mostly of unornamented brick, punctuated by a few vertical bands of stone. The stone-clad entrance portico, which projects only slightly from the plain brick wall behind it, consists of square, fluted piers crowned by incised blocks bearing patterns that hint at the elaborate capitals associated with Classical architecture. The interior is generally quite spare, though the auditorium itself is enlivened by arches over the stage and side balconies that are decorated with sunburst patterns. At the center of the arch over the stage is a sculpture of a pelican, the state bird of Louisiana.

The building was dedicated on April 2, 1940, a year after Charles's death.[54] True to the donor's intentions, the Favrot Family Papers were indeed stored in the Memorial Room for some time.[55] They were eventually moved with the family's permission to the Howard-Tilton Memorial Library, however, where they could be better protected.

World War II curtailed non-defense construction across the country, of course, but Favrot & Reed was already busy again by the late 1940s. The firm's design for the former Gus Mayer Co. store at 800 Canal Street in central New Orleans is a late Art Moderne landmark. Completed in 1948,[56] it is notable for its soaring, glassy bay over the main entrance; its gently curved corner where Canal meets Carondelet Street; its slightly projecting window frames; and its distinctive rooftop sign above one end of the Carondelet Street façade. The building is now occupied by a large pharmacy whose signage obscures the architecture, though fortunately, the key design features are still intact. The firm also designed the Joy Theater, built in 1946, just up the street at 1200 Canal. The recently renovated building is famous among locals for its jazzy neon marquee.[57] Further up the road, at 4176 Canal Street, is the Singer Sewing Machine Building of 1949, an International Style structure with industrial windows and strongly expressed horizontal banding.[58]

In 1949, the firm became Favrot, Reed, Mathes and Bergman, Architects, with the addition of Earl L. Mathes (1912–1976) and William E. Bergman

(1913–1988) as principals. The firm was thriving, completing 31 major projects that year alone, including at least 25 school buildings throughout the state of Louisiana. The largest project in the office by far at the time was the new Veterans Administration Hospital at 1601 Perdido Street in New Orleans, designed in association with the Washington, D.C., firm of Faulkner, Kingsbury & Stenhouse. The final design, though austere, has a certain elegance thanks to its two projecting wings that form an entry forecourt, as well as the thin, horizontal sunshades that lend depth and shadows to the façades.§§§§ Dozens more school buildings and other institutional projects followed in the ensuing years.

Social and Civic Affairs

Morty and his family lived at 1711 General Pershing during the 1930s,[59] before buying a house at 5824 St. Charles Avenue in 1941. The St. Charles residence is a center-hall, Italianate structure built in 1867, making it one of the oldest surviving houses in a neighborhood that was mostly developed in the late 19th and early 20th centuries.[60] Today, the house, which is sited across the avenue from the entry to Rosa Park, is almost entirely obscured from the street by lush plantings.

In 1942, Helen and Morty rented out rooms in their house to the well-known novelist Frances Parkinson Keyes (1885–1970) and her secretary.[61] Keyes (rhymes with "skies"), who had spent most of her life in New England and the Washington, D.C., area, had decided to write a novel about New Orleans society. The result, *Crescent Carnival*, published in 1942, revolved around two prominent New Orleans families—one Protestant, one Creole Catholic. Morty did pen-and-ink drawings of historic local buildings that appeared as illustrations in the original edition of the book. Keyes later occupied a second floor apartment of the house at 1113 Chartres Street where Confederate General P.G.T. Beauregard had lived briefly after the Civil War. In lieu of rent, Keyes paid for the renovation of the historic property, which is now a museum known as the Beauregard-Keyes

---

§§§§ As of this writing, the building is still in use as a hospital, but is expected to be turned over to the city government when a new veterans' medical complex is completed in the near future.

House.[62] Keyes decided to remain in New Orleans and wrote several additional novels set in Louisiana, of which the most famous is the murder mystery *Dinner at Antoine's*, originally published in 1948.

Helen remained conscious of being an outsider, both in Louisiana and among the Favrots, even as she gradually became a committed New Orleanian and a beloved member of the family. For "an only child of an only child" who grew up in a reserved Midwestern city, the intricate web of relatives, high degree of social visibility, and strong connection to place that characterized the Favrot family must have been bewildering and at times a bit overwhelming. One of her coping mechanisms was establishing the "Anti-Fav Club," consisting of all the non-Favrots who had married into the family.[63] Her in-laws were, by all accounts, in on the joke, and graciously indulged her occasional need to express her distinct identity. Any lingering doubts about Helen's love for her husband's family were surely dispelled when she wrote her thorough biographical study of Pierre-Joseph Favrot, "Don Pedro Favrot, A Creole Pepys," and her affectionate portrait of Charles Favrot, *Pops: A Memoir*.

Helen studied her new city so closely that she became qualified to give detailed public lectures about fine points of New Orleans history. As her daughter, Claire, put it in *All My Loves: Letters and Memorabilia from the 1920s*, "The scope of [Helen's] influence on New Orleans Society was remarkable for a convent bred girl and Yankee-Hoosier outsider from Indiana." Helen was a committed community activist who participated in numerous civic and philanthropic groups, serving on the boards of New Orleans' first Interracial Council and the New Orleans Opera Association, and as president of the De Paul Hospital Guild.[64]

Morty was also active in professional and civic organizations. He was the secretary of the New Orleans Chapter of the AIA in 1930, when Prohibition was the law of the land but chapter members still fully expected alcohol to be served at meetings and events. Morty sometimes had to go to unusual lengths to fulfill his secretarial responsibilities, as evident in this announcement:

> Tuesday, October 21, 1930, 6:00 p.m. sharp there will be a dinner meeting to entertain visiting architects and other distinguished visitors; as well as to discuss important topics. Sneak up

the winding stairway at Galatoire's, rap three times, then duck, but don't run. If the countersign has been directly delivered the other boys will be found waiting. . . . [65]

Morty went on to serve as the chapter's president from 1942 to 1944.[66] He was also involved with the Louisiana Historical Society and founded the Society of the War of 1812 in Louisiana.[67]

The Tulane School of Architecture faced another crisis in 1946 when its professional accreditation was revoked over concerns about the condition of the program's facilities. Tulane President Rufus Harris, while critical of the accreditation team's methods and conclusions, recognized that the school did indeed face serious challenges—as did many academic programs struggling to regroup in the immediate aftermath of World War II—and decided to appoint a committee of alumni to advise him on potential improvements. Morty was among the five architects appointed to the committee. The group submitted detailed recommendations regarding the school's facilities and faculty, which President Harris accepted gratefully and implemented as fully as possible. The committee was also instrumental in the appointment of Buford L. Pickens (1906–1995), a dynamic professor and administrator, as the new head of the department. Pickens, with the backing of Morty and his cohort, oversaw rapid progress, and the school's accreditation was restored by 1947.[68]

Morty and Helen took an extended European vacation in the spring of 1953. While they were in Interlaken, Switzerland, Morty suffered a heart attack and died. He was only 58 years old.

Helen outlived her husband by more than three decades. During that time, her reputation as a social activist continued. Her daughter Claire recalled being at home one day in 1967 when her Aunt Carmen appeared at the door demanding to know, "Where is your mother?" As Carmen well knew, Helen had taken Claire's young daughter, Elizabeth, on a Mediterranean cruise bound for Israel, when the Six-Day War broke out. Claire reassured her aunt that the ship had been redirected to Italy. "Yes, but is your mother on it?" asked Carmen. "I can just see her with a guerilla rifle getting into the thick of it and headed for Jerusalem!" Claire, astonished, asked, "With Elizabeth in tow?" Carmen responded, "Never take your mother for granted. There is no end to what she might do, given a cause!"[69] Fortunately, Helen had resisted any temptation to join the fight, and returned home safely with her granddaughter.

In 1968, Helen sent a letter to the editor of the *Times-Picayune* newspaper in response to a recent column written by the conservative historian and literary critic Russell Kirk (1918–1994). In his column, Kirk maintained that the early Christian theologian St. Augustine had been born to "an old Roman family," and was not a "black Christian" as claimed by "[s]ome Black Nationalists." Helen refuted Kirk's assertion with information widely accepted by mainstream historians:

> Reliable sources agree that the family of St. Augustine was a native African family. If one-sixteenth Negro blood makes one a Negro, then St. Augustine was undoubtedly a Negro. His mother, St. Monica, and his father Patricius, were both native Africans of Tagasta, where Augustine was born, 60 miles from Hippo, where he died. . . . I think it is worthwhile to set the record straight, both to give pagan Rome its due for a solution of its racial problem, as well as to give honor to a black nationalist.[70]

The letter was an extraordinary gesture coming from a white, well-to-do New Orleanian at a time when most members of her cohort were anxious about the rise of the Black Nationalism movement and struggling to accept the inevitability of racial desegregation.

Helen remained a devout Catholic heavily involved in church affairs. Later in life, she was asked to serve as a witness in the beatification process of Anne-Thérèse Guérin (1798–1856), known as Mother Théodore Guérin, founder of the Sisters of Providence and of St. Mary-of-the-Woods College, which Helen had attended. Helen's research uncovered information about Mother Guérin's life and activities that was previously unknown even to the leadership of the order.[71] Mother Guérin was beatified by Pope John Paul II in 1998, and canonized by Pope Benedict XVI in 2006.[72] Helen did not live to see the fruits of her labors in this regard, however, having died in 1984 at the age of 83.

Brothers in Building

Morty was not the only one of Charles and Beatrice's children to pursue a career in the building industry. His brothers, Gervais and Cliff, were both prominent in the construction field—Gervais as a general contractor and Cliff as a roofing contractor who later established a real estate development and management firm.

Gervais was, it seems, a born businessman. As a child, he was employed to turn on the lights at the entrance to Richmond Place at dusk and turn them off at 6:00 a.m., a job for which he was paid $2.00 per week. This was in addition to the typical teenager's paid chores such as mowing lawns, trimming hedges, washing cars, and sweeping sidewalks. Between the ages of 10 to 15, however, his main business was raising chickens. He owned his own incubator and sold the birds when mature.[73]

In contrast to the studious Morty, Gervais disliked school and never stayed in a particular school for very long. Helen, in her book *Pops: A Memoir*, gently poked fun at the many academic institutions her brother-in-law attended: "Gervais's talents, it had long been apparent, lay along commercial rather than scholastic lines. He collected *alma maters* as other boys collected cigar bands."[74]

Perhaps predictably, Gervais dropped out of school and went to work for George J. Glover General Contractor as a timekeeper and "clerk-of-the-works." In 1915, he announced his intention to travel to San Francisco to see the Panama-Pacific International Exposition there. He saved up money for the trip with no help from his parents and "refused to accept even a letter of introduction to any of their friends along his route." He made various stops along the way, however, each time taking a temporary job and earning enough money to complete the next leg of his trip. His first stop was Detroit, where he got a job in an automobile factory. He then worked in a garage in St. Louis, and then in the wheat fields in Colorado. After reaching San Francisco and the exposition, he decided to go on to Seattle, where he worked first as a busboy and later as a timekeeper on a construction site again. After he had been away for eight months, his father arranged for his return to New Orleans, largely to appease Beatrice, who worried about and missed her son.[75]

In 1920, Gervais launched his own general contracting firm.[76] The business suffered during the early days of the Great Depression, but recovered within a couple of years after winning several substantial projects, including a meatpacking plant for Swift Brands.[77] Initially a sole proprietorship, the firm became a partnership in 1946 and was incorporated as the Gervais F. Favrot Company in 1950. The firm built many of the most prominent commercial buildings in New Orleans, including the Sheraton Hotel on Canal Street and the One Shell Square office complex, which, at 697 feet, has been the tallest building in the state of Louisiana since its completion in 1972. By 1980, Gervais's company was the largest commercial contracting firm headquartered on the Gulf Coast between Houston and Tampa.[78]

Gervais followed in his father's footsteps as chairman of the City Planning and Zoning Commission and as a member of the Bureau of Governmental Research.[79] He served as president of the powerful and controversial Orleans Levee Board, which oversaw the parish's flood protection system from 1890 to 2006. He was also active in various construction industry associations, at least two corporate boards, and several philanthropic organizations, including the United War Fund, which operated as a branch of the Community Chest during World War II.[80]

With his first wife, Mabel Cooper Favrot, Gervais had two daughters: Beverly, who married Thorn B. Himel, and Joan, who married Cyril Geary, Jr. After Mabel's premature death in 1936, Gervais married the former Charlotte Felder. They had a son named Gervais F. Favrot, Jr.[81] The senior Gervais died in 1987 at the age of 90.

Cliff, the youngest of Morty's siblings, attended Louisiana State University for a year before transferring to Tulane, from which he received a bachelor's degree in chemical engineering in 1919. He then went to work as a chemist at the Lane Cotton Mills, but left in 1922 to establish the Favrot Roofing and Supply Company, which he headed until 1938. He was president and principal stockholder of what became the Asbestone Corporation from 1939 to 1952, when he sold it to the National Gypsum Company. He then formed the Carondelet Realty Company, a real estate development and management firm.[82]

In 1920, Cliff married Agnes Marsh Guthrie, a native of Mississippi. They had four sons: Clifford F. Favrot, Jr., Thomas B. Favrot, C. Allen Favrot, and D. Blair

Favrot. All four sons were involved with the Carondelet Realty Company at its inception, but also pursued separate careers.[83]

While Morty had inherited Charles's interest in architecture, and Gervais had succeeded him as chairman of the City Planning and Zoning Commission, Cliff also took after their father by serving on the boards of Tulane and the New Orleans Chapter of the American Red Cross. He was involved with more than a dozen other business, civic, and charitable organizations in New Orleans, and was a member of the National Advisory Board of the Federal City Council, a non-profit business league dedicated to the improvement of Washington, D.C. In 1956, Cliff again emulated his father when he received the *Times-Picayune* Loving Cup for his tireless service to the community, including his leadership of an endowment drive that raised $3.2 million for the Tulane Educational Advancement Program between 1951 and 1953.[84] That legacy of civic recognition was extended to a third generation when Cliff's son C. Allen Favrot was awarded the Loving Cup in 2002.[85]

In 1957 Cliff received what is unquestionably the greatest honor in New Orleans society when he was chosen as Rex, the King of Carnival.[86] Each year since 1872, the Rex Organization—a Mardi Gras krewe technically known as the School of Design—has selected a prominent male citizen to "reign" as king of that year's festivities. Rex's identity is kept secret until Lundi Gras, the day before Fat Tuesday, when he officially "proclaims" Carnival. On Mardi Gras night, he presides over the Rex Ball, which marks the conclusion of the annual festival. For the entire Favrot family, which had enthusiastically embraced the pageantry of Mardi Gras for generations, Cliff's reign as Rex was surely a proud moment.

Cliff died in 1989 at the age of 91, having outlived all of his older siblings.

ILLUSTRATIONS

Portrait of Joseph-Claude Favrot,
in which he is gesturing toward fortifications in the background.
According to family lore, Joseph-Claude assisted in the
construction of the fortifications at Verdun, France.
Courtesy of William Randolph D'Armond

Portrait of Claude-Joseph Favrot,
who brought the Favrot name to the Louisiana colony.
Courtesy of William Randolph D'Armond

Portrait of Pierre-Joseph Favrot,
also known as Don Pedro José Favrot during
the period of Spanish control of Louisiana.
Courtesy of William Randolph D'Armond

Portrait of Marie-Françoise Gérard Favrot,
wife of Pierre-Joseph Favrot.
Courtesy of Kay Favrot; photo by David J. Armentor

Portrait of Pierre-Louis-Étienne Favrot,
known as Louis or simply "Favrot."
Courtesy of William Randolph D'Armond

Portrait of Joseph-Philogène-Zénon Favrot,
known as Philogène or Philo, drawn by his sister
Marie-Joséphine Favrot, who was commonly called Phine.
Philogène was killed in a duel in 1822.
Courtesy of Kay Favrot

Portrait of the first Henri Mortimer Favrot,
who served as historian of Louisiana's troops
during the Civil War.
Courtesy of William Randolph D'Armond

Charles Allen Favrot,
the first Favrot to become a professional architect.
*Newspaper clipping, Louisiana Image Collection, Louisiana Research
Collection, Tulane University*

Henri Mortimer Favrot, Sr.,
known as Morty, as pictured in the 1913 Tulane Jambalaya yearbook.
*University Archives, Special Collections, Howard-Tilton Memorial
Library, Tulane University, New Orleans, LA*

Kathleen Loker Gibbons Favrot, known as Kay, with
Henri Mortimer Favrot, Jr., known as Tim,
to whom this book is dedicated.
Courtesy of Kay Favrot

Monte Vista Plantation House, West Baton Rouge,
completed in 1859. The plantation was central to
Favrot family life throughout the 19th century.
Courtesy of William Randolph D'Armond

Otis Elevator Company Building, New Orleans,
designed by Favrot & Livaudais and completed in 1912.
The Charles L. Franck Studio Collection at
The Historic New Orleans Collection, 1979.325.422

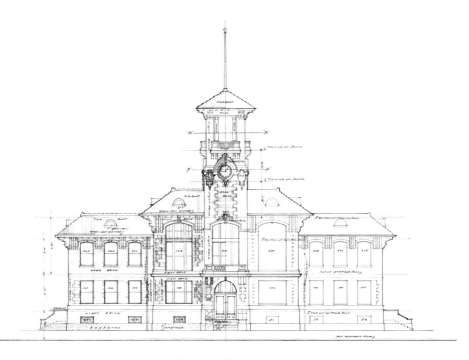

Front elevation of the City Hall in Lake Charles, Louisiana,
designed by Favrot & Livaudais and completed in 1912.
The Archives of Mathes Brierre Architects

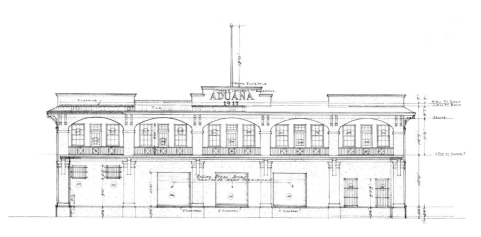

North elevation of the Custom House in La Ceiba, Honduras,
designed by Favrot & Livaudais and completed in 1917.
The Archives of Mathes Brierre Architects

Hibernia Bank Building, New Orleans,
designed by Favrot & Livaudais and completed in 1921.
It was the tallest building in the city until 1965.
*The Charles L. Franck Studio Collection at The Historic New
Orleans Collection, 1979.325.314*

Municipal Auditorium, New Orleans,
designed by Favrot & Livaudais and opened to the public in 1930.
Buildings/Government/Municipal Auditorium, Louisiana Image Collection, Louisiana Research Collection, Tulane University

McAlister Auditorium,
which was designed by Favrot & Reed, built by Gervais Favrot's contracting firm,
and financed by Amelie McAlister Upshur, a distant cousin of the Favrots.
*University Archives, Special Collections, Howard-Tilton Memorial Library,
Tulane University, New Orleans, LA*

The Parktowne Townhouses,
in Metairie, Louisiana, developed by Favrot & Shane and
designed by Tim Favrot. The project won an Honor Award
from the Louisiana Architects Association in 1971.
Courtesy of Favrot & Shane Companies, Inc.

CHAPTER 11

THE ARCHITECT AS DEVELOPER

H. Mortimer Favrot, Jr., was born in the early days of the Great Depression, when his parents were living in the duplex at 1917 Joseph Street owned by his grandfather Charles. His nickname, "Tim," which was derived from the middle syllable of his middle name, helped to distinguish him from Morty. The nickname perpetually caused confusion outside the family, however, as people often incorrectly assumed that it was short for Timothy.[1]

During Tim's youth, 18 Richmond Place was still the center of Favrot family life. Charles hosted a meal there for the extended family each Sunday afternoon, a tradition that continued under Olga after Charles's death in 1939. Tim vividly recalled being in the yard at Richmond Place playing touch football one Sunday in 1941 when his cousin ran out of the house and yelled, "We're at war! The Japanese attacked Pearl Harbor!" Tim was 11 years old at the time and had never heard of Pearl Harbor before the attack.[2] Eager to keep abreast of the course of the war, he began making models of military aircraft and carefully studying maps of the theaters of battle.[3]

Like his father, Tim seems to have been predestined for a career in architecture. He started making cartoons and other drawings at an early age,[4] and often accompanied Morty to construction sites.[5] "If I had the opportunity, I thought I'd like to be an architect," Tim recalled. "My father kind of took it for granted: 'Of course you're going to be an architect!'"[6] Tim attended Catholic schools through the 10th grade, then transferred to the Culver Military Academy in Culver, Indiana, from which he graduated in 1947. After briefly considering studying civil engineering, he decided definitively to pursue a degree in architecture, enrolling at Tulane that fall.

Tulane's architecture program in those days was still a department within the School of Engineering, and classes were held on the fourth floor of Stanley Thomas Hall. Among Tim's more noteworthy professors were Bernard Lemann (1905–2000), the venerable architectural historian and preservationist; J. Herndon Thomson (1891–1969), a former head of the architecture department who had participated in groundbreaking archaeological expeditions of Mayan sites in the Yucatan; and Herbert Levy (life dates unknown), a demanding but widely beloved structures professor.[7] Other prominent faculty members of the period included Buford Pickens, the head of the Department of Architecture, and Arthur Q. Davis (1920–2011), co-founder of the firm Curtis & Davis Architects, neither of whom taught Tim directly though each exerted a powerful influence on the character of the school.

Tim followed in his father's academic footsteps not only by joining the Delta Kappa Epsilon fraternity at Tulane, but also by participating in the summer architecture program at the Conservatoire Américain in Fontainebleau, France, in 1950. He also interned with his father's firm, Favrot, Reed, Mathes & Bergman Architects, during breaks from school. He graduated from Tulane in June 1953, the month after Morty's death in Switzerland.

While at Tulane, Tim had participated in the R.O.T.C. program, and received a commission in the Air Force upon graduation. He began a two-year tour of active duty in the fall of 1953, spending time at Patrick Air Force Base in Florida, Wright-Patterson Air Force Base in Ohio, and finally Holloman Air Force Base in New Mexico. He completed the Installation Engineer Office Basic Course, and went on to supervise several military construction projects in the United States and the Caribbean. Following his discharge in October 1955, he spent several months traveling in Europe and Morocco before returning to work at Favrot, Reed, Mathes & Bergman, which initially retained the full name despite the deaths of Alan Reed and Morty Favrot.[8]

In December 1955, 19-year-old Kathleen ("Kay") Loker Gibbons spotted the 25-year-old Tim at a debutante party. Although she never spoke to him that night, she left the party convinced that she had seen the man she was going to marry. Kay was a member of a prominent family herself. Her great uncle, T. Semmes Walmsley (1889–1942), had been the mayor of New Orleans from 1929 to 1936 and was one of Governor Huey Long's nemeses. Kay had graduated from the Academy of the Sacred Heart, a prestigious, all-girls Catholic high school on St. Charles Avenue, at the age of only 16.[9]

As fortune would have it, Kay and Tim met for the first time the following night at Bruno's bar on Maple Street. Their relatively brief courtship began with a date to the Sugar Bowl game at Tulane Stadium on January 2, 1956,[10] and ended just eight-and-a-half months later, on September 15, when they were married at the Holy Name of Jesus church on the Loyola University campus. They left almost immediately on their honeymoon, which actually consisted of a long drive to Cambridge, Massachusetts, where Tim was about to begin graduate study at the Harvard University Graduate School of Design.

The newlyweds rented an attic apartment at 14 Ellsworth Avenue in Cambridge, about seven blocks from the Harvard Yard. Tim, thanks to his military service, received a stipend from the federal government under the G.I. Bill that covered his tuition. While Tim was studying, Kay went to work at Harvard's Widener Library as a library assistant, earning $185 per month, which covered the couple's rent and most other living expenses.[11]

The dean of the Graduate School of Design at the time was Josep Lluís Sert (1902–1983), a Catalonian-born architect who had immigrated to the United States at the end of the Spanish Civil War. A disciple of the highly influential Swiss-French architect Charles-Édouard Jeanneret-Gris, better known as Le Corbusier (1887–1965), he was also the lead designer of several prominent buildings at Harvard, including the Holyoke Center (now the Smith Campus Center) and the Harvard Science Center. Sert was closely associated with the *Congrès internationaux d'architecture moderne* (CIAM), a European-based organization dedicated to codifying and promulgating the principles of the emerging Modern Movement in architecture and related fields.

Sert was widely remembered for his diminutive stature, which belied an outsize personality and fiery temper. "He was tough," said Tim. "It was the old European philosophy—you give [students] hell, and don't compliment them, because they'll get soft." Tim recalled Sert's scathing critique of one of his projects that included the question, "Are you sure you want to be an architect?" Tim was devastated immediately after the harsh review, but persevered, knowing that it was typical of Sert's interactions with students. He completed the program and received his Master of Architecture degree in June 1957. Kay, who was pregnant with their first child, James Parkhurst Favrot, and struggling with morning sickness, had already returned to New Orleans several weeks earlier. Tim attended a year-end student party hosted by Sert in New York before rejoining his wife.[12] Their first residence as a couple in New Orleans was a duplex apartment on South Rendon Street owned by Tim's cousin, Cliff Favrot, Jr. Their son James was born while they lived in that apartment.

Tim soon got a job with Curtis & Davis Architects, by then the leading firm in the city. He worked on such projects as an addition to the Ochsner Hospital complex in suburban Jefferson Parish. About a year after he joined the firm, however, the economy went into recession, and Tim, as one of the most recently hired employees, was also among the first to be laid off. "We had a brand new baby when Tim came home one night and said, 'I'm out of a job,'" recalled Kay. "And I said, 'Oh, I'm sure you'll find something. I wasn't the least bit concerned." Indeed, he was hired almost immediately by the firm of Colbert & Lowrey and Associates, which was headed by Charles Colbert (1921–2007), a local architect who later served as dean of the School of Architecture at Columbia University.

Colbert, whose body of work included some of the most innovative mid-20th-century buildings in New Orleans, was talented but difficult.[13] Within months, Tim decided to take the risk of going out on his own. He formed a partnership with Henry Grimball (life dates unknown), whom he had known as a student at Tulane. The firm lasted until 1961. Tim then had a solo practice from 1962 to 1964,[14] during which time he was the associated architect, with John

M. Lachin, Jr. (1918–2005), for the Men's Food Service Building (now Bruff Commons) on Tulane's campus.[15]

In 1964, Tim became a partner in the successor firm to Favrot, Reed, Mathes & Bergman, which was accordingly renamed Mathes, Bergman, Favrot & Associates Architects. In the intervening years since he had left, the firm had completed several significant projects, including the New Orleans City Hall, executed in association with Goldstein, Parham & Labouisse Architects, and the central Public Library, done in association with that firm and Curtis & Davis as lead designers.[16] The firm's most significant project after Tim rejoined as a partner was the Rivergate, an exhibition facility near the New Orleans riverfront designed in collaboration with Curtis & Davis and Edward B. Silverstein & Associates. The concrete structure, with its expressively sculpted roof supported by a row of slender columns, was completed in 1968 but demolished in 1995 to make way for the Harrah's Casino.[17]

During this period, Tim and Kay moved several times to successively larger houses. The first property they owned was a modest, one-story house at 7046 Camp Street, which they bought in 1958. Their second child, Kathleen Cartan Favrot, was born while they lived there in 1959. In 1960, they bought a large double house at 1737 Bordeaux Street, which Tim renovated and sold in 1963. Their third and fourth children, Timothy Semmes Favrot (who goes by his middle name) and Caroline Walmsley Favrot, were born during that time, in 1960 and 1961, respectively. The family then lived at 2135 State Street for seven years. In 1970, they moved into a new house of Tim's design at 433 Bellaire Drive, just a block east of the canal that separates New Orleans from Metairie.[18] Tim and Kay's daughter Kathleen remembers the Bellaire Drive house as being distinctly modern, with a front courtyard enclosed by a brick wall, an entrance on the side, and globe lights that were very much in vogue at the time. The Favrots sold the house in 1975, and since then it has undergone substantial alterations.[19]

Branching Out Into Development

In the mid-1960s, Tim concluded that he needed a source of income besides his salary in order to build a secure financial future for his family. Perhaps taking a cue from his grandfather, whose real estate ventures had been quite successful, he decided to try his hand at small-scale development. He approached a close friend of his father's who was a vice president at Whitney Bank to seek a loan to build a 24-unit apartment complex on a site at 1725 Delachaise Street, a block-and-a-half off St. Charles Avenue. To his surprise, the banker denied his request, arguing that Morty would not have wanted Tim to engage directly in contracting or development because it was "unprofessional." "I thanked him," said Tim, "and as I was leaving his office, I thought to myself, 'I didn't come here for advice, I came here for money.'" Tim eventually obtained financing from another bank, in addition to lining up an individual investment partner, and the project went forward.[20] Mathes, Bergman, Favrot & Associates designed the building but did not have an investment stake in the project. When completed in 1965, the simple structure was somewhat reminiscent of a modest beach resort, with wood shingle siding and an exposed, white-painted exterior staircase.[21] The building still stands, though it has been heavily remodeled and was later converted into a condominium.

After the Delachaise Apartments quickly proved to be a solid investment, Tim tried to interest his professional partners, Earl Mathes and William Bergman, to go in with him on the development of a larger residential complex on Lake Avenue in Metairie, a close-in suburb of New Orleans in eastern Jefferson Parish. Mathes and Bergman declined, so Tim proceeded again with outside investment partners.[22] This project, too, was successful, but when the time came for a second phase, the construction cost estimates were too high to be viable. At that point, Henry Shane (1937–), a Tulane graduate and a junior partner at Mathes, Bergman, Favrot & Associates who had already built several small projects on his own, offered to act as general contractor for the addition, working within the budget that the investors had set. Shane took a leave of absence from the firm in order to build the project for a set fee plus 50 percent of any cost savings he could achieve. Upon completion of the project in 1969, he announced his decision to leave the firm permanently and become an independent architect/developer.[23]

Tim resigned from Mathes, Bergman, Favrot & Associates later that year and re-established his own office, quickly picking up a few educational and other projects. Before long, however, he called Shane to express his interest in forming a partnership with him. Tim proposed a simple business model: the pair would buy parcels of land, Tim would design buildings to go on those parcels, Shane would oversee construction, and then they would rent out the properties and split the profits equally. Shane agreed, and in 1970, the two men officially established the firm of Favrot & Shane Architects, with a small office on Veterans Boulevard in Metairie.[24]

The business grew slowly at first, as the firm focused on building low-rise, medium-density residential projects—town houses and garden apartment buildings—in Metairie. The burgeoning suburb, whose population grew by over 20 percent in the 1970s alone,[25] had plenty of open lots and a steady need for new housing. Nonetheless, profits were initially modest. "When we started," said Shane, "things were different. Real estate didn't make much sense [in some ways]. We had a lot of partners who'd give us money so they'd get tax deductions—mostly lawyers and doctors who needed tax breaks. They funded us to buy land. The tax breaks were greater than the [rental] income."[26]

Favrot & Shane strove to maintain design quality while producing readily marketable residences. Tim's design for the Parktowne Townhouses on Transcontinental Drive at York Street in Metairie won an Honor Award from the Louisiana Architects Association in 1971. The complex consisted of 74 paired three-bedroom units lining the perimeter of a full city block. The most remarkable element of the project was the private, four-acre park at the center of the block, incorporating three swimming pools, play areas, and recreational pavilions with distinctive roofs evocative of tropical huts.[27] Originally sheathed in wood shingles, the town houses have been refaced, but the basic plan of the development, including the shared green space, remains intact.

Tim and Shane worked long hours—typically 10 to 12 hours a day, including Saturdays, and often a few hours on Sundays.[28] Tim's son James Favrot recalled that during his childhood, his father would leave for work on weekdays before the children woke up for school, come home in the early evening, have a single gin-and-tonic, eat dinner with the family, and then return to the office, finally coming home for the night at about 10:30 or 11:00.[29] That work ethic never changed: Tim still went to the office regularly until he was incapacitated by illness in 2014; as of this writing, Shane continues to work every day at the age of 80.

Early in the history of the company, the partners made a consequential decision never to sell any of the projects they developed. That buy-and-hold strategy began to pay off by the late 1970s and early '80s, as rental income had risen in the older properties while operating expenses remained relatively constant. Tim and Shane no longer needed investment partners to develop new properties. The company also began to expand into commercial development, and in 1980, moved into a new headquarters building on the Interstate 10 Service Road that Tim designed.[30] The building's restrained exterior offers no hint of its surprising interior feature—a lushly planted, naturally lit atrium space. The project received an Honor Award from the AIA New Orleans Chapter in 1982.

In the mid-1980s, a steep nationwide drop in energy prices caused a severe regional recession in Louisiana, whose economy depended heavily on oil production, refining, and related industries. The "oil bust" led several major corporations, including Shell, Chevron, and Amoco, to consolidate their operations, which entailed transferring most of their New Orleans-based employees to Houston. Retailers and other non-oil businesses struggled to stay afloat as the area's population shrank.

Occupancy rates in properties owned by Favrot & Shane, which by then comprised approximately 3,000 units in total, dropped precipitously. The company's cash reserves all but vanished. "We were really at death's door," said Shane. The collapse of the real estate market convinced the partners to break their buy-and-hold rule by selling two properties to the Catholic Church, thus gaining some liquidity. The company also got a break when several major banks, which had repossessed thousands of units from other owners in default, offered to pay Favrot & Shane to manage those properties. Although debt kept piling up for years, the company was able to weather the crisis, and eventually repaid all of its lenders in full. To this day, the two properties bought by the Catholic Church remain the only ones that the company has ever sold.[31]

Family Life and Professional Service

After about five years in the house that Tim designed on Bellaire Drive near the New Orleans city limit, the family missed living in Uptown. They sold the Bellaire residence in 1975 and bought an existing house at 1701 Nashville Avenue. In the early 1980s, Tim and Kay bought a large vacant lot on State Street, in an elegant neighborhood riverside of St. Charles Avenue. An earlier house on the lot had been demolished by the previous owner, who had intended to build afresh but never did. Tim divided the property into three lots, and designed a new house for his family on the corner parcel. His design, developed during the ascendancy of the postmodern movement, incorporated various allusions to historical architectural motifs, with a tall, arched entry portico and an array of round-arched and perfectly circular windows. The family moved into the new house in 1984,[32] and Kay still lives there as of this writing.

Two years earlier, Tim had sold his inherited interest in his father's former house at Favrotville to his sister Claire. He and Kay then bought a property on West Beach Boulevard in Pass Christian, Mississippi, and built a guest cottage, swimming pool, and other outbuildings based on Tim's designs. In 2000, they bought a 547-acre property near St. Francisville, Louisiana—the former "capital" of the short-lived Republic of West Florida in 1810—for which Tim designed a house and garage completed in 2003.[33]

Once Favrot & Shane was well established, Tim felt able to devote more time to the architectural profession, continuing the tradition set by his grandfather and father. He served as president of the New Orleans Chapter of the AIA in 1982–1983, and as president of the Louisiana Chapter in 1984–1985.[34] According to one source who asked not to be named, "Tim Favrot might deny this, but he practically single-handedly saved the AIA chapters, both in New Orleans and Louisiana. People weren't joining, but when Tim became president, he turned it around." Indeed, Tim was instrumental in developing the local chapter's long-range plan, hiring its first executive director, establishing its first permanent headquarters, and creating its first Honor Awards program. During his tenure, the membership ranks grew by 40 percent. He oversaw similar strides at the state chapter level, including the creation of a statewide Medal of Honor for service to the profession, and the development of the annual Louisiana Design Festival. He also formed a partnership to buy a building for the state chapter to lease, allowing the organization to have a permanent home without dramatically increasing its expenses. In 2001, Tim was awarded the Medal of Honor himself in recognition of his many contributions to the profession in Louisiana.[35] The New Orleans Chapter honored him as a "Legend of Architecture" in 2012.[36] He was elevated to Fellowship in the AIA at the organization's national convention in Denver in 2013. "That," said Kay, "was the proudest accomplishment of Tim Favrot's life."[37]

Hurricane Katrina and Its Aftermath

On Friday, August 26, 2005, Kay and Tim headed to their house in Pass Christian to spend the weekend. They were well aware that a hurricane named Katrina had just struck South Florida and was moving into the Gulf of Mexico, but having both lived in New Orleans virtually all their lives, they had endured many such storms and were not overly concerned.[38] As of that morning, the storm was only a Category 1 hurricane[39]—certainly capable of causing serious damage, but a relatively common meteorological event for the Gulf Coast. Besides, the last report they had heard before leaving home indicated that the storm was likely moving toward Cuba. Assuming that the risk was minimal, they went out to dinner and barely gave the weather another thought.[40]

Not long after they got back to the house, the telephone rang. It was their daughter Kathleen, who asked, "What the heck are you all doing there? Don't you know there's a storm?" Kay turned on the television and quickly learned that over the course of the day, Katrina had gathered strength rapidly and was now likely to strike the Gulf Coast, leading the governors of Louisiana and Mississippi to declare states of emergency. Kay and Tim decided that they would leave the next morning, return to New Orleans to pack some more clothes and supplies, and head to their house in St. Francisville, which was roughly 60 miles from the nearest large body of water and therefore likely safe from storm surges or major flooding. They had plenty of room in the car even after loading their suitcases, but did not think to pack up important personal mementos, such as family photographs and their children's artworks, that were kept at the Pass Christian house. "We all thought, 'We've been through hurricanes before,'" said Kay. "This looks pretty bad, but we'll be back next week."

The house at St. Francisville was already teeming with family members by the time Kay and Tim arrived. Three of their four children were there along with their spouses and children, plus several friends. "When we got there it was almost like a party," said Kay. The festive atmosphere quickly subsided, however, as the reports of the hurricane's power and path became increasingly ominous that Sunday.[41] That day, the mayor of New Orleans issued an unprecedented order for all residents to evacuate the city.

At about 3:00 a.m. on Monday, August 29, Katrina made landfall as a Category 3 hurricane near the mouth of the Mississippi River, bringing torrential rain and damaging winds to the New Orleans metropolitan area. At 7:00 a.m. came the first reports that water was overtopping a levee by the city's Lower Ninth Ward, causing severe flooding in the low-lying neighborhood. Four hours later, it was reported that a levee along the Industrial Canal in eastern New Orleans had failed, allowing water from Lake Pontchartrain to flow unchecked into New Orleans East, the Lower Ninth Ward, and adjacent St. Bernard Parish. Then at 2:00 p.m. came the shocking news that a levee along the 17th Street Canal, which divides New Orleans from Metairie, had been breached. Water began pouring into the Lakeview neighborhood—one of the city's wealthiest—as well as Mid-City, Gentilly, and other areas. By the time floodwaters reached equilibrium with the level of the lake, upwards of 80 percent of the land within the city limits was inundated.[42] There was also significant flooding from the heavy rain in Jefferson Parish, where nearly all of Favrot & Shane's properties were located. In just three days, a routine storm had turned into an unfathomable catastrophe.

Kay, Tim, and their extended family remained safe in the St. Francisville house, where at one point after the storm as many as 24 people were living on an extended basis. They watched helplessly as television news reports documented the struggles of people who had been unable or unwilling to evacuate the city, and the full extent of the physical damage to buildings and infrastructure. Soon it became clear that a swath of relatively high ground along the Mississippi, widely known as the "Sliver by the River," had not flooded. Kay and Tim's house on State

Street was within that zone, but that fact was of limited comfort, as they knew that many friends, family members, businesses, and important institutions had suffered tremendous losses.

For Labor Day, which fell just a week after Katrina hit New Orleans, Kay and Tim decided to take a break from the barrage of alarming news out of their hometown and visit their daughter Caroline in Austin, Texas. "When we were driving from St. Francisville to Austin," Kay recalled, "we stopped to get coffee somewhere, and when we came out, a state policeman offered us some food stamps, because he saw the Louisiana license plate. We said, 'Well, thank you so much, we really appreciate it, but save those for someone who really needs them—we don't need them.'"

She continued: "I was in a grocery store in Austin, and a lady heard me talking to somebody, and she came up to me, she said, 'I heard you say you're from New Orleans, and I'm going to give you a hug whether you want one or not.' It was just amazing. People could not do enough for you. It was very humbling. It was very inspiring. We were so grateful that people recognized what had happened to our city. And then some of these idiot commentators would come on: 'New Orleans isn't worth saving, it's below sea level,' and oh, we got so angry with that."

Kay and Tim returned to St. Francisville and began adapting to temporary life away from their primary home. Meanwhile, Tim and James, who had been working with his father at Favrot & Shane since 1980, were already actively developing a recovery plan for the business and the properties that the company owned and managed. They were eager to get to work, but with all of the entry points to the New Orleans metropolitan area closed indefinitely, they knew that drastic—and creative—action was required.

James went online, copied the Jefferson Parish logo from the official government website, and managed to produce official-looking reentry passes for the recovery team the company had assembled. He also borrowed magnetic signs from a friend who owned an environmental company and placed them on his car. It is unclear whether the police officers who were guarding the reentry points truly believed that these credentials were real, but they clearly accepted that the team's purpose was legitimate. "Our explanation was, 'Look, we have thousands of residents,'" said James. "We have to get back here and fix this so that they have a place to live."

"We were [among] the first people back," said James. "I personally drove a 24-foot travel trailer across the [Lake Pontchartrain] Causeway the wrong way in a caravan being escorted by two Jefferson Parish police deputies with a convoy of vehicles from [subcontractors] and suppliers and other people." The company set up a temporary base in Elmwood, an area of Jefferson Parish near the river, which was largely spared of flooding. From there, smaller teams were dispersed to specific properties to begin cleanup and repair work.[43]

Henry Shane, who never evacuated his house during the storm, recalls that the total damage to all of the company's properties came to approximately $90 million. The total insurance claim, which included non-physical losses, was closer to $100 million.[44]

Tim went back to work at the company's headquarters as soon as he could. Initially, he was commuting back to St. Francisville every night—a trip that would normally take about two hours, but which was now running to four hours each way due to greatly increased traffic into and out of the city. When the strain of the commute became too much to bear, he began staying in one of the apartments owned by the company. He eventually moved back into the State Street house. Kay did not return permanently from St. Francisville until the first week of November. The State Street house suffered no flooding and no wind damage. Tim and Kay's house in Pass Christian, however, was destroyed. They later bought another house in Pass Christian on East Scenic Drive. "The current house has been there since 1885," said Kay. "We decided that if it had withstood [hurricanes] Camille and Katrina, and everything in between, that it was probably not going anywhere."[45]

The physical recovery of New Orleans in the aftermath of Hurricane Katrina was infamously slow and inconsistent, and remains incomplete as of this writing more than a decade later. Given the scope of the damage, however, the very fact that the city was essentially functional again within a few months of the storm was rather remarkable. Without the rapid work of key companies such as Favrot & Shane, that would have been impossible.

After the recovery was well under way, James and his colleagues informed the Jefferson Parish authorities of the ruses they had employed to get back into the metropolitan area immediately after Katrina. Not only were parish officials understanding, they also recognized that, in the event of a future natural disaster, the company should be able to gain access to its properties without hindrance. "We're now Tier One First Responders," said James, "so if it happens again, we get back in at the same time as any other first responders."[46]

Favrot & Shane and its subsidiary companies, including 1st Lake Properties, now own more than 9,500 residential units, along with a number of office buildings, shopping centers, and other commercial structures. Most are still in Jefferson Parish, which includes Metairie, but the company has begun to expand its geographical scope in order to reduce the risk from localized economic and natural hazards. Roughly 18 percent of the company's holdings are now outside of Jefferson Parish, including several in Mississippi. Long-term plans call for expansion throughout the Gulf South.[47] The company employs nearly 350 people, and has been named one of the "Best Places to Work in New Orleans" for four years running by *New Orleans CityBusiness* newspaper.[48]

Community Engagement and Philanthropy

Even as Favrot & Shane was growing rapidly and Tim was routinely working 10- or 12-hour days, he found time to participate in civic and cultural affairs. Beginning in 1970, he spent 14 years as a member of the New Orleans City Planning Commission—one of the successor agencies to the City Planning and Zoning Commission on which both his grandfather Charles and his Uncle Gervais had served—including two years as chairman. He was also a member of the Mayor's Design Review Committee under Mayor Maurice Edwin ("Moon") Landrieu (1930–) from 1974 to 1978.[49]

Tim was active with several non-profit cultural organizations, including the Preservation Resource Center of New Orleans (PRC). In the 1980s, he led a joint initiative of the PRC and the AIA New Orleans Chapter under which architects volunteered to produce renderings of blighted buildings in the city's Lower Garden District. The PRC used the drawings to attract buyers for the properties, many of which were then restored through the organization's Operation

Comeback program, which facilitates the renovation and sale of vacant historic structures. Tim was president of PRC in 1994 and 1995, during which time the organization successfully fought the demolition of the Sanlin Building, actually a series of antebellum commercial buildings on Canal Street just below Magazine Street, across from the Custom House. Now obscured by a modern metal screen added in the 1950s, the underlying buildings were built in the Greek Revival style in the 1840s by a pair of African American entrepreneurs. Tim later led the capital campaign for the purchase of the Leeds-Davis Building, a historic, cast-iron, Gothic Revival landmark built as a foundry in 1853. The building was restored and became the PRC's headquarters in 2000.[50]

The New Orleans Museum of Art was another of Tim's favorite cultural institutions. He served on the museum's Board of Trustees from 1986 to 1992, and again from 2009 until 2014, and was vice president of the board from 1990 to 1992. During the 1980s, he played a substantial advisory role in the construction of a major addition to the museum designed by the firm of Clark & Menefee Architects in association with Eskew, Vogt, Salvato & Filson. Completed in 1991, the addition won design awards from the New Orleans and Louisiana chapters of the AIA. More recently, Tim and Kay established the Favrot Architecture and Design Endowment, which encourages the museum to develop exhibitions and programming related to these fields. The museum honored Tim with the Isaac Delgado Award, named for the institution's founder, in 2014.[51]

The National WWII Museum, located in the New Orleans Warehouse District, has grown rapidly and dramatically since it opened as the National D-Day Museum in 2000. The direct impetus for the museum's establishment was the vital role that Higgins Boats—landing craft manufactured in New Orleans by the thousands—played in the Invasion of Normandy and many other key battles of World War II. Tim was a founding member of the museum, and made a pre-opening donation that supported the Mr. and Mrs. H. Mortimer Favrot, Jr., Orientation Center, a multipurpose space in the original building. He went on to serve on the museum's National Board of Trustees beginning in 2004, and while chair of the Facilities Committee, he was closely involved in the early phases of a major expansion designed by Voorsanger Architects, a prominent New York firm.[52] Working in association with Mathes Brierre Architects, the successor to

Mathes, Bergman, Favrot & Associates, Voorsanger designed a series of dramatically angular pavilions sheathed in interlocking panels of ribbed, precast concrete. The addition has given the museum a clear architectural identity and helped to turn it into one of the most popular tourist attractions in New Orleans.[53]

Kay and Tim's generosity has extended to the Academy of the Sacred Heart, from which Kay graduated in 1953, and which Tim also attended briefly as a young child when the school still accepted boys. They provided lead funding for the 2011 conversion of part of an existing building on the St. Charles Avenue campus into the Favrot Arts Center, which includes a dance studio, art studio, and music rooms. Kay is a member of the academy's Board of Trustees and its Alumnae Board, which supports academic and social programming at the school.[54]

Tim was an avid supporter of Tulane University throughout his life. Named Outstanding Alumnus of the School of Architecture in 1985, he was a member of the Board of Tulane from 1986 to 2000, and served on the Tulane School of Architecture Board of Advisors under several deans. In addition to funding multiple endowed professorships in the School of Architecture, he and Kay made significant donations to support the Tulane City Center, Richardson Memorial Hall, and other programs of the school.

Tim was not reluctant to speak out, however, when the university was considering actions with which he disagreed. In 1999, the university administration proposed demolishing Cunningham Observatory—a tiny architectural gem designed by Favrot & Reed and built in 1941 near McAlister Auditorium—to make way for an expansion of the School of Business. According to a source who prefers to remain anonymous, Tim argued for the observatory's preservation, and offered to raise the necessary money to have the building moved to another spot on campus. Despite his personal pledge to make up any difference if the fund raising fell short, the university proceeded with the demolition of the observatory in 2001.

In the wake of Hurricane Katrina, the university announced plans to merge Newcomb College—then a semi-autonomous women's college under the Tulane umbrella—with the School of Arts and Sciences. Tim was among the few prominent figures in the Tulane community to question the decision publicly. "I spoke up to make sure there was sufficient, serious reason" for the move, said Tim.[55] Ultimately, the administration proceeded with the merger as part of a series of organizational changes intended to stabilize the university's finances following the Katrina disaster.

Despite such differences of opinion with the Tulane leadership, Tim remained an unwavering champion of his *alma mater*. In the years just before his death, he served as a key adviser to the dean of the School of Architecture and the university president regarding plans for the renovation of, and addition to, Richardson Memorial Hall, which has housed the architecture program since it moved from Stanley Thomas Hall in the 1970s. Tim and Kay Favrot have provided substantial financial support for the early phases of the design and planning process. During several interviews for this book, Tim's affection and reverence for Tulane were always evident.

Tim's health declined rapidly in early 2014. He had already been hospitalized for throat ailments when he suffered a stroke that left him unable to communicate. After 51 days in the hospital, he was brought home, where Kay and a dedicated team of caregivers tended to him. He died peacefully in May 2015.

EPILOGUE

The story of the Favrot family over the past three centuries would be virtually unimaginable in any setting other than Louisiana. The state's exotic culture, peculiar geography, and often-turbid history have infused the family members' lives and shaped their destinies. It is a story of place as much as people.

I was movingly reminded of this during one of my research visits to New Orleans. After spending a day poring through the family papers at the Howard-Tilton Memorial Library, I took a walk through Audubon Park, just across St. Charles Avenue from the Tulane University campus. The weather was nice, and most of the benches along the lagoon that winds its way through the park were occupied. As I approached the first empty bench I saw, I noticed that it faced a small memorial, which I decided to investigate. I discovered that it had been placed there in honor of Kelsey Ann Bradley Favrot, James Favrot's first wife, who had died of brain cancer in 2009 at the age of only 49. Fresh flowers rested atop the small monument. With a lump in my throat, I marveled at the odds of coming across a previously unknown memorial to a Favrot family member whose tragic story I had learned only a few weeks earlier. Then, adding to the coincidence, two people walked by on the path behind me, and as they passed, I overheard them sympathetically noting the Favrot family's dedication to keeping fresh flowers on the memorial.

The Favrots today are widely known and well regarded in New Orleans. Many locals, upon hearing about this book project, expressed an acquaintance with, and affection for, one or more Favrot family members. A surprisingly large number of people were at least somewhat familiar with the family's deep roots in Louisiana, dating back to the early days of the colonial period.

There are already at least three generations of Favrots beyond Tim's. As of this writing, Kay has twelve grandchildren and two great-grandchildren. Of her four children, three live in New Orleans with their families—the exception being Caroline, who still lives with her husband Harry John Trube and their daughter in Austin, Texas. James Favrot is now married to Sheila Favrot. They live with James's four children by his first wife. Kathleen and her husband Charles Van Horn have three children, and Semmes and his wife Catherine have four.

Tim's sister Claire married W. Harvey Killeen, who is now deceased. They had eight children, seven of whom are still living, and many grandchildren. Claire, who wrote a popular and humorous column for the Loyola University *Maroon* while she was a student there in the early 1950s, is also the author of *Eardrums of the Heart: Empowering the Disadvantaged: Dr. Bertha Mugrauer and the Caritas Way*, published by the University Press of America in 2000. She retired as the administrator of the Francis House, a shelter for homeless families in New Orleans. Tim and Claire's brother, James Freret Favrot (not to be confused with James Parkhurst Favrot, Tim's son) died young in 1961 and did not marry or have children.

The business now known as Favrot & Shane Companies, Inc., continues to thrive and is still controlled by the two founding families. James is now president, and he and Henry Shane serve as co-chairmen of the companies. Shane's daughters, Michele Shane L'Hoste and Stacey Shane Schott, also hold executive positions within the business.

Members of the other branches of the Favrot family tree, including the descendants of Louis's brother Bouvier; Charles's brothers Henry, Edgar, William, and Leo; and Morty's brothers Gervais and Cliff, now number at least in the dozens. There are also probably hundreds of descendants of female Favrot family members who married and took their husbands' last names. Cursory research suggests that the vast majority still lives in Louisiana.

The Favrots have made an indelible imprint on the history and character of their state. Four generations—led by Claude-Joseph, Pierre-Joseph, Louis, and Henri—participated directly in many of Louisiana's formative events. The three succeeding generations—including Charles, Morty, and Tim—have left a physical legacy in the form of noteworthy buildings and communities. Their collective bequest to subsequent generations is a remarkable, centuries-long heritage that both reflects and illuminates the history of Louisiana.

ENDNOTES

PREFACE

1. Guillermo Náñez Falcón, ed., *Transcriptions of Manuscript Collections of Louisiana, No. 1, The Favrot Papers,* vol. XVII, 1861–(1865)–1885 (New Orleans: Tulane University, 1984), iii.

2. Maggy Carof, letter to Thomas B. Favrot, January 19, 1966, Favrot Family Papers, Louisiana Research Collection, Tulane University.

3. Kay Favrot, interview with author, November 21, 2013.

INTRODUCTION

1. Henri Sée, *Economic and Social Conditions in France During the Eighteenth Century,* trans. Edwin H. Zeydel (Kitchener, Canada: Batoche Books, 2004), 17.

2. Thomas B. Favrot, "Recap of the Favrot family from 1575 to 1695, compiled by T.B. Favrot from his research," undated, Favrot Family Papers, Louisiana Research Collection, Tulane University.

3. Institut national de la statistique et des études économiques. "25263—Gellin: Populations légales 2013 de la commune." Accessed April 8, 2016. http://www.insee.fr/fr/ppp/bases-de-donnees/recensement/populations-legales/commune.asp?depcom =25263.

4. Thomas B. Favrot, "Recap of the Favrot family from 1575 to 1695, Favrot Family Papers, Louisiana Research Collection, Tulane University."

CHAPTER 1: Origins in France

1   Guillermo Náñez Falcón, ed., *The Favrot Family Papers: A Documentary Chronicle of Early Louisiana*, vol. I, 1690–1782 (New Orleans: Tulane University, 1988), 3.

2   Náñez Falcón, *The Favrot Family Papers*, vol. I, 1–2.

3   Thomas B. Favrot, "Genealogy of the Favrot Family of Louisiana," undated, Favrot Family Papers, Louisiana Research Collection, Tulane University.

4   Náñez Falcón, *The Favrot Family Papers*, vol. I, xxx.

5   Ibid., 4–5.

6   Ibid., 27.

7   Ibid., xxviii–xxix.

8   Ibid., xxxviii.

9   Ibid., 6.

10   Ibid., 7–8.

11   Ibid., 9.

12   Ibid.

13   Ibid., 12.

14   Ibid., 10.

15   Ibid., 13–15.

16   Ibid., 15–16.

17   Ibid., 27. (This letter may have been misdated, as it was written after Joseph-Claude's death, which is consistently dated elsewhere to October 28).

18   Ibid., 24–25.

19   Ibid., 34–37.

20   Ibid., 40–41.

21   Ibid., 29.

22   Ibid., 31–32.

23   Ibid., 27.

24   Ibid., 34–37.

CHAPTER 2: Early Years in Louisiana

1   Stanley C. Arthur and George Campbell Huchet de Kernion, *Old Families of Louisiana* (Baltimore: Genealogical Publishing Company, 2009), 375. (Although this source lists only four children, several documents in the Favrot Family Papers indicate that there were five at the time of Joseph-Claude's death. Nonetheless, family lore supports the contention that Claude-Joseph was the youngest.)

2   Guillermo Náñez Falcón, ed., *The Favrot Family Papers: A Documentary Chronicle of Early Louisiana*, vol. I, 1690–1782 (New Orleans: Tulane University, 1988), 27.

3   Arthur and Huchet de Kernion, *Old Families of Louisiana*, 375.

4   Náñez Falcón, *The Favrot Family Papers*, vol. I, 27. See also pp. 28–34: "Inventory of the Estate of Joseph-Claude Favrot," December 31, 1709, which mentions his "minor children" who are his "heirs, each for one-fifth of their said deceased father."

5   Ibid., 40.

6   Fayçal Falaky (associate professor of French, Tulane University), email to author, July 2, 2015.

7   Náñez Falcón, *The Favrot Family Papers*, vol. I, 174.

8   Ibid., 40–41.

9   Ibid., 41.

10 Dunbar Rowland and A.G. Sanders, trans. and eds., *Mississippi Provincial Archives: French Dominion*, Vol. III (Jackson: Press of the Mississippi Department of Archives and History, 1927), 618.

11 Náñez Falcón, *The Favrot Family Papers*, vol. I, 42.

12 Ibid., xvii.

13 Ibid., 172. Although this petition by Claude-Joseph Favrot states that he was wounded in 1735, it is likely that this actually occurred during the main French-Chickasaw conflict in 1736.

14 Ibid., 48.

15 Ibid., 47.

16 Ibid., 43–46.

17 Ibid., 49–50.

18 Ibid., xviii.

19 Ibid., 60–68.

20 Ibid., 68.

21 Ibid., 69–70.

22 Ibid., 73–75.

23 Ibid., 76–77.

24 Ibid., 79.

25 "Ancestors of Chevalier Alexandre François Joseph de Clouet Liet. [*sic*] Colonel," accessed April 10, 2016, http://www.declouet.net/pedigree/58.html

26 Náñez Falcón, *The Favrot Family Papers*, vol. I, 81.

27 Ibid., 91.

28 Ibid., xix.. See also: Rien T. Fertel, ed., *The Favrot Family Papers: A Documentary Chronicle of Early Louisiana*, vol. VI, 1817–1839 (New Orleans: Tulane University, 2012), 337.

29 Náñez Falcón, *The Favrot Family Papers*, vol. I, 131–32.

30 Ibid., 129.

31 Ibid., 138–39.

32 Ibid., 195–97.

33 Ibid., 147–48.

34 Ibid., 148.

35 Ibid., 174.

36 Ibid., 150–53.

37 Ibid., 209–10.

CHAPTER 3: The Spanish Colonial Era
---

1 Guillermo Náñez Falcón, ed., *The Favrot Family Papers: A Documentary Chronicle of Early Louisiana*, vol. I, 1690–1782 (New Orleans: Tulane University, 1988), 55.

2 Ibid., 78.

3 Ibid., 90.

4 Ibid., 91.

5 Ibid., 111–12.

6 Ibid., 129.

7 Ibid., 166–67.

8 Ibid., 143–44.

9 Ibid., 146–47.

10 Ibid., 149.

11 Ibid., 154.

12 Ibid., 155.

13 Ibid., 156.

14 Ibid., 157–59.

15 Ibid., 164–65.

16 Ibid., 161–64.

17 Ibid., 165.

18 Ibid., 160–61.

19 Lawrence N. Powell, letter to author, January 10, 2016.

20 Náñez Falcón, *The Favrot Family Papers*, vol. I, 166.

21 Ibid., 167.

22 Ibid.

23 Ibid., 186.

24 Ibid., 185.

25 Ibid., 186.

26 Ibid.

27 Ibid., 188–90. The published translations of the Favrot Family Papers estimate the date of the report as May 10, 1777, but the content of subsequent documents suggests that it was actually submitted to d'Argout upon Pierre-Joseph's arrival in Martinique, which would have been around December of 1776.

28 Ibid., 191–92.

29 Ibid., 192–93.

30 Ibid., 193–95.

31 Ibid., 210–11.

32 Ibid., 211.

33 Ibid., 215.

34 Ibid., 206–7.

35 Ibid., 226.

36 Ibid., 226–27.

37 Helen Parkhurst [Favrot], "Don Pedro Favrot, A Creole Pepys," *The Louisiana Historical Quarterly*, vol. 28, no. 3 (July 1945): 694.

38 Náñez Falcón, *The Favrot Family Papers*, vol. I, 235.

39 Ibid., 236–37.

40 Ibid., 248.

41 Ibid., 249–50.

42 Gwendolyn Midlo Hall, *Africans in Colonial Louisiana: The Development of Afro-Creole Culture in the Eighteenth Century* (Baton Rouge: Louisiana State University Press, 1992), 312.

43 Parkhurst, "Don Pedro Favrot, A Creole Pepys," 697–98.

44 Náñez Falcón, *The Favrot Family Papers*, vol. I, 280.

45 Ibid., 285–87.

46 Ibid., 296 and 298.

47 Ibid., 299–301.

48 Ibid., 290.

49 Ibid.

50 Guillermo Náñez Falcón, ed., *The Favrot Family Papers: A Documentary Chronicle of Early Louisiana*, vol. II, 1783–1796 (New Orleans: Tulane University, 1988), 5.

51 Ibid., 14.

52 Ibid., 33–36.

53 Ibid., 26–28.

54 Ibid., 64–65.

55 Ibid., 50.

56 Ibid., 57–58.

57 Ibid., 69–70.

58 Ibid., xiv.

59 Ibid., 91.

60 Ibid., 3–5.

61 Ibid., 59–60.

62 Guillermo Náñez Falcón, ed., *The Favrot Family Papers: A Documentary Chronicle of Early Louisiana*, vol. III, 1797–1802 (New Orleans: Tulane University, 1988), 99–100.

63 Náñez Falcón, *The Favrot Family Papers*, vol. II, 87–90.

64 Ibid., 90.

65 Ibid., 119.

66 Ibid., 126.

67 Ibid., 142.

68 Ibid., 158–59.

69 Ibid., 161.

70 Náñez Falcón, *The Favrot Family Papers*, vol. III, 100.

71 Náñez Falcón, *The Favrot Family Papers*, vol. II, 155.

72 Ibid., 172.

73 Ibid., 200–204.

74 Ibid., 251.

75 Ibid., 207.

76 Ibid., 214.

77 Ibid., 228.

78 Ibid., 266–68.

79 Ibid., 238–39.

80 Ibid., 242–44.

81 Náñez Falcón, *The Favrot Family Papers*, vol. III, 16–17.

82 Ibid., 26.

83 Ibid., 25.

84 Ibid.

85 Ibid., 58.

86 Ibid., 54.

87 Ibid., 96.

88 Ibid., 260.

89 Ibid., 100.

90 Ibid., 154.

91 Ibid., 173–74.

92 Ibid., 183.

93 Ibid., 185.

94 Ibid., xvi.

95 Ibid., 48.

96 Ibid., 214.

97 Ibid., 229.

98 Ibid., 260–61.

99 Ibid., 302.

100 Pierre Clément de Laussat, *Memoirs of My Life*, trans. Agnes-Josephine Pastwa, ed. Robert D. Bush (Baton Rouge: Louisiana State University Press, 1978), 12–13.

101 Wilbur E. Meneray, ed., *The Favrot Family Papers: A Documentary Chronicle of Early Louisiana*, vol. IV, 1803–1809 (New Orleans: Tulane University, 1997), 19.

102 Laussat, *Memoirs of My Life*, 15.

103 Ibid., 17.

104 Meneray, *The Favrot Family Papers,* vol. IV, 21–24.

CHAPTER 4: The Americanization of Louisiana

---

1 Wilbur E. Meneray, ed., *The Favrot Family Papers: A Documentary Chronicle of Early Louisiana*, vol. IV, 1803–1809 (New Orleans: Tulane University, 1997), 32–35.

2 Ibid., 15.

3 Ibid., 35–36.

4 Ibid., 37–38.

5 Ibid., 42–43.

6 Ibid., 61–62.

7 Ibid., 76.

8 Alcée Fortier, *A History of Louisiana*, vol. II (New York: Manzi, Joyant & Co., 1904), 246.

9 Meneray, *The Favrot Family Papers*, vol. IV, 114–16.

10 Ibid., 123.

11 Ibid., 118–19.

12 Ibid., 121–22.

13 Ibid., 133.

14 Ibid., 90.

15 Ibid., 92–93.

16 Pierre Clément de Laussat, *Memoirs of My Life*, trans. Agnes-Josephine Pastwa, ed. Robert D. Bush (Baton Rouge: Louisiana State University Press, 1978), 91.

17 Ibid., 76.

18 Meneray, *The Favrot Family Papers*, vol. IV, 154.

19 Ibid., 158.

20 Ibid., 158–59.

21 Ibid., 160.

22 Ibid., 162–63.

23 Ibid., 167.

24 Ibid., 169–70.

25 Ibid., 216–17.

26 Ibid., 239.

27 Ibid., 238.

28 Ibid., 256.

29 George Dargo. *Jefferson's Louisiana: Politics and the Clash of Legal Traditions*, Revised Edition (Clark, New Jersey: The Lawbook Exchange, Ltd., 2009); 246–253.

30 Meneray, *The Favrot Family Papers*, vol. IV, 265–67.

31 Ibid., 251.

32 Ibid., 271.

33 Wilbur E. Meneray, ed., *The Favrot Family Papers: A Documentary Chronicle of Early Louisiana*, vol. V, 1810–1816 (New Orleans: Tulane University, 2001), 38–40.

34 Ibid., 45–46.

35 Ibid., 55.

36 Ibid., 66.

37 Ibid., 77.

38 Ibid., 79.

39 Ibid., 83–84.

40 Ibid., 91.

41 Ibid., 111.

42 Ibid., 122.

43 Ibid., 154.

44 Ibid., 163–64.

45 Ibid., 127.

46 Ibid., 133.

47 Ibid., 176.

48 Ibid., 176–77.

49 Ibid., 189.

50 Ibid., 193–94.

51 Ibid., 213.

52 Ibid., 205.

53 Ibid., 225–27.

54 Ibid., 200–01.

55 Ibid., 216–17.

56 Ibid., 227.

57 Ibid., 219.

58 Ibid., 169.

59 Ibid., 221.

60 Ibid., 218.

61 Ibid., 221–22.

62 Ibid., 219.

63 Ibid., 230–31.

64 Ibid., 232.

65 Ibid., 242–44.

66 Ibid., 268.

67 Ibid., 246–47.

68 Ibid., 288.

69 Ibid.

70 Ibid., 293.

71 Guillermo Náñez Falcón, ed., *Transcriptions of Manuscript Collections of Louisiana, No. 1, The Favrot Papers*, vol. XVII, 1861–(1865)–1885 (New Orleans: Tulane University, 1984), 228.

72 Meneray, *The Favrot Family Papers*, vol. V, 252.

73 Ibid., 274.

74 Ibid., 287.

75 Ibid., 291–92.

76 Ibid., 296.

77 Ibid., 300.

78 Ibid.

79 Ibid., 308.

80 Ibid., 316–17.

81 Rien T. Fertel, ed., *The Favrot Family Papers: A Documentary Chronicle of Early Louisiana*, vol. VI, 1817–1839 (New Orleans: Tulane University, 2012), 7.

82 Ibid., 68.

83 Ibid., 82.

84 Ibid., 74–76.

85 Ibid., 87–88.

86 Ibid., 148.

87 Ibid.

88 Ibid.

89 Ibid., 152.

90 Ibid., 149.

91 Ibid., 152.

92 Ibid., 165.

93 Ibid., 152–53.

94 Ibid., 153–54.

95 Helen Parkhurst [Favrot], "Don Pedro Favrot, A Creole Pepys," *The Louisiana Historical Quarterly*, vol. 28, no. 3 (July 1945).

96 Fertel, *The Favrot Family Papers*, vol. VI, 174–76.

97 Ibid., 242.

98 Ibid., 244–46.

99 Ibid., 250–53.

100 Ibid., 254–55.

101 Ibid., 256–62.

102 Ibid., 265–75.

103 Ibid., 318.

104 Ibid., 316–17.

105 Ibid., 297–98.

106 Mike Miller, "Favrot, Henry Louis; West Baton Rouge Parish, Louisiana," accessed April 11, 2016, http://files.usgwarchives.net/la/westbatonrouge/bios/favrot.txt.

107 Fertel, *The Favrot Family Papers*, vol. VI, 346.

CHAPTER 5: The Fragile Union

1 Guillermo Náñez Falcón, ed., *Transcriptions of Manuscript Collections of Louisiana, No. 1, The Favrot Papers,* vol. XVI, 1840–1859 (New Orleans: Tulane University, 1983), 7.

2 Ibid., 27.

3 Ibid., 28.

4 Ibid., 30–31.

5 Rien T. Fertel, ed., *The Favrot Family Papers: A Documentary Chronicle of Early Louisiana,* vol. VI, 1817–1839 (New Orleans: Tulane University, 2012), 2.

6 Náñez Falcón, *Transcriptions*, vol. XVI, 76.

7 Ibid., 76–77.

8 Ibid., 126.

9 John M. Sacher, "The Sudden Collapse of the Louisiana Whig Party," *The Journal of Southern History*, vol. 65, no. 2 (Athens, Georgia: Southern Historical Association, 1999), 221. See also: John M. Sacher, *A Perfect War of Politics: Parties, Politicians, and Democracy in Louisiana,* 1824–1861 (Baton Rouge: Louisiana State University Press, 2003), 163–170.

10 Sacher, "The Sudden Collapse of the Louisiana Whig Party," 224.

11 Wilbur E. Meneray, ed., *The Civil War Diaries of H.M. Favrot, 1860* (New Orleans: Tulane University, 2002), xiii.

12 Sacher, "The Sudden Collapse of the Louisiana Whig Party," 245.

13 Náñez Falcón, *Transcriptions*, vol. XVI, 163–64.

14 Meneray, *The Civil War Diaries of H.M. Favrot*, xvii.

15 Ibid., 142.

16 Ibid., xiii.

17 Ibid., xv.

18 Ibid., 31.

19 Ibid., 95.

20 Ibid., xv.

21 Ibid., 106, 107, and 128.

22 Ibid., 157.

23 Ibid., 170.

24 Guillermo Náñez Falcón, ed., *Transcriptions of Manuscript Collections of Louisiana*, No. 1, The Favrot Papers, vol. XVII, 1861–(1865)–1885 (New Orleans: Tulane University, 1984), 1–2.

25 Ibid., 5.

26 Ibid., v–vi.

27 William Preston Johnson, *The Life of General Albert Sidney Johnston* (New York: D. Appleton and Company, 1878), as quoted in Náñez Falcón, *Transcriptions*, 240.

28 Náñez Falcón, *Transcriptions*, vol. XVII, 238–39.

29 Ibid., 12–15.

30 Ibid., 16.

31 Ibid., vi.

32 Ibid.

33 Ibid., 34.

34 Ibid., 24.

35 Ibid., 27–28.

36 Ibid., 37–38.

37 Ibid., 29–30.

38 Ibid., 38–39.

39 Ibid., 42–43.

40 Ibid., 44.

41 Ibid., 47–48.

42 Ibid., 42.

43 Ibid., 51.

44 Ibid.

45 Ibid., 58.

46 Ibid., 59.

47 Ibid., 62.

48 Ibid., 51–52.

49 Ibid., 60.

50 Ibid., 63.

51 Ibid., 67.

52 Ibid., 52.

53 Ibid., 83.

54 Ibid., 52.

55 Ibid., 76.

56 Ibid., 88.

57 Ibid, 88 and 91–92.

58 Ibid., 77.

59 Ibid., 115.

60 Henry Watkins Allen, "Annual Message of Governor Henry Watkins Allen, to the Legislature of the State of Louisiana, January 1865," electronic edition, accessed April 10, 2016, http://docsouth.unc.edu/imls/lagov/allen.html.

61 Náñez Falcón, *Transcriptions*, vol. XVII, 115.

62 Ibid., 202.

63   Ibid., 187.

64 Andrew B. Booth, "Records of Louisiana Confederate Soldiers," accessed April 10, 2016, files.usgwarchives.net/la/state/military/wbts/booths-index/f.txt; also Michelle Favrot Heidelberg, email to author, October 13, 2017.

65 Henry Watkins Allen, "Farewell Address," accessed April 10, 2016, http://library.duke.edu/digitalcollections/broadsides_bdsla20583/.

66 Náñez Falcón, *Transcriptions*, vol. XVII, 212.

67 Ibid., 233.

68 Helen Parkhurst Favrot, *Pops: A Memoir* (New Orleans: Tulane University, 1964), 6.

69 Jara Dubroca Roux and Ron Shawhan, "The Dubroca Family of Louisiana," accessed April 10, 2016, http://files.usgwarchives.net/la/pointecoupee/history/family/dubroca.txt.

70 Mike Miller, "Leo M. Favrot, W. Baton Rouge Parish, Louisiana," accessed April 10, 2016, http://files.osgwarchives.net/la/westbatonrouge/bios/favrot3.txt.

71 Helen Parkhurst Favrot. *Pops: A Memoir,* 12.

72 Náñez Falcón, *Transcriptions*, vol. XVII, 232–33.

CHAPTER 6: Pierre-Joseph Favrot's Education Manual For His Sons

1. Guillermo Náñez Falcón, ed., *The Favrot Family Papers: A Documentary Chronicle of Early Louisiana*, vol. III, 1797–1802 (New Orleans: Tulane University, 1988), 279.

2. Guillermo Náñez Falcón, ed., *Pierre-Joseph Favrot's Education Manual for His Sons* (New Orleans: Tulane Howard-Tilton Memorial Library, 1988), 1.

3. Ibid., 5–6.

4. Ibid., 11–12.

5. Ibid., 13–14.

6. Ibid., 15–16p.

7. Ibid., 17–20.

8. Ibid., 21–22.

9. Ibid., 23–24.

10. Ibid., 3–4.

11. Guillermo Náñez Falcón, ed., *Transcriptions of Manuscript Collections of Louisiana*, No. 1, The Favrot Papers, vol. XVII, 1861–(1865)–1885 (New Orleans: Tulane University, 1984), 229.

CHAPTER 7: Domestic & Social Life in the 19th Century

1. Wilbur E. Meneray, ed., *The Favrot Family Papers: A Documentary Chronicle of Early Louisiana,* vol. V, 1810–1816 (New Orleans: Tulane University, 2001), 148.

2. Ibid., 9.

3. Guillermo Náñez Falcón, ed., *Transcriptions of Manuscript Collections of Louisiana, No. 1, The Favrot Papers,* vol. XVI, 1840–1859 (New Orleans: Tulane University, 1983), 142–43.

4. Meneray, *The Favrot Family Papers*, vol. V, 149–50.

5. Ibid., 159–61.

6. Náñez Falcón, *Transcriptions*, vol. XVI, 37–38.

7. Rien T. Fertel, ed., *The Favrot Family Papers: A Documentary Chronicle of Early Louisiana*, vol. VI, 1817–1839 (New Orleans: Tulane University, 2012), 3–4.

8. Ibid., 5.

9. Ibid., 11.

10. Wilbur E. Meneray, ed., *The Civil War Diaries of H.M. Favrot, 1860* (New Orleans: Tulane University Howard-Tilton Memorial Library, 2002), 35, *inter alia*.

11. Fayçal Falaky (associate professor of French, Tulane University), email to author, July 2, 2015.

12 *San Francisco Chronicle*, "After Death: A Woman Does an Act of Justice," June 15, 1889, accessed December 19, 2015, https://www.newspapers.com/image/27338727/?terms=Mrs.%2BHenry%2Bfavrot %2Bchronicle.

13 Guillermo Náñez Falcón, ed., *Transcriptions of Manuscript Collections of Louisiana, No. 1, The Favrot Papers,* vol. XVII, 1861–(1865)–1885 (New Orleans: Tulane University, 1984), 70.

14 Célestine Dubroca Favrot, letter to Charles Allen Favrot, July 29, [1891?], Favrot Family Papers, Louisiana Research Collection, Tulane University.

15 Wilbur E. Meneray, ed., *The Favrot Family Papers: A Documentary Chronicle of Early Louisiana*, vol. IV, 1803–1809 (New Orleans: Tulane University, 1997), 212.

16 Mary Ann Sternberg, *Along the River: Past and Present on Louisiana's Historic Byway* (Baton Rouge: Louisiana State University Press, 2013), 212.

17 Guillermo Náñez Falcón, ed., *The Favrot Family Papers: A Documentary Chronicle of Early Louisiana*, vol. III, 1797–1802 (New Orleans: Tulane University, 1988), xviii.

18 Ibid., 283.

19 Meneray, *The Favrot Family Papers*, vol. IV, 180.

20 Ibid., 195–96.

21 Ibid., 282–91.

22 Meneray, *The Civil War Diaries of H.M. Favrot, 1860*, viii.

23 Meneray, *The Favrot Family Papers*, vol. V, 87 and 110.

24 Ibid., 150.

25 Fertel, *The Favrot Family Papers*, vol. VI, 44–45.

26 Ibid., 57.

27 Ibid., 59.

28 Ibid., 57.

29 Ibid., 61.

30 Ibid., 55–56.

31 Ibid., 69.

32 Ibid., 81.

33 Ibid., 89–90.

34 Ibid., 84.

35 Ibid., 92.

36 *World Atlas*, "Most Populated Cities in Cuba," accessed December 3, 2015, http://www.worldatlas.com/na/cu/cities-in-cuba.html.

37 UNESCO, "Urban Historic Centre of Cienfuegos, accessed December 3, 2015, http://whc.unesco.org/en/list/1202.

38 Michelle Favrot Heidelberg, email to author, October 17, 2017.

39 Elizabeth Kellough and Leona Mayeux, *Chronicles of West Baton Rouge* (Baton Rouge: Kennedy Print Shop, 1979), no page number (reproduction), Favrot Family Papers, Louisiana Research Collection, Tulane University.

40 Sternberg, *Along the River*, 212.

41 Helen Parkhurst Favrot, *Pops: A Memoir* (New Orleans: Tulane University, 1964), 6.

42 Célestine Dubroca Favrot, letter to Charles Allen Favrot, January 11, [1886?], Favrot Family Papers, Louisiana Research Collection, Tulane University.

43 Helen Parkhurst Favrot, *Pops: A Memoir*, 8.

44 Célestine Dubroca Favrot, letter to Charles Allen Favrot, June 3, [1888?], Favrot Family Papers, Louisiana Research Collection, Tulane University.

45 Célestine Dubroca Favrot, letter to Charles Allen Favrot, January 11, [1886?], Favrot Family Papers, Louisiana Research Collection, Tulane University.

46 Henry Louis Favrot, letter to Charles Allen Favrot, June 6, 1888, Favrot Family Papers, Louisiana Research Collection, Tulane University.

47 Henri Mortimer Favrot, letter to Charles Allen Favrot, July 26, 1885, Favrot Family Papers, Louisiana Research Collection, Tulane University.

48 Célestine Dubroca Favrot, letter to Charles Allen Favrot, July 29, [1891?], Favrot Family Papers, Louisiana Research Collection, Tulane University.

49 Helen Parkhurst Favrot. *Pops: A Memoir*, 19.

50 Ibid., 21.

51 Ibid., 22.

52 Kellough and Mayeux, *Chronicles of West Baton Rouge*, no page number.

53 Guillermo Náñez Falcón, ed., *The Favrot Family Papers: A Documentary Chronicle of Early Louisiana*, vol. I, 1690–1782 (New Orleans: Tulane University, 1988), 81.

54 Ibid., 151.

55 Meneray, *The Favrot Family Papers*, vol. IV, 180–82.

56 Ibid., 285–87.

57 United States Census, 1810, accessed November 10, 2015, https://familysearch. org/ark:/61903/ 3:1:33SQ-GYY1-LF7?mode= g&i=5&wc=QZZC-1TW% 3A1588180603% 2C1588181739%2C1 588179902%3Fcc% 3D1803765&cc= 1803765.

58 Fertel, *The Favrot Family Papers*, vol. VI, 223.

59 Meneray, *The Civil War Diaries of H.M. Favrot, 1860*, 167.

60 Náñez Falcón, *Transcriptions*, vol. XVII, 130.

61 Ibid., 203.

62 Helen Parkhurst Favrot. *Pops: A Memoir*, 9.

63 Ibid., 6.

64   Ibid., 22.

65   Helen Parkhurst Favrot and Claire Favrot Killeen, *All My Loves: Letters and Memorabilia from the 1920s* (Covington, LA: Francis House Press, 1992), A:2.

66   Nánez Falcón, *The Favrot Family Papers*, vol. III, 206, *inter alia*.

67   Ibid., 210.

68   Ibid., 212.

69   Ibid., 235.

70   Meneray, *The Favrot Family Papers*, vol. IV, 299–303.

71   Meneray, *The Favrot Family Papers*, vol. V, 99–100.

72   Nánez Falcón, *Transcriptions*, vol. XVI, 55.

73   Nánez Falcón, *Transcriptions*, vol. XVII, 229–30.

74   Fertel, *The Favrot Family Papers*, vol. VI, 206–11.

75   Ibid., 329–36.

76   Ibid., 341.

77   Ibid., 344–46.

78   Nánez Falcón, *Transcriptions*, vol. XVI, 43.

79   Meneray, *The Favrot Family Papers*, vol. IV, 177–78.

80   Meneray, *The Favrot Family Papers*, vol. V, 5.

81   Ibid., 10.

82   Ibid., 19.

83   Fertel, *The Favrot Family Papers*, vol. VI, 213–21.

84   Ibid., 229–30.

85   Nánez Falcón, *Transcriptions*, vol. XVI, 116–24.

86   Nánez Falcón, *Transcriptions*, vol. XVII, 230.

87   Ibid., 78.

—— **CHAPTER 8:** Civic Engagement & Domestic Life in the Early 19th Century ——

1   Helen Parkhurst Favrot, *Pops: A Memoir* (New Orleans: Tulane University, 1964), 30–31.

2   *New Orleans Times-Picayune*, February 22, 1918.

3   Helen Parkhurst Favrot and Claire Favrot Killeen, *All My Loves: Letters and Memorabilia from the 1920s* (Covington, LA: Francis House Press, 1992), A:2.

4   Henry E. Chambers, "East Baton Rouge County Louisiana Archives Biographies—Favrot, Joseph," accessed April 18, 2016, http://files.usgarchives.net/la/eastbatonrouge/bios/favrot51gbs.txt.

5   Michelle Favrot Heidelberg, email to author, October 13, 2017.

6   "Biographical Directory of the United States Congress—Favrot, George Kent," accessed April 18, 2016, http://bioguide.congress.gov/scripts/biodisplay.pl?index+F000048.

7   *Journal of the American Medical Association*, vol. 47, no. 22, December 1, 1906, accessed April 18, 2016, https://books.google.com/books?id=m6khAQAAMAAJ&pg=PA1845&lpg=PA1845&dq=robert+aldrich+journal+of+the+american+medical+1906&source=bl&ots=S1udocnNN1&sig=9UUqd0eE199LzRFgWYEM1ALYtV0&hl=en&sa=X&ved=0ahUKEwinzOXnu5fMAhWI2T4KHXEsBd8Q6AEIHDAA#v=onepage&q=robert%20aldrich%20journal%20of%20the%20american%20medical%201906&f=false

8   *The Washington Post*, April 12, 1907, 1.

9   "Biographical Directory of the United States Congress—Favrot, George Kent."

10 *New Orleans Times-Picayune*, Tuesday, March 8, 1921.

11 Favrot and Killeen, *All My Loves*, A:14.

12 Mike Miller, "Leo M. Favrot, W. Baton Rouge Parish, Louisiana," accessed April 18, 2016, http://files.usgwarchives.net/la/westbatonrouge/bios/favrot3.txt.

13 Rockefeller Archive Center, *A Guide to the Leo M. Favrot Papers* (Sleepy Hollow, New York: Rockefeller Archive Center, 2009), 5.

14 "Better Schools for Negroes in Louisiana," *The Southern Workman*, vol. XLVII, no. 12 (Hampton, Virginia: The Press of The Hampton Normal and Agricultural Institute, December 1918), 567–8.

15 Leo M. Favrot, "A Study of County Training Schools for Negroes in the South," *The Journal of Social Forces*, vol. 1, no. 5 (Oxford: Oxford University Press, 1918), 585, accessed April 18, 2016, http://www.jstor.org/stable/3005140?seq=1#page_scan_tab_contents.

16 Leo M. Favrot, speech to the National Association for the Advancement of Colored People, June 25, 1919, from the Thomas B. Favrot Collection, printed from microfilm at the Library of Congress on June 23, 1982, Favrot Family Papers, Louisiana Research Collection, Tulane University.

17 Adam Fairclough, *A Class of Their Own: Black Teachers in the Segregated South* (Cambridge, MA: Harvard University Press, 2007), 320–331.

18 The Rockefeller Foundation, "The General Education Board," accessed April 18, 2016, http://rockefeller100.org/exhibits/show/education/general_education_board.

19 Fairclough, *A Class of Their Own*, 320–331.

20 Lynne Marie Getz, "Extending the Helping Hand to Hispanics: The Role of the General Education Board in New Mexico in the 1930s," *Teachers College Record*, vol. 93, no. 3, Spring 1992; 500–515, accessed March 30, 2016, http://eric.ed.gov/?id=EJ443788.

21 "Statement on the Appointment of Members to the President's Commission for the Study and Review of Conditions in the Republic of Haiti, February 7, 1930," accessed March 30, 2016, http://www.presidency.ucsb.edu/ws/?pid=22512.

22 *The Afro-American*, Saturday, July 5, 1930.

23 Rockefeller Archive Center, *A Guide to the Leo M. Favrot Papers*, 5.

24 Helen Parkhurst Favrot, *Pops: A Memoir*, 24–25.

25 Ibid., 30.

26 Ibid., 40.

27 Ibid., 41.

28 Ibid., 41.

29 Favrot and Killeen. *All My Loves*, A:6.

30 Helen Parkhurst Favrot, *Pops: A Memoir*, 42.

31 Favrot and Killeen, *All My Loves*, unnumbered page at beginning of document.

32 Helen Parkhurst Favrot. *Pops: A Memoir*, 47.

33 Favrot and Killeen. *All My Loves*, A:3.

34 Ibid., X:15.

35 Ibid., A:6–7.

36 Helen Parkhurst Favrot. *Pops: A Memoir*, 42.

37 Ibid., 43–44.

38 Kathleen Van Horn, telephone conversation with author, June 29, 2015.

39 David Conradsen, et al., *The Arts & Crafts of Newcomb Pottery* (New York: Skira Rizzoli Publications, Inc., 2013), 235, 237, 241, 270, 292, & 302.

40 Beatrice M. Field and Amanda R. Rittenhouse, *Potpourri: An Assortment of Tulane's People and Places*, 1983 (updated 2002), accessed December 5, 2015, https://tulane.edu.alumni/upload/potpourri.pdf.

41 Clarence L. Mohr and Joseph E. Gordon, *Tulane: The Emergence of a Modern University, 1945–1980* (Baton Rouge: Louisiana State University Press, 2001), 130–135.

42 Ibid., 130–136.

43 Ibid., 130–141.

44 Field and Rittenhouse, *Potpourri*.

45 Tulane University, Department of Sociology, "History of Tulane Sociology," accessed December 5, 2015, https://tulane.edu/liberal-arts/sociology/history.cfm.

46 Tulane School of Architecture, "The Favrot Chair, honoring Charles A. Favrot of Favrot & Livaudais and H. Mortimer Favrot of Favrot and Reed," brochure, 1996.

CHAPTER 9: Louisiana in the Gilded Age

1   Helen Parkhurst Favrot, *Pops: A Memoir* (New Orleans: Tulane University, 1964), 6–8.

2   Antoinette J. Lee, *Architects to the Nation: The Rise and Decline of the Supervising Architect's Office* (New York: Oxford University Press, 2000), 142–47.

3   Thomas B. Favrot?, "A Sketch on the activities of James Freret," undated, Favrot Family Papers, Louisiana Research Collection, Tulane University.

4   Gary Van Zante, "James Freret," in *KnowLA: The Encyclopedia of Louisiana History, Culture and Community*, edited by David Johnson, Louisiana Endowment for the Humanities, 2010-, article published May 18, 2011, http://www.knowla.org/entry/967/&view=summary.

5   Immaculate Conception Jesuit Church, "The Church," accessed December 4, 2015, jesuitchurch.net/learn/the-church.

6   Federal Writers' Project of the Works Project Administration, *New Orleans City Guide 1938* (New Orleans: Garrett County Press, 2009), 305.

7   Gary Van Zante, "James Freret."

8   Helen Parkhurst Favrot, *Pops: A Memoir*, 2.

9   Beatrice Freret, letter to Charles A. Favrot, October 8, 1886, Favrot Family Papers, Louisiana Research Collection, Tulane University.

10 Nette Freret, letter to Charles A. Favrot, October 28, 1886, Favrot Family Papers, Louisiana Research Collection, Tulane University.

11 James Freret, letter to Charles A. Favrot, October 29, 1886, Favrot Family Papers, Louisiana Research Collection, Tulane University.

12 Helen Parkhurst Favrot. *Pops: A Memoir*, 5.

13 J.C. Sunderland, letter to Charles A. Favrot, June 18, 1887, Favrot Family Papers, Louisiana Research Collection, Tulane University.

14 Abner J. Haydel, letter to Charles A. Favrot, December 30, 1887, Favrot Family Papers, Louisiana Research Collection, Tulane University.

15 C. Francis Osborne, letter to Charles A. Favrot, June 24, 1887, Favrot Family Papers, Louisiana Research Collection, Tulane University.

16 Thomas B. Favrot?, "A Sketch on the activities of Charles Allen Favrot, Architect," undated, Favrot Family Papers, Louisiana Research Collection, Tulane University.

17 Helen Parkhurst Favrot. *Pops: A Memoir*, 17.

18 Ibid., 17.

19 Ibid., 18.

20 Ibid., 22.

21 Ibid., 18.

22 Gary Van Zante, "James Freret."

23 National Park Service, "Old Courthouse Museum," accessed November 15, 2015, http://www.nps.gov/nr/travel/caneriver/old.htm.

24 Robert J. Cangelosi, Jr., AIA, and Dorothy G. Schlesinger, eds., *New Orleans Architecture, Volume VIII: The University Section* (Gretna, LA: Pelican Publishing Company, 2011), 173–74.

25 Robert J. Cangelosi, Jr., AIA, and Dorothy G. Schlesinger, eds., *New Orleans Architecture, Volume VII: Jefferson City* (Gretna, LA: Pelican Publishing Company, 2010), 166.

26 *The Bankers' Magazine*, vol. LXVIII, January to June 1904, 234.

27 Cangelosi and Schlesinger, *New Orleans Architecture, Volume VIII*, 102, 175.

28 Ibid., 176.

29 Karen Kingsley, *Buildings of Louisiana* (New York: Oxford University Press, 2003), 127.

30 Cangelosi and Schlesinger, *New Orleans Architecture, Volume VIII*, 139.

31 Helen Parkhurst Favrot. *Pops: A Memoir*, 29.

32 Ibid., 28.

33 Ibid., 31–32.

34 Cangelosi and Schlesinger, *New Orleans Architecture, Volume VIII*, 77.

35 Helen Parkhurst Favrot. *Pops: A Memoir*, 32.

36 Cangelosi and Schlesinger, *New Orleans Architecture, Volume VIII*, 78.

37 Helen Parkhurst Favrot. *Pops: A Memoir*, 31–32.

38 Ibid., 33.

39 Ibid., 32.

40 Ibid., 31–32.

41 *New Orleans Times-Picayune*, February 22, 1918.

42 Helen Parkhurst Favrot. *Pops: A Memoir*, 44.

43 Helen Parkhurst Favrot and Claire Favrot Killeen, *All My Loves: Letters and Memorabilia from the 1920s* (Covington, LA: Francis House Press, 1992), A: 2.

44 Helen Parkhurst Favrot. *Pops: A Memoir*, 48.

45 Ibid., 34.

46 Tulane University, Southeastern Architectural Archive, "Architecture Research," accessed October 15, 2015, http://southeasternarchitecture.blogspot.com/search/label/Favrot%20and%20Livaudais.

47 Ibid.

48 Kingsley, *Buildings of Louisiana*, 235–36.

49 Ibid., 365.

50 Ibid., 302.

51 Calcasieu Historical Preservation Society, "Article Commemorating the Great Fire of 1910," accessed October 15, 2015, http://www.calcasieupreservation.com/index.php?option=com_content&view=article&id=81:the-great-fire-of1910&catid=24&itemid=18.

52 Lake Charles *American Press*, August 9, 1912.

53 Kingsley, *Buildings of Louisiana*, 294–95.

54 Mathes Brierre Architects, design and construction drawings of the Lake Charles City Hall, 1911–1912.

55 Society of Architectural Historians, Archipedia, "Historic City Hall Arts and Cultural Center," accessed April 18, 2016, http://sah-archipedia.org/detail%2Fcontent%2Fentries%2FLA-01-CC2.xml?q=section%3ALA-01

56 Calcasieu Historical Preservation Society, "Article Commemorating the Great Fire of 1910."

57 Kingsley, *Buildings of Louisiana*, 295–96.

58 Helen Parkhurst Favrot. *Pops: A Memoir*, 35.

59 Favrot and Killeen. *All My Loves*, II–19.

60 XplorHonduras, "Aduana de La Ceiba Honduras Video," accessed October 15, 2015, http://www.xplorhonduras.com/aduana-de-la-ceiba-honduras-video/.

61 Mathes Brierre Architects, design and construction drawings of the La Ceiba Custom House (Aduana), undated.

62 Mathes, Bergman, Favrot and Associates Architects, corporate brochure, ca. 1964.

63 Hospital y Clínicas Vicente D'Antoni, "Antecedentes Históricos," accessed April 18, 2016, http://hospitalvicentedantoni.com/pagina.php?id=10. See also: http://hospitalvicentedantoni.com/index.php.

64 Mathes, Bergman, Favrot and Associates Architects, corporate brochure, ca. 1964.

65 Google Maps and related online images from Bluefields, Nicaragua.

66 National Register of Historic Places, "New Orleans Cotton Exchange Building Nomination Form," June 1977, accessed October 15, 2015, http://focus.nps.gov/pdfhost/docs/NHLS/Text/77000675.pdf.

67 Mathes Brierre Architects, design and construction drawings of the New Orleans Cotton Exchange, 1920.

68 Emporis, "Capital One Bank Building," accessed October 15, 2015, http://www.emporis.com/buildings/122846/capital-one-bank-building-new-orleans-la-usa.

69 Jessie Poesch and Barbara SoRelle Bacot, *Louisiana Buildings: 1720–1940: The Historic American Buildings Survey* (Baton Rouge: Louisiana State University Press, 1997), 313.

70 Helen Parkhurst Favrot. *Pops: A Memoir*, 49. See also: Tulane University, "New Orleans Preservation Timeline Project," accessed October 15, 2015, http://arch itecture.tulane.edu/preservation-project/ entity/343.

71 Helen Parkhurst Favrot. *Pops: A Memoir*, 49.

72 Cangelosi and Schlesinger, *New Orleans Architecture, Volume VIII*, 176–77.

73 Kingsley, *Buildings of Louisiana*, 132.

74 Cangelosi and Schlesinger, *New Orleans Architecture, Volume VIII*, 137.

75 *Ruston Leader* (Ruston, Louisiana), Wednesday, February 5, 1930.

76 Albert C. Ledner, et al., *A Guide to New Orleans Architecture* (New Orleans: American Institute of Architects, New Orleans Chapter, 1974), 58.

77 Helen Parkhurst Favrot. *Pops: A Memoir*, 46.

78 Ibid., 46–47.

79 The American Institute of Architects, "The AIA Historical Directory of American Architects," accessed October 16, 2015, http://public.aia.org/sites/hdoaa/wiki/ Wiki%20Pages/ahd1013397.aspx.

80 *Architectural Art*, VI, January 6, 1911, as quoted in Bernard Lemann, Malcolm Heard, Jr., and John P. Klingman, eds., *Talk About Architecture: A Century of Architectural Education at Tulane* (New Orleans: Tulane University School of Architecture, 1993), 45.

81 Lemann, Heard, and Klingman, *Talk About Architecture*, 48–49.

82 Ibid., 61–65.

83 The American Institute of Architects, "List of Chapters of the American Institute of Architects," 1913, 1914, 1915, and 1916.

84 The American Institute of Architects, "AIA Directory," 1962.

85 Helen Parkhurst Favrot. *Pops: A Memoir*, 48.

86 *Journal of the American Institute of Architects*, vol. XI, no. 9, September 1923, 275.

87 Helen Parkhurst Favrot. *Pops: A Memoir*, 51–52.

88 Ibid., 52.

89 Ibid., 53.

90 Ibid., 52–55.

91 Bureau of Governmental Research, "History of BGR," accessed April 18, 2016, http://www.bgr.org/about/history/.

92 Helen Parkhurst Favrot. *Pops: A Memoir*, 55.

93 Ibid., 38.

94 Ibid., 59–60.

95 Ibid., 64–65.

96 Ibid., 1.

CHAPTER 10: The Emergence of the Modern Era

1   Helen Parkhurst Favrot, *Pops: A Memoir* (New Orleans: Tulane University, 1964), 22.

2   Helen Parkhurst Favrot and Claire Favrot Killeen, *All My Loves: Letters and Memorabilia from the 1920s* (Covington, LA: Francis House Press, 1992), A:16.

3   Eeva-Liisa Pelkonen and Donald Albrecht, eds., *Eero Saarinen: Shaping the Future* (New Haven: Yale University Press, 2006), 33.

4   Bernard Lemann, Malcolm Heard, Jr., and John P. Klingman, *Talk About Architecture: A Century of Architectural Education at Tulane* (New Orleans: Tulane University School of Architecture, 1993), 45.

5   Lemann, Heard, and Kilngman, Talk About Architecture, 53–59.

6   Favrot and Killeen, *All My Loves*, II:22.

7   Tulane University College of Technology, Bachelor of Engineering degree awarded to Henri Mortimer Favrot, June 2, 1915.

8   H. Mortimer Favrot, Jr., and Kay Favrot, interview with author, November 21, 2013.

9   Helen Parkhurst Favrot. *Pops: A Memoir*, 39.

10 Ibid., 40.

11 Ibid., 44.

12 Favrot and Killeen, *All My Loves*, II:5.

13 Ibid., II:5–7.

14 Ibid., Intro:3–4.

15 Ibid., I:4–5.

16 Ibid., I:16–18.

17 Ibid., II:9–14.

18 Ibid., II:9.

19 Ibid., II:14–17.

20 Ibid., II:17–20.

21 Ibid., III:3–4.

22 Ibid., III:13.

23 Ibid., III:24.

24 Ibid., VI:9.

25 Ibid., VII:3.

26 Ibid., III:2–4.

27 Ibid., IV:2–3.

28 Ibid., V:15–6.

29 Ibid., VI:1.

30 Ibid., VI:21–23.

31 Ibid., VI:25–30.

32 Ibid., VII:6.

33 Ibid., VII:6–7.

34 Ibid., VII:8.

35 Ibid., VII:9–11.

36 Ibid., VII:17.

37 Ibid., VIII:7–12.

38 Ibid., VIII:30.

39 Ibid., IX:1–2.

40 Ibid., IX:10.

41 Ibid., X:2.

42 Ibid., X:17.

43 Robert J. Cangelosi, Jr., AIA, and
    Dorothy G. Schlesinger, eds., *New Orleans
    Architecture, Volume VIII: The University
    Section* (Gretna, LA: Pelican Publishing
    Company, 2011), 148. See also: Favrot and
    Killeen, *All My Loves*, A:26.

44 Cangelosi and Schlesinger, *New Orleans
    Architecture, Volume VIII*, 146.

45 Mathes, Bergman, Favrot and Associates
    Architects, corporate brochure, ca. 1966.

46 Robert D. Leighninger, Jr., *Building
    Louisiana: The Legacy of the Public Works
    Administration* (Jackson, MS: University
    Press of Mississippi, 2007), 228.

47 Downtown Development Authority,
    accessed December 5, 2015, "http://www.
    developlafayette.com/about/contact.html.

48 Leighninger, *Building Louisiana*, 226–28.

49 Ibid., 187–268.

50 H. Mortimer Favrot, Sr., memorandum
    regarding McAlister Auditorium Memorial
    Room, March 15, 1940, Favrot Family
    Papers, Louisiana Research Collection,
    Tulane University.

51 Helen Parkhurst Favrot. *Pops: A Memoir*,
    63.

52 John Hix, "Strange As It Seems," United
    Feature Syndicate, December 9, 1939.

53 Mathes Brierre Architects, design and
    construction drawings of McAlister
    Auditorium, 1939.

54 Helen Parkhurst Favrot. *Pops: A Memoir*,
    63–64.

55 Ibid., 34.

56 Tulane University, Southeastern
    Architectural Archive, "Architecture
    Research," accessed December 15, 2015,
    http://southeasternarchitecture.blogspot.
    com/2008/07/gus-mayer-company-ltd-
    800-804-canal.html.

57 The Joy Theater, "About Us," accessed
    December 15, 2015, http://www.the-
    joytheater.com/about-us.

58 Docomomo-Nola, *Modernism on Canal
    Street: A Streetcar Tour of Endangered
    Buildings* brochure, 2010.

59 Favrot and Killeen, *All My Loves*, unnum-
    bered page at the beginning of the book.

60 Cangelosi and Schlesinger, *New Orleans
    Architecture, Volume VIII*, 174.

61 Vigo County Public Library, "Scrapbooks," accessed December 15, 2015, http://www.vigo.lib.in.us/archives/inventories/wars/WWII/Scrapbooks/Digital_Images/DC3/Scrapbook1M/Folder08/page046.pdf.

62 The Beauregard-Keyes House and Garden Museum, "Learn," accessed December 15, 2015, http://www.bkhouse.org/#!learn/chg5.

63 Favrot and Killeen, *All My Loves*, P:2.

64 Ibid., P:1–2.

65 AIA New Orleans, "History," accessed December 15, 2015, http://www.aianeworleans.org/history/.

66 The American Institute of Architects, "List of Chapters of the American Institute of Architects," 1942, 1943, and 1944.

67 Tulane School of Architecture, "The Favrot Chair, honoring Charles A. Favrot of Favrot & Livaudais and H. Mortimer Favrot of Favrot and Reed," brochure, 1996.

68 Lemann, Heard, and Klingman, *Talk About Architecture*, 107 and 110.

69 Favrot and Killeen, *All My Loves*, P:5.

70 Helen Parkhurst Favrot, "St. Augustine," *Times-Picayune*, December 21, 1968 (courtesy of Lawrence N. Powell).

71 Favrot and Killeen. *All My Loves*, A:23.

72 Catholic Online, "St. Mother Theodore Guerin," accessed December 15, 2015, http://www.catholic.org/saints/saint.php?saint_id=6984.

73 Helen Parkhurst Favrot. *Pops: A Memoir*, 36.

74 Ibid.

75 Ibid., 38–39.

76 *The Story of Louisiana, Volume II: Biographical* (New Orleans: J.F. Hyer Publishing Co., 1960), 261.

77 Beverly Himel, telephone interview with author, July 13, 2015.

78 Gervais F. Favrot Company, Inc., brochure, undated (but after 1980), Favrot Family Papers, Louisiana Research Collection, Tulane University.

79 Helen Parkhurst Favrot. *Pops: A Memoir*, 65.

80 *The Story of Louisiana, Volume II*, 262.

81 Ibid.

82 Ibid., 63.

83 Ibid.

84 Ibid., 65.

85 Times-Picayune, "Previous Loving Cup Winners," accessed December 3, 2015, http://www.timespicayune.com/MainArt/tp-lovingcup.pdf.

86 *The Story of Louisiana, Volume II*, 65.

CHAPTER 11: The Architect As Developer

1 Kay Favrot, interview with author, September 27, 2013.

2 H. Mortimer Favrot, Jr., interview with author, September 27, 2013.

3 National World War II Museum, "Featured Donor," accessed December 15, 2015, http://www.nationalww2museum.org/expansion/featured-donor.html.

4 H. Mortimer Favrot, Jr., interview with author, November 21, 2013.

5 H. Mortimer Favrot, Jr., September 27, 2013.

6 H. Mortimer Favrot, Jr., November 21, 2013.

7 Ibid.

8 "Biography of Henri Mortimer Favrot, Jr.," provided by the Tulane School of Architecture, 2014.

9 Kay Favrot, September 27, 2013.

10 H. Mortimer Favrot, Jr., interview with author, January 23, 2014.

11 Kay Favrot, interview with author, November 21, 2013.

12 H. Mortimer Favrot, Jr., November 21, 2013.

13 Ibid.

14 "Biography of Henri Mortimer Favrot, Jr."

15 Beatrice M. Field and Amanda R. Rittenhouse, *Potpourri: An Assortment of Tulane's People and Places*, 1983 (updated 2002), accessed December 5, 2015, https://tulane.edu.alumni/upload/potpourri.pdf.

16 Mathes, Bergman, Favrot and Associates Architects, corporate brochure, ca. 1964.

17 Tulane School of Architecture, "New Orleans Preservation Timeline Project," accessed December 5, 2015, http://architecture.tulane.edu/preservation-project/place/307.

18 Kay Favrot, telephone conversation with author, April 7, 2016.

19 Kathleen Van Horn, telephone conversation with author, June 29, 2015.

20 H. Mortimer Favrot, Jr., September 27, 2013.

21 Mathes, Bergman, Favrot and Associates Architects, corporate brochure, ca. 1966.

22 "Biography of Henri Mortimer Favrot, Jr."

23 Henry Shane, telephone interview with author, November 1, 2015.

24 Ibid.

25 United States Census Bureau, "Census of Population and Housing," accessed December 5, 2015, http://www.census.gov/prod/www/abs/decennial/.

26 Shane, November 1, 2015.

27 Albert C. Ledner, et al., *A Guide to New Orleans Architecture* (New Orleans: American Institute of Architects, New Orleans Chapter, 1974), 145.

28 Shane, November 1, 2015.

29 James Favrot, interview with author, November 21, 2013.

30 Shane, November 1, 2015.

31 Ibid.

32 "Biography of Henri Mortimer Favrot, Jr."

33 Ibid.

34 Ibid.

35 Nomination of H. Mortimer Favrot, Jr., AIA, for Fellowship in the American Institute of Architects, 2012, courtesy of the Tulane School of Architecture.

36 "Biography of Henri Mortimer Favrot, Jr."

37 Kay Favrot, April 7, 2016.

38 Kay Favrot, November 21, 2013.

39 Times-Picayune, "Katrina Timeline," accessed December 1, 2015, http://www.nola.com/katrina/timeline/.

40 Kay Favrot, November 21, 2013.

41 Ibid.

42 Times-Picayune, "Katrina Timeline."

43 James Favrot, November 21, 2013.

44 Shane, November 1, 2015.

45 James Favrot, November 21, 2013.

46 Ibid.

47 Ibid.

48 1st Lake Properties, "About 1st Lake Properties," accessed December 1, 2015, http://1stlake.com.

49 Nomination of H. Mortimer Favrot, Jr., AIA, for Fellowship.

50 Patricia Gay, telephone conversation with author, December 17, 2015.

51 Brooke A. Minto, email to author, December 15, 2015.

52 National World War II Museum, "Featured Donor," accessed December 1, 2015.

53 National World War II Museum, "About the Museum," accessed December 1, 2015, http://www.nationalww2museum.org/about-the-museum/.

54 Academy of the Sacred Heart, "Campus Tour," accessed December 1, 2015, http://www.ashrosary.org/page.cfm?p=507.

55 H. Mortimer Favrot, Jr., November 21, 2013.

INDEX